EMILY DICKINSON

A MEDICINE WOMAN FOR OUR TIMES

Emily Dickinson

A MEDICINE WOMAN FOR OUR TIMES

Steven Herrmann

Published in the United States of America by Fisher King Press, an imprint of Fisher King Enterprises. For information on obtaining permission for use of material from this work, submit a written request to:

permissions@fisherkingpress.com

Fisher King Press
www.fisherkingpress.com
+1-307-222-9575

Many thanks to all who have directly or indirectly provided permission to quote their works, including: *The Poems of Emily Dickinson*, edited by Thomas H. Johnson, Cambridge, Mass.: The Belknap Press of Harvard University Press, Copyright © 1951, 1955 by the President and Fellows of Harvard College. Copyright © renewed 1979, 1983 by the President and Fellows of Harvard College. Copyright © 1914, 1918, 1919, 1924, 1929, 1930, 1932, 1935, 1937, 1942, by Martha Dickinson Bianchi. Copyright © 1952, 1957, 1958, 1963, 1965, by Mary L. Hampson.

Every effort has been made to trace all copyright holders; however, if any have been overlooked, the author will be pleased to make the necessary arrangements at the first opportunity.

This book is lovingly dedicated to Jean Kirsch.

ACKNOWLEDGEMENTS

I am very grateful to those who have helped inspire me along the way towards the birthing of this book. Firstly, I would like to thank Harvard University Press for giving me permission to quote from the poetry of Emily Dickinson. Secondly, I would like to thank former Jungian analyst Donald F. Sandner for reading an early seventy-page draft of this book-in-progress in 1995 and for offering his remarkable support, inspiration, and critical feedback over two decades ago.[1] Jungian analyst John Beebe helped to edit an early draft of my manuscript in 1995 as well, and offered his insightful feedback and corrections. Nineteen years later, Dr. Beebe aided me again by substantially editing the first three chapters, and also a part of the Conclusion section in my now revised and expanded version of this book.[2] John has been a mentor of mine and a source of wisdom for over twenty years and an invaluable editor and consultant. I'd like to thank Andrew Harvey for encouraging me to complete this work. Thanks are also due to Clark McKowen for our conversations about Dickinson. I'd like to especially thank Jungian analyst Jean Kirsch for her helpful insights about the mystery of the anonymous Master Letters and for her encouragement of my vocation as a Jungian psychotherapist and writer. I'd also like to extend many warm thanks to Matthew Fox for his encouragement and personal support while I was in the process of completing this manuscript. Matt has been a great inspiration over the past eight years and he was particularly helpful during my period of explication of Dickinson's religious ideas as a post-Christian poetess. Special thanks go to my wife Lori Goldrich, Ph.D., who ongoingly discussed

---

1 See Endnote A.
2 See Endnote B.

the ideas in this book, read the entire manuscript from front to back, and offered valuable critical comments and editorial feedback. A warm thanks to Mel Mathews at Fisher King Press for enthusiastically taking on the publication of this book. I also want to thank Patty Cabanas in her capacity as copy-editor and proofreader. I am extremely pleased with her sensitivity to my style of writing and attention to fine detail. Her expertise and eloquence ensured the integrity of my work throughout the entire process. It was a pleasure to work with her! Finally, my deepest gratitude goes to our great national poet, Emily Dickinson. She is the real champion of this book.

CONTENTS

Footnotes in this publication consist mostly from the following five principal sources:

1. *The Complete Poetry* of Emily Dickinson, with J and the numerical order representing the poem's number in the Johnson edition, and F in the R.W. Franklin edition;

2. *The Letters of Emily Dickinson* in 3 Volumes;

3. *The Life of Emily Dickinson*;

4. *Cosmos A Sketch of the Physical Description of the Universe* Volume I;

5. *The Collected Works* of C.G. Jung, with ¶ representing the paragraph number as in standard English use in all Jungian journals published internationally;

All five of these principal sources may be quickly identified with the following abbreviations:

J/F   *The Complete Poems of Emily Dickinson*, (Thomas Johnson, Ed.). New York: Little Brown and Company, 1951; *The Poems of Emily Dickinson: Variorum Edition*, (R.W. Franklin, Ed.). Cambridge Massachusetts: The Belknap Press of Harvard University Press, 1998.

L   *The Letters of Emily Dickinson*, 3 Volumes, (Thomas H. Johnson and Theodora Ward, Eds.). Cambridge Mass.: Harvard University Press, 1958.

S   *The Life of Emily Dickinson* by Richard Sewall, Cambridge, Mass.: Harvard University Press, 1980.

CS1   *Cosmos: A Sketch of the Physical Description of the Universe*, Vol. 1. by Alexander Von Humboldt, Baltimore: John Hopkins, 1997.

CW   *Collected Works of C.G. Jung,* in 20 Volumes, (William McGuire, Ed.). Princeton: Bollingen.

INTRODUCTION

The last fifteen years in the USA were a virtual battleground between people favoring marriage equality across the nation and those who opposed it primarily on religious grounds. This ethical movement favoring democracy was pitted against the religious right, Catholics, Mormons, and many other non-liberal Christian denominations, which tried to oppose what would become in late June 2015, a national celebration for many American citizens. Countless people who were in favor of the institutionalization of same-sex marriage felt vindicated in the victory and I myself personally rejoiced that Spiritual Democracy had triumphed over the forces of oppression and darkness.[3]

In my home State of California, this movement in good conscience began to heat up when proposition 22 was passed, banning same-sex marriage equality. Many sentient souls were incensed. This was followed in 2003, when the Massachusetts—Emily Dickinson's home State—Supreme Judicial Court became the nation's first State to legalize same-sex marriage. The following year, in February 12, 2004, San Francisco mayor, Gavin Newsome defied California law by issuing marriage licenses to same-sex couples. The rest, as everyone knows, is in our history books. For on June 26, 2015, in a historic victory for gay rights and human rights, the U.S. Supreme Court ruled 5-4 to grant gays and lesbians the constitutional right to marry their chosen partners, whomever they might be, regardless of gender, religious beliefs, or sexual orientations. It is not enough remembered today, moreover, that one of our national leaders, who spoke up for human rights at Moscow, Russia, was our former Secretary of State, Hillary Rodham Clinton. Clinton was present at the placement of the statue of Walt Whitman at Moscow Uni-

---

3 Steven B. Herrmann, *Walt Whitman: Shamanism, Spiritual Democracy, and the World Soul.*

versity on October 14, 2009. The statue was a reciprocal gift given 10 years prior by the Russian government of Alexander Pushkin and placed on the campus of George Washington University in Washington D.C. At the base of the Whitman statue are inscribed the following words: "You Russians and we Americans, so far apart from each other, so seemingly different, and yet in ways *that* are most important, our countries are so alike." Clinton added: "Just as Pushkin and Whitman reset poetry we are resetting our relations for the 21ˢᵗ century."

Many people today have their own public or private views, religious or scientific or secular on the meaning of marriage equality. Yet, often in the news, the significance of marriage as a *spiritual phenomenon in a very real and deep psychological sense* is completely overlooked. Looking to the Old and New Testaments of the Bible and the Koran, Bhagavad Gita, or any other religious text amongst the world's great religions, it is hard to see how they provide sufficient answers to an issue that was always at its roots, a doctrinal dispute filled mostly with male bias. Even in our outdated psychology texts, the progressives were slow to speak out about this ethical principle of human rights.

When we place ourselves back in the context of Amherst, Massachusetts, New England in 1861 at the time of the outbreak of the Civil War, when another contradiction in our American democracy was plaguing our nation and pressing for racial equality, we can see that justice won the battle for human rights, and will again and again until all ethnicities, cultures, and nations are made whole. I have written two books on Walt Whitman. As the unveiling of the statue in Russia shows, he is without any doubt our great poet of democracy. Yet, what about Dickinson? Can Dickinson be treated with the same national dignity? Will she ever rise to the stature of the male bards who reset American poetry? Will she ever be regarded in our American Universities as an equal to Whitman, or Herman Melville?

Melville's and Whitman's and Dickinson's voices are still speaking to us today.[4] They speak up for the same core freedom of religious liberty. It is out of religious schisms, in fact, that Dickinson came into her

---

4 S.B. Herrmann, *Spiritual Democracy: The Wisdom of Early American Visionaries for the Journey Forward.*

full poetical power. Her aim in life was to "Tell all the Truth but tell it slant—" as she famously said for "Success in Circuit lies" (J 1129/F 1263). One of these lies in American politics was the lie about gender equality. Dickinson told the Truth about equal rights but she told it slant. In this book, I see her as an intellectual and compassionate genius who was far ahead of her times. She may be even more relevant to the climate of our current world affairs and the struggle for human rights than when she was alive. This book is about women's rights as human rights, as Hilary Clinton has said, and the rights of all people across the globe. In the following pages, I draw out some of best themes of Dickinson's poetry and demonstrate how she speaks to us now, at a time when we need to listen most carefully to what she has to say.

Melville and Whitman helped form the cornerstone for what I'm calling spiritual democracy. But little known to the world of white male privilege in their day was an unacknowledged poetess of Amherst who published only seven poems in her lifetime, with 1,775 of them now in print in Thomas Johnson's authoritative text. Despite her virtual anonymity during her relatively short lifetime (she died at 55 years of age) she has risen, nevertheless, to the very pinnacle of American poetry and in some respects, she may even surpass the intellectual brilliance of her male contemporaries, if only because she chose her words more precisely, and also proves to be more scientifically minded in her themes of nature and the Cosmos.

Whereas the men in Emily's family, along her father-line, all believed in the Puritan doctrine of original sin, Emily said in fierce rebellion against this patriarchal inheritance: "I do not respect 'doctrines.'"[5] Hers was a natural theology of love to the world of nature and the Goddess, not one of damnation and sin. Taking the national violence inwards, her fight was not with Native Americans, like her ancestors, but with traditional Christianity, and all of its creeds, which became her interior battleground. "My Life had stood—a Loaded Gun" (J 754/F 764) she wrote, and "My Wars are laid away in Books—" (J 1549/F 1579). For her revolution in theology, she confronted outworn doctrines that had

---

5 Emily Dickinson, *The Letters of Emily Dickinson*, p. 346.

been written by faded men in that campaign inscrutable of her own powerful interiority.

As the great Prussian scientist of the 19ᵗʰ century, Alexander von Humboldt, once said about himself, the one feat he prided himself on most and that sustained his writings most during his lifetime of international fame was the feat of scaling what he thought to be the highest summit in the world: Chimborazo, in Ecuador. All of the great American men of letters from Emerson, to Thoreau, to Melville, to Whitman, knew about Humboldt's book *Cosmos*, which made him the most famous man in the world by the time of his death in 1859. Dickinson scaled her own interior summits of famous volcanic peaks. She had read about them in her geology books. Today, she is the rave on University and College campuses in programs specializing in feminist studies and American literature. Yet, the images we have of her in the general public today are of a shy and reclusive woman who wrote poetry in personal letters to friends and family, but who was a bit mad, and did not care much for publication. In her lifetime, she was ironically a "Nobody!" "I'm Nobody! Who are you?" (J 288/F 260) she asked sixty years before women were granted the right to vote. The fact of her anonymity was painful for her and she suffered much anguish when her desires for a successful publishing career were dashed because publishers could not properly understand, nor appreciate, the depths of her feminine wit and wisdom. This wisdom is a *medicine* that Dickinson has to offer us today.[6] We can thank her sister, Lavinia, or Vinnie, for ensuring that her poems were put into the right hands for posthumous publication.

In Amherst, where she lived almost her whole lifetime in her father's house, she once said to a female friend: "I find I need more vail."[7] Today, of course, the veil has become a symbol for religious oppression of women's freedoms in Iran and across the world, and women are throwing off their veils to become who they are. I see her as one of the greatest advocates for women's voices that has ever lived, and this includes the voices of the injured feminine in men, and women alike.

---

6 See Endnote C.

7 *L*, I, p. 229.

Today, many literary critics agree that Dickinson is unequalled by anyone writing in American English. Her lack of recognition and sense of outer failure, in the traditional male sense, must have nearly drove her to feel the pain of an entire generation of women and this depth of feeling is what makes her voice so vital and important for us to hear again today. As we will see in this book, no one in the world of literature grasped the significance of human equality and equal rights for women's voices in the 19th century as completely and as powerfully as Emily did. What did it mean to her to love men and women in her generation with equal body, equal heart, and equal voice? How did she arrive at the foundation of American democracy that insists on the principle of human freedom?

By going through a subliminal door, deep inside her own psyche, Emily entered the mythopoetic realm that was a main domain of study of such explorers of the unconscious as Frederick Myers, Theodore Flournoy, William James, Sigmund Freud, and C.G. Jung. Long before such pioneers of the new dynamic psychiatry helped give birth to modern psychology, Dickinson had already mapped out the terrain of the mythopoetic imagination in stupendous metaphorical images and she had arrived at the domain where human rights are also natural rights.

Her fight for women's rights was an interior battleground with traditional male stereotypes with a long pre-history in theology, philosophy, and politics. Such religious biases had been inherited from her grandfather, Samuel Fowler Dickinson (1775-1838), who died when Emily was seven years old. Samuel was born a year before the Declaration of Independence was drafted. He entered Dartmouth in 1791. He was made famous by having founded Amherst College. As Edward Hitchcock, a pious scientist and President of Amherst College from 1845-1854 said of Samuel: he was "urged by the command of our divine Savior to preach the gospel to every creature."[8] It was from Hitchcock that Emily was introduced to what would become her favorite chapter in the King James Bible, Revelation 21. Chapter 21: 2 reads: "And I John saw the Holy city, new Jerusalem, coming down from God out of heaven, prepared as a bride adorned for her husband." In Revelation 21: 9, the

---

8 *S*, 1: 35.

bride is referred to as the "the Lamb's wife." In his vision, John is carried away to a great and high mountain by the seventh angel who descends out of Heaven and where he is shown a mystical light, which was said to be "like jasper stone, clear as crystal" (Revelation 21: 11). It is a vision that describes the New Jerusalem in great detail; it is constructed from foundation to top by gold, pearls, and twelve precious stones. This chapter of Revelations gives us a stupendous image of the Holy city and its foundation in the Hebrew-Christian Bible, which is wonderfully set forth in grand archetypal imagery.

Even there, however, the meaning of women's voices as an archetypal reality in the human soul, which might make us all equal, was not made sufficiently conscious for us in scripture or "doctrine" by any woman or man. It is true that we have had many Christian Saints that were women and who wrote mystical poetry in the Christ tradition, and that many churches of Europe were erected to the Virgin Mary. In a deep *feeling* of love that transcends sex and gender and gets outside the Christ myth, however, there have been no sacred texts written by women that have elicited much veneration. With the exception of the great mother religions, which were wiped out by the patriarchies, men have written all of the major religions of the world. No major female voice has risen in the world to inspire the nations with a spiritual message such as Dickinson's.

As we will see in the pages ahead, in the field of modern psychology and in the psychology of religions, it was only Jung who fully grasped the significance of the feminine in theology and its spiritual significance for world culture as a whole. We need to fill in some of the missing pieces, however, that Jung himself could not mine as a European. By turning to an authentic trailblazer who anticipated the social and political movements of Spiritual Democracy that are currently afoot, my hope is that I can help to show how Dickinson succeeded in writing her own version of a new sacred text for the world. We will proceed to examine her full credentials herein, with all of the appropriate modesty such a task entails by telling her simple and wonderful story in a psychobiography. In doing so, I will view her as a Medicine Woman, a poet-shaman,[9]

---

9 S. Herrmann, "Whitman, Dickinson and Melville—American Poet-Shamans: Forerunners of Poetry Therapy," *Journal of Poetry Therapy*, Vol. 16, No. 1.

whose chief aim was to bring *healing* to a one-sidedly patriarchal and heterosexual culture of white privilege during a time when women were just beginning to find their voices after the secret meeting of a group of incensed women assembled together at Seneca Falls and spoke out through their feminist rebellion in 1848.

Emily's grandfather, Samuel, her father Edward, and brother, Austin, were all men of privilege and worldly affairs. Her father, Edward, was the treasurer of Amherst College. In their very home, however, was a child of remarkable genius, a girl of unsurpassed wit and scintillating brilliance, who dropped out of Mount Holyoke Female Seminary, yet, who soared to become "Wife" not only to a single nation, but to become a "Bride" of unlimited possibilities in the world and Cosmos.

She had the instinctive intelligence of "Nature's God" inborn in her. Her calling as a poet was given to her from birth. It is out of the well of natural wisdom that she spoke to the world with a "Voice" of authority about the news of the universe, which was at that very moment being said to be infinite by astronomers.

> If the foolish, call them *"flowers"*—
> Need the wiser, *tell?*
> If the Savants "Classify" them
> It is just as well!
>
> Those who read the "Revelations"
> Must not criticize
> Those who read the same Edition—
> With beclouded Eyes!
>
> Could we stand with that Old "Moses"—
> "Canaan" denied—
> Scan like him, the stately landscape
> On the other side—
>
> Doubtless, we should deem superfluous
> Many Sciences,
> Not pursued by learned Angels
> In scholastic skies!

> Low amid that glad Belles lettres
> Grant that we may stand,
> *Stars*, amid profound *Galaxies*—
> At that grand "Right hand"!   J 168/F 179

What she is saying here is that the new Revelation in 1860, the year after Alexander von Humboldt died, was the spiritual science of an infinite Cosmos. I think she believed that poets are sometimes wiser than those who merely classify nature into scientific categories because they have a wider vision from the "other side" in "scholastic skies!" By this she means astronomy and the angelic realm, or archetypal psyche, where the whole infinite universe can be beheld in the beauty and symmetry of a single flower. Classification, such as in the science of botany, can narrow one's cosmic vision and close one off thereby to the Infinite.

> The Life we have is very great.
> The Life that we shall see
> Surpasses it, we know, because
> It is infinity.
> But when all Space has been beheld
> And all Dominion shown
> The smallest Human Heart's extent
> Reduces it to none.   J 1162/F 1178

This mature Voice of a "Bride of God" who respected no doctrines and claimed to have written a "Diagnosis of the Bible" scored a major victory for her destiny-pattern, for women the world over, and modern art by providing us with her own theory of truth, told with forthrightness and great conviction: "Estranged from Beauty—none can be—/ For Beauty is Infinity—" (J 1474/F 1515). To keep a vision of the Cosmos ever in her mind was the poet's main task:

> The Infinite a sudden Guest
> Has been assumed to be—
> But how can that stupendous come
> Which never went away?   J 1309/F 1344

We will try in this book therefore to take a modest role, as many feminist critics have before, of speaking up for Dickinson as an advocate for what she taught in a down-to-earth psychobiography that puts her in cultural context as a disseminator of a new vision of women's rights in a patriarchal society that could not understand her because they failed to appreciate the beauty of her poetry in its natural eloquence, just the way she wrote it. We will do this in two primary ways: 1) from a *psychological angle,* we will attempt to explain what she means by equality and show how her poetry relates to freedom, liberty, and equal rights for everyone (animals, plants, reptiles and amphibians included). 2) from a *spiritual angle,* we will try and demonstrate how her aims as a Medicine Woman were to administer a shamanic cure to a creedal and male-dominant culture that could not agree on doctrinaire matters, and that desperately needed and still needs to be questioned today.

Dickinson's voice-as-Wife is one of the most *powerful* voices in American poetry. This may sound contradictory since power is typically measured in our culture in a career sense, by the impact of one's vocation upon the world in one's lifetime. Yet by the cherishment of her own introverted power and fierce protection of her style, Emily gave birth to *the explosive power of her calling* as a poet of the Infinite. "To see the Summer Sky / Is Poetry", she said (J 1472/F 1491). "Expanse cannot be lost—/ Not Joy, but a Decree / Is Deity— / His Scene, Infinity—" (J 1584/F 1625). As a poet-shaman, Dickinson's vision of God subsumed the entire Universe with all of its galaxies. This is the image of God that she married. Such a stupendous vision that rendered not only many of the sciences, but religious doctrines superfluous was vouchsafed to her through a *syzygy* (an alchemical term for union) with an infinite Deity, embracing the whole Cosmos. She made such a vision possible in her generation through the newest developments in geology, astronomy, and natural sciences from her place of sacred worship: "Vesuvius at Home."

"Perhaps you laugh at me!" she wrote in a letter to her friends in defiance against the typically sexist attitude of America, "Perhaps the whole United States are laughing at me too! *I* can't stop for that! *My* business is to love."[10] Her business was to love for the sake of her own and

---

10 *L*, II, p. 413.

humanity's Immortality. This was not a doctrine of prayer to a heavenly Father who demanded of his flock a faith in God, but a natural *theology of love* for the nations of the world that she hoped to disseminate her wisdom-medicine to: "This ecstatic Nation / Seek—it is Yourself" (J 1354/F 1381), she said. "Of Course—I prayed—" she cried out and then answered ironically: "And did God Care?" (J 376/F 581).

In a society that prided itself on the principles of human freedom and equal rights for everyone, did it matter that her voice be heard in the press in the 1860s? Does it matter today that we publish another book on her? What can we learn from a feminist poet who saw herself as an equal with men, a second Jacob? What can a nation founded on religious liberty learn from her when human rights are still being threatened with patriarchal oppression and condemnation by chauvinist forms of government? That she felt such bigotry from her fellow men in the field of her art is without a doubt: "When they dislocate my Brain! / Amputate my freckled Bosom! / Make me bearded like a man!" (J 1737/ F 267). Despite the attempts that were made to amputate the style of her feminine poetry in her lifetime, she never compromised her integrity. This conviction to stay true to her natural voice is what gives her singular power today to speak to women and men in all nations of the world and to hopefully help it to become a more civil and humane place for all of us to live in.

I

EMILY DICKINSON: A MEDICINE WOMAN FOR CHALLENGING TIMES

This book is about Emily Dickinson, whom I regard as one of America's foremost poet-shamans—an intuitive take on who she was, what she thought, and what (from my perspective) she is really about. To think of her as a poet, an honor that eluded her in her lifetime, because her work remained all but unpublished at the time of her death, is not new. Yet to think of her as also a shaman is, and so that description, which will be applied to her in this book, does need some unpacking at the start. I call her a *poet-shaman.* This is a bit heretical, even in the literature on shamanism, which is now a budding library.

For a long time, anthropologists maintained that shamans were the epileptics, neurotics, or schizophrenics of the tribes. Such pathologizing views of their personal styles have since been dispelled by cross-cultural and ethnographic studies, which have revealed them as deliberate wounded healers. It is also clearer than ever today that what some of our most extraordinary-personality-poets like Dickinson was doing, along with her contemporaries, Walt Whitman and Herman Melville, is with aesthetic force paving a way for Spiritual Democracy and using Western American poetry pragmatically to promote that idea.

In this opening chapter, I will stress the intuitive, psychological side of Dickinson as a forerunner of the apotheosis in American thought of an analytical depth-psychology, which opens access to the spirit more democratically than traditional religions by drawing on a therapeutic, shamanistic level of psychological experience common to all. Such shamanism finds religious mystery in everyday human experience and can be compared to the way Native American religion celebrates life as actually lived in extended families and tribes. Such a homespun spiritual attitude infuses Dickinson's poetry.

Like shamans and not unlike C.G. Jung, who coined the term "analytical psychology" for his approach to understanding the human psyche, anyone who is called to separate from the collectivity and follow an urge to personal spiritual individuation runs the risk of being viewed by the majority of humanity as insane, psychotic, or deranged, if not also condemned as a heretic. Historically, there are reasons for this, and it is evident that many who have followed the shaman's path into as yet unknown registers of spiritual exploration have found that the hostile forces of traditional civilization and culture punish them severely for their liberties. It requires caution to embark on an endeavor that is not commonly undertaken by most people and survive.

If, however, the few who are called by the shamanic archetype[11] to move along such a path, perhaps more deeply *do* by luck and good fortune happen to make it back to the safe shores of the known world, they become initiators of new perspectives in their cultures and (like Dickinson, Whitman, and Melville) tutelary figures within the cultural milieu they have enriched. They illustrate, in their poetic triumph that shamans *are* uncommon, but absolutely necessary for a culture to survive. Where would American literature be without them—if we had only Cooper, Irving, Hawthorne, Longfellow, Emerson, and Twain to show for the 19th Century? The shaman-poet is even more than Shelley knew the unacknowledged legislator of a worldview.

The price paid by anyone who embraces shamanism in the course of a modern life is usually quite high. For instance, some of the psychoanalysts who congregated around Sigmund Freud during the apostasy with C.G. Jung in 1912, declared that Jung was insane ("As regards Jung he seems all out of his wits, he is acting quite crazy" wrote Freud to his later biographer, the English psychoanalyst Ernest Jones. Jones regarded Freud as his Viennese master at the time).

---

11 S. Herrmann, "Donald Sandner: The Shamanic Archetype." In *The San Francisco Jung Institute Library Journal*, Vol. 21, No. 2.

Similar claims were also made about Emily Dickinson in her day. By pre-psychological standards, the reclusive female poet appeared to some of her privileged contemporaries as a bit crazy. Her mentor and spiritual advisor, Thomas Wentworth Higginson, a former Harvard divinity student and radical Unitarian minister actually called her "my partially cracked poetess of Amherst," and Higginson's wife is reported to have asked this literary man who meant so much to Dickinson as her one hope for publishing her work, "Oh why do the insane so cling to you?"[12]

Despite such attempts to categorize her in her own time as a sort of mad woman in the attic, Emily Dickinson was in fact mastering her literary vocation as they spoke, by incorporating into her work the shamanic technique of inducing ecstasy with the hope of ministering to ministers. Half a century later, the literary critic, Yvor Winters put words to the now-common view that she is "one of the greatest lyric poets of all time."[13] What Dickinson herself said, however, is more instructive with regard to the shamanic root of her lyricism:

> Take all away from me, but leave me Ecstasy,
> And I am richer than all my Fellow Men—
> Ill it becometh me to dwell so wealthily
> When at my very Door are those possessing more,
> In abject poverty—   J 1640/F 1671

Unfortunately, depth psychology has done precious little to help us understand either Dickinson's personality or her poetry from *inside* her Door. In a later chapter, we will make an attempt to crouch within her Door to comprehend what she meant when she said she was "richer" than all her "Fellow Men."

Under the spell of Tennessee Williams' portraits of fragile heroines, Julie Harris' performance as "The Belle of Amherst" only reified the image of the schizoid, emotionally inadequate "highly sensitive" Dickinson, who could only retreat from life. By our present, diagnosing-prone mental health establishment (no less prejudiced toward her than the 19th

---

12 *S*, 1: 6.

13 Y. Winters, "Emily Dickinson and the Limits of Judgment." In *Emily Dickinson: A Collection of Critical Essays*, p. 40.

century) she has been misdiagnosed with such pejorative labels as bipolar disorder, paranoia, agoraphobia, panic disorder, and schizotypal personality.[14] Such labels do nothing to inform us about the extraordinary nature of her exceptional mental states, which are actually shamanic ecstasies, revealing her vocation as a *healer*.

In this book, we will examine her calling and urge to life as a Medicine Woman, that is, someone in whom the technique of ecstasy can evoke in the reader, no less than in the poet herself, a shamanic state of mind. As any of us can attest, the simple act of reading her is enough to adjust one's spiritual orientation to the present moment of life. That, as a poet, is all that matters for Dickinson, for *that* level of communication is all there is for a poet to impart. As she said to Higginson during their first meeting at her Amherst home: "I find ecstasy in living; the mere sense of living is joy enough."[15] She meant, she was telling him to make that experience available to all in her poems.

During her states of ecstasy from childhood to the very end of her life at the age of 55, she centered her mind on her subjective states of consciousness as specifying her vocation, i.e., what she had to tell the world. When outer success was denied to her, the disappointment in her justified ambition to write a "letter to the World / That never wrote to Me—" (J 441/F 519) led her to an excruciating experience that could be compared to the alchemical tortures depicted in the visions of Zosimos.[16]

Not to be able to communicate passion and be heard is one of the most painful human experiences. In the language of shamanism, such agonies are referred to as dismemberment journeys, wherein the shaman's body is cut open and filled with quartz crystals. The aim is to achieve the attitude that is superordinate to any outward blows of fate after leaving the safe shores of traditional religion behind for Ecstasy. In *Shamanism,* Eliade states: "the shaman, and he [she] alone, is the great master of ecstasy. A first definition of this complex phenomenon, and

---

14 S. Winhusen, "Emily Dickinson and Schizotypy." In *The Emily Dickinson Journal*, Vol. 13, No. 1, pp. 77-96.

15 *L*, p. 264.

16 C.G. Jung, *CW* 13: ¶¶ 85-144. (Note: *CW* refers throughout this book to *The Collected Works of C.G Jung*.)

perhaps the least hazardous, will be: shamanism = *technique of ecstasy*…the shaman specializes in a trance during which his [her] soul is believed to leave his [her] body and ascend to the sky or descend to the underworld."[17] Ecstasy is an experience that can include different types of emotions, joy and agony, sorrow and happiness, grief and rapture, etc. And Dickinson was, no less than any successful shaman, a master of it. We need to recognize her robustness in this regard.

One has to be robust to be religious in the context of modernism. The first depth psychologist to take on the modern problem of holding onto a sense of the sacredness, rather than just the secularity of individual experience was Jung, fully a half-century after Dickinson, with his active imaginations in the wake of the death of the heroic image of Siegfried, son of Sigmund, mirroring his own break with Freud. For Jung, the task of finding a new religious attitude during the passage at midlife was one of risking what he had inherited from birth as a parson's son.

On January 5, 1922, for instance, Jung had a conversation with his soul concerning his vocation and the fate of *Liber Novus,* or the *Red Book,* in which an inner feminine voice said to him: "You should listen: to no longer be a Christian is easy. But what next? For more is yet to come. Everything is waiting for you" and "above all your calling comes first." "But what is my calling?" Jung asked her. "The new religion and its proclamation" she said. "Oh God," Jung answered reluctantly "how should I do this?"[18]

But astonishingly, Dickinson had already "done this" through her poetry. We might do well to cross-reference them, therefore, for they illustrate each other and shared a common interest in the transformation of the traditional Judeo-Christian God-image. As both Jung and Dickinson teach, there is no way to arrive at the goal of spiritual transformation except through an experience of symbolic death. Death is the great liberator and no poet teaches us about the importance of temporary moments of ego death as eloquently and as brilliantly as Dickinson. "Do we die— / Or is this Death's Experiment— / Reversed—in Victory?" (J 550/F 666) Emily asks us to consider.

---

17 Mircea Eliade, *Shamanism: Archaic Techniques of Ecstasy,* pp. 4-5.
18 C.G. Jung, *The Red Book,* p. 211.

Dickinson's mythopoetic descriptions of dying to her former self, so that a new religious attitude, a new state of consciousness that is acutely aware, could be born in her are at times a painful process to experience at first, yet as we follow her we will be led into states of liberation. Her death to her former life and rebirth into a Medicine Woman is one of the clearest poetic renderings of a shamanic journey in the annals of American poetry.

In her poetry, Dickinson wrestles fiercely with historical Christianity and Judaism and emerges transformed with a new religious revelation, a shamanic evocation of a new religious attitude that the new democracy of world-readers can share: the same global religion Whitman, at just the same time, and without the benefit of her example, was calling Religious Democracy.

In Emily's year of study at Mount Holyoke Seminary in 1847, when it was in vogue to devote one's life to traditional creeds of faith, she broke away from a conventional path of religious piety and heeded the shaman's call[19] to assume a new dress. As Dickinson wrote to an Amherst friend from her childhood years in 1850 at the age of 20: "The shore is safer, Abiah, but I love to buffet the sea—I can count the bitter wrecks here in these pleasant waters, and hear the murmuring winds, but oh, I love the danger!"[20]

What Dickinson experienced through listening to her inner voices is what Jung describes (in his book *Aion*) as an experience of the syzygy, the union of masculine and feminine opposites, on the road to a full realization of the Self. Jung writes:

> There are far more people who are afraid of the unconscious than one would expect. They are even afraid of their own shadow. And when it comes to the anima and animus [the masculine and feminine soul-images] this fear turns to panic. For the syzygy [or spiritual marriage] does indeed represent the psychic contents that irrupt into consciousness in a psychosis (most clearly of all in the paranoid forms of schizophrenia). The overcoming of this fear is often a moral achievement of

---

19 S. Herrmann, *William Everson The Shaman's Call.*
20 *L*, I, p. 102.

unusual magnitude, and yet it is not the only condition that
must be fulfilled on the way to a real experience of the self.[21]

Dickinson overcame her fears and panic by turning to an elixir within. Rather than shutting her inner voices off with Western medicines,
she conducted an experiment in active visioning techniques through
verse, in a straightforward style she invented that is uniquely her own.
Jung was not amiss when he used the words "fear" and "panic" above to
describe the conjunction of masculine and feminine opposites that come
together during the inner marriage of the soul with God (or the Self).
It is a fate that cannot be escaped on the road to full Self-realization and
the symbols that do emerge during the process of confrontation with
the unconscious form a central piece of individuation.

Anyone who enters the seas of the collective unconscious is faced
with a fear that may border on terror, not unlike a child who enters the
ocean for the first time and then learns not only how to swim, but to
find great joy in it.[22] Indeed, *Joy* is a hallmark of the shaman's way of
being. Had she met Walt Whitman before she died in May of 1886,
she might have found a kindred spirit and a brother to sympathize with
her in verse: "The ship is clear at last, she leaps! / She swiftly courses
from the shore, / Joy, shipmate, joy."[23] Without a doubt, Dickinson was
by nature an ecstatic, and when she wrote her poem about Ecstasy to
Helen Hunt Jackson in 1885 above, she was thinking of the night sea
journey, for Jackson was in Santa Monica, California at the time, and
looking across the vast Pacific towards Japan from California shores, the
very spot Walt Whitman had looked to as the place where his dream of
Religious Democracy might be fulfilled in the Far West.

"But what next?" What is "to come?" What is the "new religion?" In
a sense, Dickinson, who died of kidney failure (Bright's Disease) at the
age of 55, had this to say in a letter to Mrs. Edward Tuckerman, who
was grieving over the recent loss of her husband: "'Eye hath not seen nor
ear heard.' What a recompense! The enthusiasm of God at the reception

---

21 Jung, *CW* 9.2: ¶ 62.
22 S. Herrmann, "The Transformation of Terror into Joy," *Journal of Sandplay Therapy*, Vol. XVI, No. 2, pp. 101-113.
23 Walt Whitman, *Leaves of Grass*, p. 608.

of His sons! How ecstatic! How infinite! Says the blissful voice, not yet a voice, but a vision, 'I will not let thee go, except I bless thee'"![24] What she is saying is that she is convinced beyond any doubt that her husband will be received as a son by God on the other side of death's door in ecstasy. On the other hand, for much of her lifetime she wrestled with this burning question of immortality. Holding these opposites for herself and readers keep this question vitally alive for all of us.

Not unlike Whitman and Melville, Emily Dickinson was strongly influenced by science. Her life was self-described as experimental. As Dickinson puts it, her life was one of an intense "internal / Experience between / And most profound experiment / Appointed unto Men—." This experimental attitude towards her spiritual experiences was viewed as an "Adventure" into the secret of her "own identity" (J 822/F 817).

Dickinson admits that in such states, she did indeed skirt madness, but her capacity for metaphor led her to articulate, and not psychotically mind you, the *aims of her spiritual individuation*. "Had Madness," she said "had it once or twice / The yawning Consciousness" (J 1323/F 1325). By "Consciousness" she means not ego's awareness but what Jung would have called a Self-experience: the vast consciousness of the Cosmos, the very same unity of being that the great geologist and world-explorer Alexander von Humboldt had probed in his scientific writings starting in 1844, when he published the first of five volumes that are known in German as *Kosmos*. Emily says in a description of the objective psyche: "The Brain—is wider than the Sky— / For—put them side by side— / The one the other will contain / With ease—and You—beside—" (J 632/F 598).

The expansion of Consciousness is the aim of human life, a Consciousness as we shall see in Chapter 11 that is Aware. This is the realization she puts forth as a central article of her faith, an experiential sense of *knowing* the ultimate meaning of life, which is to be Resurrected—like Christ—in body, soul, and spirit. We will learn much from her about the meaning of Resurrection in what follows.[25]

---

24 *L*, III, p. 898.
25 See Endnote D.

In the face of death, Dickinson is often fearless. She *knows.* This is the knowledge of immortality born of the experience of having died and been resurrected while still living. This is not the conventional view of Christianity that was being disseminated at Mount Holyoke in the "Bride-of-Christ" tradition; hers was a "Queen's endeavor" (J 617/F 681) to disseminate the "vital light" that inheres "as do the Suns—": the resurrected light of "Circumference—" (J 883/F 930), and by Circumference she means the Cosmos.

What we will demonstrate herein is what happens to Dickinson when she allows herself to pass beyond her fears of insanity, and assumes full responsibility for her fate and destiny in space and time as a Medicine Woman. As a bearer of a new American myth, Dickinson joins Whitman and Melville in celebrating the new American-born—and borne—vision of Spiritual Democracy.

In Mircea Eliade's view, "it is unacceptable to assimilate shamanism to any kind of mental disease,"[26] so to use psychopathological terms such as Higginson and his wife did above to describe Dickinson in her shaman-poet-aspect, is far from satisfactory, psychologically speaking. We will therefore use a Jungian method of interpretation to examine her "irrational" vocation and the poetic discipline she brings to performing it.

As we will see, what Jung would describe as a *Mysterium Coniunctionis,* a spiritual marriage is at the heart of Dickinson's own claim to authority as a poet-shaman (though of course she found her own way of describing her poetic identity); as "Wife" of the Cosmos. I would like to introduce one of her many poems that takes us straight into the psychic atmosphere of the "syzygy," the conjunction or inner marriage of opposites, and describes the fears, which Dickinson eventually overcame. I do this now because it will take us into the main subject of my book, which is spiritual marriage and its supreme meaning for our time.[27]

Upon first reading, the following is a poem that may leave readers feeling uneasy, because of its stark resemblance to schizophrenia, a "splitting" of the mind, and an entry into the darkness of unreason, not

---

26 M. Eliade, *Shamanism,* pp. xi-xii.
27 See Endnote E.

unlike the "eclipse" of consciousness that the astronomical syzygy, the passage of moon against the sun, so awesomely produces. Yet it is just such a darkening conjunction in the subconscious that makes possible the supreme integrity of the Self in the process of artistic creation. I find it helpful and relevant to remember Jung's interpretation of the syzygy, which he says "does indeed represent the psychic contents that irrupt into consciousness in a psychosis (most clearly of all in the paranoid forms of schizophrenia)."

No person who attempts to integrate psychic opposites, such as solar and lunar consciousness, within a single person recognizing these as a *union of sames* even though they are apparent opposites, can rush the process of Self-realization or individuation of integrity that eventually emerges. For as in alchemy, the opposites must be separated first before they can be combined:

> I felt a Cleaving in my Mind—
> As if my Brain had split—
> I tried to match it—Seam by Seam—
> But could not make them fit.
>
> The thought behind, I strove to join
> Unto the thought before—
> But Sequence raveled out of Sound
> Like Balls—upon a Floor.   J 937/F 867 (b)

The "Balls" may be likened, in the thread we're following, to round images of the Self's original wholeness. The poetess is making a heroic attempt to unite the opposites through poetry, but since the opposites have already been united in her by this point, she must be describing a more *integral* process here, something that has only become Self-aware since the dawning of neuropsychology, with its emphasis on integration of the two hemispheres of the cerebral cortex and its central axis of interhemispheric communication at the corpus callosum.

Language becomes the vehicle that seams the two sides of the brain (imaging the metaphor a hundred and fifty years before it became popular through neuroscience!) together into a single unit. The pay off, the "gold," as Dickinson might put it, was won by diligent work at her craft: "I never told the buried gold / Upon the hill—that lies—/ I saw the sun—his plunder done / Crouch low to guard his prize/…Whether to keep his secret—/ Whether to reveal—/…Atropos decide!" (J 11/F 38). Atropos was one of the three goddesses of fate and destiny. Known as "inflexible" or "Inevitable," Atropos chose death to end each life of humans by cutting their mortal thread with her "abhorred shears." Along with her two younger sisters, the three fates were called by some, Daughters of the Night, or *Nyx*. We'll hear more about the Fates in what lies ahead.

There is of course a certain quality about "I felt a Cleaving in my Mind—" that might rightly lead a reasonable reader to question the poet's sanity, and indeed, to postulate that she herself was "half-cracked," as did Thomas Higginson to his wife. But since the poem dates from 1864, and is cast in the past tense, I believe she is looking back at a cleavage that took place *earlier* in her life and, even in the life of a now divided nation engaged in Civil War. She was, in other words *meditating* (and recollecting in relative tranquility) on an experience of psychic opposites that had occurred earlier in her own and her nation's history and now was already capable of at least poetic resolution.

As a national and transnational poet of Spiritual Democracy, she is writing out of the nation almost to culminate Civil War. She knew by then opposites can be contained in the mind. Let us recall her 1862 poem above about the brain: "The Brain—is wider than the Sky—(J 632/F 598). Though she writes of a time when the cleaving in her mind that "split" her brain in two and was now splitting the nation could not be seamed, or "yoked" together, there is a larger sense that her poem is equal to the task of bringing them together as aspects of her own embodied consciousness—her Brain—through an image that however rending shows them present in one and the same mind.

Dickinson suffered out her solitary fate as a *literary* Wife whose destiny was to become wife to "nations to come."[28] In fact, she does appear to have seen herself as a "Bride" of the nations, holding a bouquet of flowers between the USA and other world countries, with Emily, as their eloquent minister of a post-Christian vision of equality between all reli-

---

28 *L*, I, p. 115.

gions, all races, and all sexual orientations. Flowers negotiated in her poetic imagination between her world of experience and the true spirit of Democracy that is potentially realizable in all lands.

> Between My Country—and the Others—
> There is a Sea—
> But Flowers—negotiate between us—
> As Ministry.   J 905/F 829

No doubt the loss of women and men whom she deeply loved *equally* with endless fire took its toll on her, and Dickinson herself had retreated into a solitude that would enable her to contemplate without challenges what she had in fact experienced pragmatically in the quiet of her own room. She had, after all, only herself to turn to and to the few she loved to communicate her quenchless passion.

The following passage comes from an 1870 letter to a friend: "I never had a mother. I suppose a mother is one to whom you hurry when you are troubled."[29] Jung understood that individuation begins with the realization, "I am an orphan" and I am all alone. It was Emily's fate and destiny to suffer that kind of aloneness in a patriarchal age that failed to understand what a spiritual marriage between opposites and sames can *be*, and since Dickinson did not marry the mystery man she pined after for a short time (the "Master"), we need to ask moreover what she meant by "*Wife?*"

As we shall see, Emily's references to being married, a housewife, and betrothal are not reflective of any superficial thinking on Dickinson's part, but anticipate by 160 years where we are today in political debates regarding the marriage question. The question of who should be granted the right to marry entered the courtrooms of America and marriage equality won, and the world may in time follow. Why is it, we might ask, that Whitman, Melville, and Dickinson *all* foresaw this change in our Civil Rights? We might chalk it up to the fact that they were all visionary geniuses, intuiting in their poetry what would one day be a political position that could prevail and recently in 2015 has become a reality, but there is something much deeper to their simulta-

---

29 *L*, II, p. 517.

neous claims for the value of a *union of sames* and opposites (both being *equals*) that requires a more intrapsychic and penetrating reading. That is the impulse to follow the way of the shaman: an archetypal dynamism with a pre-history that extends back 70,000 years, requiring of the shaman a marriage of opposites within the Self of the *healer*, and not infrequently married in same-gender relations with those who could accept such a bi-erotic man-woman or male-female identity.

Dickinson's own integral identity was not one familiar to traditional Western societies, nor was she referring to herself, in a Puritan sense, as a "Bride of Christ." As we will see, Dickinson's notion of marriage is quite exceptional, extraordinary, really, and is patterned upon an archaic, shamanistic archetype: the *typos* of bi-erotic marriage. As the late American poet and Dickinson scholar Adrienne Rich said about Emily: "I have come to imagine her as somehow too strong for her environment, a figure of powerful will, not at all frail or breathless."[30]

According to anthropological evidence the typos of bi-erotic marriage has been preserved as a marriage custom in historical documents and is based on an *archetype that is timeless*; bi-erotic marriages were widespread throughout societies in Tibet, China, and the Far East.[31] How old these marriage customs really are cannot be confirmed fully by anthropology, ethnography, or social science. Yet dreams of a collective nature provide us with some clues of its longevity. One of the best surveys of anthropological and ethnographic literature to date is Mircea Eliade's book *Shamanism*.

Eliade tells us that in Japan for instance girls destined for shamanhood often received shamanic instructions from adult shamanesses from the remarkable age of three, to seven years! Often there would be, after the four-year initiation period culminating in a new "birth," a mystical marriage to a tutelary god. This (3-7-year-old stage of development) is a period when a girl-child also has a close connection to her unconscious. Such future female shamans were put through an excruciatingly exhausting, physical ordeal, whereby the girl novice fell to the ground,

---

30 Adrienne Rich, "Vesuvius at Home: The Power of Emily Dickinson," *Parnassus: Poetry in Review*, V, No. 1, p. 51.

31 Eliade, *Shamanism*, p. 463.

in a state of unconscious Ecstasy, rapt in trance. They were then visited by a spirit-husband and became thereby a Spirit-Wife.

The states of mental and physical exhaustion in these rituals led to the novice's initiatory experiences of death and "rebirth," whereby she died and then *married* her tutelary deity, thereafter donning wedding garments. In the Far East, such "spirit-women" were commonly referred to as shamanesses, "Divine Mothers," or "Holy Mothers."[32]

The remarkable thing about Dickinson in this regard is that she followed this same archaic initiatory pattern through her own imaginal processes, processes Eliade described as "spontaneous election," and election (a metaphor Dickinson uses for spiritual marriage is the *White Election*) was based solely on her dreams, visions, and ecstatic experiences. Such visions led Dickinson, like shamans in all world cultures, to soar to vistas of her spiritual vocation, or her *call to shamanhood*, and as well to a conscious androgyny made possible through a bi-erotic channel.

Dickinson's experiences of spontaneous Election were, in my view, the catalyst for her now famous "Master Letters": three letters which didn't emerge until they were released in 1955 for public viewing. (We'll return to the subject of these letters in the chapters that lie ahead.) To follow the idea I am developing about Dickinson's exceptional experience of the syzygy—as bi-erotic: homoerotic[33] and heteroerotic—it doesn't matter who the Master Letters were actually addressed to. What's most important is that we *see* the therapeutic value of the relationship between her Master and the mature Dickinson as protégé-poetess in *transferential terms*. By transferential we mean in Jungian terms the psychology of the transference, which as Freud and Jung agreed, forms the alpha and omega of analysis.

Although the precise dates of the three Master Letters are not known, it has been generally assumed that they were written between 1858 to

---

32 Eliade, *Shamanism*, p. 463.

33 For a discussion on the homoerotic imagination as it applies to the poetry of Whitman, see Herrmann, S. (2007b). "Walt Whitman and the Homo-erotic Imagination," *Jung Journal: Culture and Psyche*, Vol. 1, No. 2, pp. 16-47.

1862, which seems to be consistent with the emotional tone of many of her poems during this time; particularly regarding recurrent themes of the West ("Sundown,") literary greatness, Love, marriage, explosive force, cosmic Consciousness ("New Horizons" of the Universe that were boundless and tremendous), healing ("Balm,") and a death to her puerile ego; accompanied by the losses of significant love-objects on the outside; and to some kind of real imaginary death within herself (i.e., to a death *in* her "Brain,") which suggests not only the temporary loss of her *logos*-function, but a real life-embodied experience.

In the poems and letters we will examine up close, we'll see that she had an extra-ordinary experience of a shamanic dismemberment, followed by the Ecstasy of spiritual marriage, evidenced in her question to her anonymous Master: "What would you do with me if I came 'in White'?"

In some of Dickinson's best poems the marriage symbolism is clothed in conventional Judeo-Christian metaphors, which has led some critics to conjecture that she was merely repeating the "Good News" of the Gospels, but in others she parts with convention altogether to create her own completely *new images* of God. These images, we'll be exploring the meaning of form portraits of instinctive dynamisms patterned on shamanic structures of the objective regions of the collective psyche.

Dickinson takes us beyond traditional interpretations of what it means to be a "Bride of Christ" (sometimes mistaken for the meek and mild historical Jesus spoon-fed to us by fundamentalist interpretations of the King James Bible) to new Cosmic visions of spiritual marriage that are shamanistic at their fiery core and show us how stunningly progressive she truly was in her religious thinking. She writes in one of her gems: "Given in Marriage unto Thee / Oh thou Celestial Host— / Bride of the Father and the Son / Bride of the Holy Ghost" (J 817/F 818).

The Holy Ghost is not a masculine symbol of Jesus. It is, for her, Trinity, yet perhaps especially the Holy Spirit, which is inclusive of the Divine Feminine, the male friend and lover and female friend and lover *combined* a truly bi-erotic union that leads her to experience an anguish and rapture that connect her through death to the life of the very Cosmos, Sun, Moon, Awe and Night, all of which are synonymous in her lexicon with the Beloved.

As a little girl, she tells us she was taught Immortality, which she referred to as her "Flood subject." From that point onward she followed the call of her Snake and other medicine-animals as her spirit-guides. Snake was her tutelary-helper, an animal *power*, and one of her most powerful poems is addressed to him in adoring Fellowship. Medicine powers such as Snake, Butterfly, and especially Hummingbird endowed her with a capacity for cultural *healing*; she transformed language from the very foundations of her shamanistic personality into a genre that can have no imitators because her style is the signature of the "columnar Self," the axis of her art that can never be broken by reductive diagnoses or pathologizing. Her marriage with Christ was to a Cosmic Divinity, transcendent of gender categories, and this is the "simple News" she wishes to convey to her readers:

> This is my letter to the World
> That never wrote to Me—
> The simple News that Nature told—
> With tender Majesty
>
> Her message is committed
> To Hands I cannot see—
> For love of Her—Sweet—countrymen—
> Judge tenderly—of Me.   J 441/F 519

Calling Nature "Her" is also a reference to her own erotic nature, to which she had by this time become married; though in my opinion this was a bi-erotic nature. The inner marriage Dickinson had accepted was to the deep feminine, which is not infrequently realized as bisexual Eros. "News" she has to share with the world is the News of "Nature's God," or the God our founding fathers preserved in the Declaration of Independence. In Dickinson's view, Immortality is everywhere—in trees, woods, sky, moon and sun: "The only News I know / Is Bulletins all Day / From Immortality" (J 827/F 820).

How different Dickinson's tropes are from the King James Bible that she had on her writing desk! Like Whitman and Melville, Dickinson moved beyond Judeo-Christian images of God into an "Undiscovered Continent." "The Bible is an antique Volume—" she wrote wryly, "Written by faded Men" (J 1545/F 1577). The "News" she has to share is shamanistic and aims to put an end to fundamentalist feuding about whose religion is better than whose or what creed or what marriage equality means according to Scripture. Says Emily: "Soto! Explore thyself! / Therein thyself shalt find / The 'Undiscovered Continent'— / No settler had the Mind" (J 832/F 814).

Before white Christian settlers came to North America there was an age-old practice that filled the land and Dickinson tapped into this: the spirit of shamanism. The medicine she dispenses for our benefit and blessing is not traditional; her marriage goes deeper to include the Feminine, the vulva of the flower, and Night. She is Bride of the Holy Spirit that comes after Christ, in preparation for the Age of Aquarius.

Dickinson's spiritual marriage takes the Judeo-Christian dispensation and the teachings of the monotheisms far, far further to include all people in the ritual of betrothal. For the "Other Betrothal shall dissolve—" (J 817/F 818) she asserts. She gives birth to a new symbol of wedlock, which is older than the historical teachings of Moses, Jesus, or the Prophet. She goes beyond these Sons of the Father and the Messenger, to include the News Nature told—of sleeping with her sisters, female friends, and lying down on the grass of her Volcano—Vesuvius—with the Goddess.

What Dickinson is after in her *ecstatic questing* for a theory of truth is to provide a vision of psychological and spiritual transformation for everyone; children included—as she is the only poet whose verse is still commonly read by school children! Her aim is to put forth a new spiritual dispensation, where everyone is valued, as equivalents. Traditional notions of "Wedlock of Will, decay—" she foresees. "Only the Keeper of this Ring" will "Conquer Mortality—" (J 817/F 818). Dickinson's aim is to disseminate "a Theme stubborn as Sublime" (J 1221/F 1210) and that is theme of being spiritually married to God and Goddess, Christ and Cosmos, Sun and Night.

What is the "Ring" Dickinson seeks to bequeath to us? As we shall see the gold of spiritual marriage is bi-erotic, a style of feminine expression that is neither heterosexual nor homosexual. It is inclusive of and transcendent of these psychic opposites, yet it is not the same. I would not even call it bisexual. It is *bi-erotic*, in the sense that it is transcendent of both genders and particular sexual "orientations" as to object choice. Such bi-eroticism does not demand a partner, for it may also serve as a prototype for a celibate nun, or a brother in monastic life, who never marries, and it also subsumes the *union of sames*. About this state of marriage that is open to everyone, she writes: "And now, I am different than before, / As if I breathed superior air— / Or brushed a Royal Gown—" (J 506/F 349).

When Dickinson says "superior" air here, she means she is breathing in an advance of previous notions of marriage, an air of Spiritual Democracy that has always been present on this beautiful planet spinning in space. Here is another example of her suggestive meanings: "The Soul's Superior instants / Occur to Her alone" (J 306/F 630). I think Dickinson felt she was alone because she was at least a century and a half in advance of her times; perhaps she really felt she was a pioneer, because no other woman in her century was bold enough to write a new version of the Bible that could revolutionize Christianity and still maintain her adhesion to its main article of faith while diagnosing it.

The Christ she wedded was not the traditional image of God that was being taught in the Churches. Whitman and Melville were putting forth images of same-sex marriage, but who were the women who were brave enough to do this with a spiritual attitude as robust as theirs? "What this one had to do" writes Adrienne Rich, "was to retranslate her own unorthodox, subversive, sometimes volcanic propensities into a dialect called metaphor: her native language."[34] Dickinson breathed superior air because she had found a new way. "Superiority to Fate" she wrote, "Is difficult to gain / 'Tis not conferred of Any / But possible to earn" (J 1081/F1043). That fate included having in life to remain a spinster (the adult form of being "an orphan" and all alone) and yet to be ever at risk of exposure as an eccentric who was passionately in love with *both* women and men in enduring friendship and loyalty.

---

34 A. Rich, "Vesuvius at Home," p. 51.

Emily Dickinson, who published merely seven poems in her lifetime, one of which was her "Snake," shows that it is only by staying true to one's destiny, one's *vocation*, that the attitude of superiority to fate can be achieved; by refusing to change her style at the hands of male editors who insulted her brilliance, she followed the powerful hand of her destiny. The real irony is that she wrote 1,775 poems, 1,049 letters and 124 prose fragments in her lifetime, and was the only 19th century American poet who was in her own way as powerful as Whitman! How could she have endured her incredible isolation from her national audience, which became so huge after her death that it even surpassed Whitman's in his own lifetime? What gave her the strength and immense power to endure her suffering without much bitterness, resentment, or envy creeping into her poetry? Sure, she felt such fleeting emotions, as we all do at times, but they did not stop her from fulfilling her destiny-pattern as a Medicine Woman.

The idea of superiority to Fate appears in the ancient wisdom-text from China (the *I Ching* or *Book of Changes*) in Hexagram # 11 *T'ai* or "Peace," and we have just seen what Dickinson had to say about it in (J 1081/F1043) from *The Complete Poems of Emily Dickinson*.[35] Under changing line number three, in Hexagram # 11 of the *I Ching*, it is written: "As long as man's inner nature remains stronger and richer than anything offered by external fortune, as long as he [she] remains superior to fate, fortune will not desert him [her]."[36] Dickinson, who represents this attitude, more supremely perhaps, than any other poet writing in America, wrote simply and eloquently that becoming superior to Fate is an attitude that may in fact be *earned* through practical devotion to her spiritual inheritance, which in her case was her Art. It is not conferred on one; it must be earned pragmatically through the only means we have and that is our vocation to *sacred action*: our call to spiritual activity.

Hence, we need to inquire what type of healing follows the emotional distress within herself and her Puritan culture when Dickinson

---

35 Emily Dickinson, *The Complete Poems of Emily Dickinson*.
36 Richard Wilhelm translation rendered into English by Cary F. Baynes, *The I Ching or Book of Changes*, p. 51.

withdrew into seclusion at the age of thirty, all dressed in white, and began to act differently from the majority. What is the psychological meaning of her withdrawal from the world into her dreams, visions, and ecstasies? Her donning of a white wedding dress signifies a *living symbol* of betrothal, I hypothesize, to the spirit of her shamanistic art and it will be my aim, as author of this book and as a marriage and family psychotherapist, to make its meaning translucent for the reader.

2

A WOMAN WHITE TO BE

> A solemn thing—it was—I said—
> A woman—white—to be—
> And wear—if God should count me fit—
> Her blameless mystery—
>
> A hallowed thing—to drop a life
> Into the purple well—
> Too plummetless—that it return—
> Eternity—   J 271/F 307

Like Walt Whitman and Herman Melville, Emily Dickinson is a mediator between the world of the living and the world of the dead during a time in our nation when grief and death was everywhere knocking at democracies hallowed door. "Death," she writes, "is a dialogue between / The Spirit and the Dust. / 'Dissolve' says Death—The Spirit 'Sir / I have another Trust'—" (J 976/F 973). This dialogue of the human spirit with death may be the most important theme in all of Dickinson's art. "A woman—white—to be—" is a symbol for Dickinson's spiritual transformation. The colloquy that emerges does indeed have a goal it can "trust"—*spiritual* marriage, which transcends the inevitable evolution of flesh into dust. We have to inquire in this chapter what the symbol of white meant to Emily. On one hand, it means death to the ego, while on another hand, it might represent death's apotheosis, which is immortality.

What the causal origins of the poet's pre-occupations with death as a path to immortality were, has long been a puzzle to Dickinson scholars.

Even more mysterious is the symbol of whiteness, which can be found at the convergence point of her spiritual center. "Each Life," she writes, "Converges to some Centre— / Expressed—or still— / Exists in every Human Nature / A Goal—" (J 680/F 724).

Convergence towards a center is an idea we find in many parts of the world and in practically all world religions, the center is usually seen as a symbol of the goal of Self-fulfillment.[37] In sacred geometric diagrams from alchemy, this is known as the quintessence of the work, and the center is placed in the middle of a four-cornered square, where diagonals may cross. Dickinson is thus expressing a perennial truth when she claims that the fear of death can be overcome through accepting a vocation to become centered in the course of transforming development, and for her, such acceptance came through a submission to the practice of her art. Her donning of a white wedding dress at some time in 1860, or thereabouts, near the outset of the Civil War, suggests, moreover, that she was in the process of mourning for the many loves that would be lost in the War; as well as for her own personal losses; and her whiteness is an insignia of her function as a poet-shaman who administers the medicine of fearlessness towards an event that is typically terrifying to the ego.

In her center is the sacred marriage to herself that seems to have replaced, or internalized her youthful passion for other women, in gender like herself, whom she found within as her own "society," as well as her passion for a number of different men. Thus, a same-sex union as well as a heterosexual union became the path to an ever-burning bi-erotic spiritual marriage, an outcome that left Dickinson not just a reclusive New England single, but also a true "Bride of Awe"—"Awe" being the appropriate feeling toward such an unexpected, but fully satisfying inner outcome that culminated in *whiteness* as a permanent part of her daily dress.

> Circumference thou Bride of Awe
> Possessing thou shalt be
> Possessed of every hallowed Knight
> That dares covet thee   J 1620/F 1636

---

37 See Endnote F.

By "Circumference," she means the universe. As "Bride" to a new nation dressed in white, she sought to convey pride in a country that concentrated the best intellectual unity of her century in a language that grasped the great phenomena of the infinite universe through a free exercise of thought that saw power and love as the most forceful influences over the destinies of nations. By then Dickinson had married her poetry to her own country of Spiritual Democracy, America, which was no less important to her than it was to her male contemporaries, Whitman and Melville. By "Bride of Awe" she means, therefore, that she has married the entire Cosmos.

Like Whitman and Melville, who more openly chafed at the limitations of his homeland, Dickinson took into account the "higher point of view" of the idea of the Cosmos that was made possible by Alexander von Humboldt in his book *Cosmos: A Sketch of the Physical Description of the Universe*.[38] Humboldt's "rational empiricism" which the New England transcendentalists embraced, concerned "facts registered by science,"[39] but Dickinson took that notion of a cosmic order into the domain of spiritual ideas in an effort to expand the God-concept in Christian theology. She would challenge the traditional notions of faith with the new knowledge of science.

Dickinson's reflections on the unity of the Cosmos pervading the diversity of Creation convey the alchemical idea of the *unus mundus*, one world, that Jung rediscovered in the 20th century for modern psychology. She was without any doubt influenced by Humboldtian science. The language of Humboldt's vision is too close to hers to be merely coincidentally significant. Her "Circumference" being "wider than the Sky" clearly suggests Humboldt's *Cosmos*.

To be sure, Dickinson's vision truly echoes Humboldt: "earnest and solemn thoughts awakened by a communion with nature" and like him, she intuits "a presentiment of the order and harmony pervading the whole universe."[40] This is the vision that informs "A solemn thing—it

---

38 Alexander von Humboldt, *Cosmos: A Sketch of the Physical Description of the Universe*, Vol. 1, pp. 56-57.

39 *CS1*, p. 49.

40 *CS1*, p. 25.

was—I said— / A woman—white—to be—" and of "the size" of her "small" life swelling "like Horizons" in her "vest" (J 271/ F 307). Dickinson means here *horizons of the whole Cosmos.*

Her poetry is a celebration of what Humboldt called "an image of infinity revealed on every side, whether we look upward to the starry vault of heaven, scan the far-stretching plain before us, or seek to trace the dim horizon across the vast expanse of ocean."[41] Her scope of visionary seeing was from the shoulders of Humboldt, who, as we've seen, had scaled Chimborazo. That Dickinson had encountered Humboldt, along with Melville, Emerson and Whitman is more than likely because she names Chimborazo in a poem and had in her library four volumes of the geological works of the Reverend professor and president (from 1845 to 1854) of Amherst College, George Hitchcock, one of Humboldt's main disciples in the United States, and who spoke at Mount Holyoke Female Seminary in the fall of 1847, during Dickinson's first term there.

Dickinson employed the "term *volcanic,* in the widest sense of the word" possible to describe not only every "action of the interior of the planet on its exterior crust" or "surface of our globe," as Humboldt had done,[42] but widened its horizons to include *circles of commotion* that emanate from the very depths of the human psyche, whether in individuals, cities, or nations. Humboldt in *Cosmos* was enabled to transport readers to see everything in the universe as *equivalents.*[43]

Riding on these Humboldtian currents, Dickinson soared to meet her destiny as a Bride of Awe, who dispenses her awareness of Circumference as a World-teacher of "an intimate connection existing among all phenomenon."[44] "Dare you dwell in the *East* where we dwell?" (Dickinson asked one of her female friends, Kate Scott Anthon in a letter from around 1859), "Are you afraid of the Sun?"[45] The Sun was Dickinson's favorite symbol for ecstasy and its rising symbolized the energetic warmth of what Dickinson clearly enough referred to as the joy of consummated marriage: "A Wife—at Daybreak I shall be— /

---

41 *CS1*, p. 25.
42 *CS1*, p. 45.
43 *CS1*, p. 51.
44 *CS1*, p. 50.
45 *L*, II, p. 349.

Sunrise—Hast thou a Flag for me? / At Midnight I am but a Maid, / How short it takes to make it Bride—" (J 461/F 185). We can see how much these two men of science meant to Dickinson in the following poem, but we should keep in mind her own feminine way of integrating their knowledge into her own melodies that contain many insights that transcend science.

> I have never seen "Volcanoes"—
> But, when Travellers tell
> How those old—phlegmatic mountains
> Usually so still—
>
> Bear within—appalling Ordnance,
> Fire, and smoke, and gun,
> Taking Villages for breakfast,
> And appalling Men—
>
> If the stillness is Volcanic
> In the human face
> When upon a pain Titanic
> Features keep their place—   J 175/F 165

The "fire, and smoke, and gun" (an echo of the "right to bear arms" in our second Amendment to the Constitution) could be seen as a working trope in our national discourse in 1860 on the verge of Civil War. Dickinson was fascinated with the volcanic force at the earth's fiery core (J 1705/F 1691). Dickinson loved volcanic metaphors. Everywhere in Humboldt's reflections on volcanoes[46] are his own meditations on the "manifestation of force in the interior of our planet, or the upheaval of strata" that are "manifested in craters."[47] Scattered throughout this 28 page tour de force section on "Volcanoes" in his *Cosmos,* moreover, are numerous reflections on Chimborazo, Vesuvius, Etna, Tenerife, the Andes of Quito, Popocatepetl, the snow-capped Himalaya, and the crowned summits of the Cordilleras, all of which Dickinson mentions in her poetry and letters, and that she is enabled through her knowledge

46 *CS1*, pp. 227-245.
47 *CS1*, p. 226.

of Greek mythology to transform into working metaphors on the meaning of fate and human destiny.

When Dickinson writes in a letter to Higginson: "I had no Monarch in my life, and cannot rule myself, and when I try to organize—my little Force explodes—and leaves me bare and charred,"[48] this is surely an embodied, sexual metaphor for an internal eruption from her emotional core; she is, as a woman poet breaking out as an American literary heroine who is writing powerfully with volcanic force from her own home and her transformed body. She has become a bride of the nation who alights on a still and active volcano that can erupt at any time as an incarnation of Gaia, the Earth Mother, who bears the boiling heat of the Cosmos in her womb.

> Volcanoes be in Sicily
> And South America
> I judge from my Geography—
> Volcanoes nearer here
> A Lava step at a time
> Am I inclined to climb—
> A Crater I may contemplate
> Vesuvius at Home.   J 1705/F 1691

Here, she makes it clear that she finds enough variety in her private world, contemplating the geography of her inner Cosmos' central-most-point, whose eruptions she traced with the same intent as any Humboldtian explorer of the Americas to the origins of all life, which is fire and its blazing *whiteness* at the forge of her poetic vocation. With "No Monarch" to rule her life, this poetically embodied woman was indeed *volcanic.* Yet, to be sure, the source of her inner fire was far more than sexual. It was, at its psychobiological core, *force,* pure and simple: explosive, ecstatic, mythopoetic, emotional. The time of the monarchies of Europe, Russia, and the Middle East had since passed and an age of Spiritual Democracy, ruled by the feminine world soul and able to realize itself in bi-erotic ways, and not simply through masculine conquest of the feminine, or female body, had dawned to the pleasure of Ameri-

---

48 *L*, II, p. 414.

can poets.[49] Yet to the nation that was descending into the madness of the Civil War, her words fell on deaf ears. Writes the Medicine Woman:

> Much Madness is divinest Sense—
> To a discerning Eye—
> Much Sense—the starkest Madness—
> 'Tis the Majority
> In this, as All, prevail—
> Assent—and you are sane—
> Demur—you are straightway dangerous—
> And handled with a Chain—   J 435/F 620

To be sure, Higginson and his wife were amongst the "Majority" of writers, friends, and critics in her century who failed to understand her. Such "Madness" also pertains to Higginson's views of Whitman. In an 1871 essay in the *Atlantic,* Higginson wrote, for instance: "It is no discredit to Walt Whitman that he wrote 'Leaves of Grass,' only that he did not burn it afterwards and reserve himself for something better."[50] This statement's own value lies in the way it exposes the prudishness and shallowness of Higginson's mind. Dickinson herself complained to Higginson in 1866 that one of her most prized poems, "The Snake" (J 986/F 1096), one of only seven published in her relatively short life-time, had been "robbed" of her in the way it had been edited for publication.[51] "Much Madness" was in a way its own "volcano," because it exposed and exploded the lack not only of insight, but of empathy in Higginson's attempts to appreciate her "Snake" amongst other poems.

The "Snake" demonstrates that Dickinson in fact knew her mythology quite well, as is evidenced from her wide reading of Greek myths and poetry. She knew from her geography that Mount Vesuvius was a stratovolcano on the Gulf of Naples that had erupted many times and could easily lift its lid again, with massive hydrothermal pyroclastic flows to engulf the "new city" of Pompeii. In another poem, she had

---

49 The Self of the poet can be seen as an image of the world soul, or what Emily Dickinson called "The Ethiop within" (J 422/F 415). "Ethiop" was a term in common usage in the mid-19th century and had become more or less synonymous with "African."

50 *S*, p. 574.

51 *S*, p. 6.

written, "If some loving Antiquary, / On Resumption Morn, / Will not cry with joy 'Pompeii!'" (J 175/F 165). Settled by the Greeks, Pompeii was long used to the power of Vesuvius' *violence* (one derivation for the word Vesuvius is "hurling violence") that testifies to the unimaginable force of the Cosmos to level entire cities of man in an instant, "Taking Villages for breakfast / And appalling Men—" (J 175/F 165) and this force was portrayed in decorative frescoes in many household shrines as a Serpent.

Thus, the "Snake" she felt had been stolen from under her white wedding dress was one of Dickinson's best symbols for great *shamanic power*. No doubt she had suffered an eruption of authorial outrage at having her poem so conventionally edited. But, there was a spiritual issue as well for the now mature poet-shaman who had burned pure in the fires of her Andean *Whiteness*. To tamper, even a little, with its style or syntax was to insult the sacred and set off an earthquake from the "little Force" of her "Universe," her righteous indignation and Himalayan "Flags of Snow" (J 481) she could evince.

Her "Consciousness that is aware" (J 822/F 817) as an artist of its source as the center and circumference of a Cosmos reacting to human intervention could blow red hot or freezing white cold. Dickinson's fascination with Circumference and being a "Bride of Awe" dressed in white may have its origins in the sense of boundlessness that was conveyed to her as a little girl at the age of 2, when she beheld the spectacle of the Lightning and called it "the *fire.*" As a child, the future poet must have had a passionate nature, furthermore, because her parents wanted her "still." She writes for instance: "They shut me up in Prose— / As when a little Girl / They put me in a Closet— / Because they liked me "still—" (J 613/F 445).

Thus, in "A still—Volcano—Life—" her "Solemn—Torrid—Symbol—" is written in "A quiet—Earthquake Style—" (J 601/F 517). Another verse reads as follows: "I never spoke—unless addressed— / And then, 'twas brief and low— / I could not bear to live—aloud— / The Racket shamed me so—" (J 486/F 473). She speaks further of "A loss of something ever felt I— / The first that I could recollect / Bereft I was—of what I knew not / Too young that any should suspect" (J 959/F 1072). The loss left her an orphan of the Cosmos and a child of the fiery

Abyss. "The reticent volcano keeps / His never slumbering plan— / … Can human nature not survive / Without a listener?" (J 1748/F 1776). To disseminate her "vital Light" of Consciousness to humanity, Dickinson was impelled to write: "I work to drive the awe away, yet awe impels the work."[52]

Awe was Dickinson's parent, for as she said: "We were never intimate Mother and Children while she was our Mother—" and only "when she became our Child, the Affection came—"[53] Despite Dickinson's mother-and-father-wounding in infancy and childhood, she soothed her childhood complexes throughout her art and arrived at the realization of her creative destiny. No wonder that when she was fully mature as a poet, she refused to let any critic, editor, or mentor change her.

> Me, change! Me, alter!
> Then I will, when on the everlasting Hill
> A Smaller Purple grows—
> At sunset, or a lesser glow
> Flickers upon Cordillera—
> At Day's superior close!   J 268/F 281

Seeing Dickinson as an American explorer who was destined to "climb the Hill of Science" (J 3/F 2), I will show how she summons her poetic thunder to release a lightning bolt of shamanic Ecstasy to awaken us from our slumber. If we attune our ears to her sonorous and solemn tones and fill our minds with her "Bolts of Melody" (J 505/F 348), we may be led to understand precisely what she means by spiritual marriage, as a wedding to the *All-in-White*: "Take your Heaven further on— / …An Eternity—put on— / …Dressed to meet You— / See—in White!" (J 388/F 672).

> The Himmaleh was known to stoop
> Unto the Daisy low—
> Transported with Compassion
> That such a Doll should grow
> Where Tent by Tent—Her Universe
> Hung out its Flags of Snow—   J 481/F 460

---

52 *L*, II, p. 500.
53 *L*, III, pp. 754-755.

Dickinson knew her source of power was the volcanic Word, which could be either searing hot or cold-white as snow, and which she felt was needed to ignite a revolution in human consciousness. "Dare you see a Soul *at the White Heat?*" she asks "Then crouch within the door—" (J 365/F 401). Dickinson, like other shaman-poets, sometimes imagined that *sacred violence* had produced her own voice.

> Nor Mountain hinder Me
> Nor Sea—
> Who's Baltic—
> Who's Cordillera?   J 1029/F 1041

As we shall see, Dickinson's preoccupation with death, violence, and metamorphosis (change or transformation symbolized by *whiteness*) was not morbid or pathological in the least. As she wrote to Kate Scott Anthon in 1859: "Insanity to the sane seems so unnecessary—but I am only one, and they are 'four and forty,' which little affair of numbers leaves me impotent…I am pleasantly located in the deep sea."[54] Dickinson saw death as a semblance of the only reality, which is to become immortal like snow-capped mountains: "'Is immortality true?' I believe that it is true—the only reality—almost; a thousand times truer than mortality, which is but a semblance after all."[55] What was the basis for this fascination with immortality, whiteness, and death in the poet's childhood and early adolescence?

As Richard Sewall tells us, Dickinson's mother, Emily Norcross Dickinson, had a "tremulous fear of death" that she could not help convey to her children.[56] Such fears were not uncommon in 1830, when Dickinson was born. Infant mortality was quite high on both sides of the Dickinson family, especially along her maternal line. Yet, the poet's mother appears to have had intense anxieties in the face of death bordering on acute panic.

In 1844, when Emerson was calling for a national bard in his essay "The Poet" and Humboldt's *Cosmos* had just been published in its origi-

---

54 *L*, II, p. 356.
55 *L*, III, p. 731.
56 *S*, 79, p. 80.

nal German, Dickinson was still an adolescent girl, beyond her years at age 14. In this fateful year, she experienced four consecutive deaths in her family that traumatized her youthful and playful psyche and led her to feel deep sorrow on one hand, and a secret gladness over the certainty of immortality on the other. For the third of these deaths was the devastating death of her second cousin, Sophia Holland, who died of typhus, and Dickinson was present, just before the moment of her untimely death. "It seemed to me I should die too," Emily wrote the following year at fifteen, "if I could not be permitted to watch over her or even look at her face." Emily apparently took off her shoes and went to the doorway and peered in as Sophia "lay mild & beautiful as in health & her pale features lit up with an unearthly—smile."[57] Dickinson let herself be led away, but that golden "smile" that lit up on Sophia's face formed an indelible impression on the poet's mind, a memory-imprint that stayed with her, until she herself stepped through the door and became a "Soul at the White Heat."

Dickinson's consolatory letters on the death of little children and the immortality of the soul are quite remarkable; one in particular was sent to her sister-in-law, Susan Gilbert, after the death of Dickinson's little nephew, Thomas Gilbert Dickinson, who lived with her brother Austin and Sue next door, and was affectionately called by them "Gilbert," or little "Gib." This was a horrible death for everyone in the Dickinson family to have *felt*, for the latency-aged boy Gib had just turned eight years old. In 1883 the boy contracted typhoid fever. Emily, who had not been in her brother's and Sue's home for fifteen years, was present at the lad's bedside the terrible night he died. She stayed with him until 3 A.M., began to feel ill, went home and vomited, and was violently ill for weeks. Dickinson wrote to the boy's grieving mother, her dear friend Sue, that little Gib's death had been a triumph, a transcendent and heroic soaring of his spirit into Eternity: "Gilbert rejoiced in Secrets—/ His Life was panting with them.../ No crescent was this Creature— He traveled from the Full— / Such soar, but never set.../ Without a speculation, our little Ajax spans the whole..."[58] Ajax, a mighty warrior in

---

57 Alfred Habegger, *My Wars Are Laid Away in Books: The Life of Emily Dickinson*, p. 172.

58 *L*, III, pp. 800-801.

the *Iliad,* was a figure of great strength and power. But in another letter about Gib, also to Sue, Dickinson uses the gentler, though no less force-ful American metaphor of a spirit boat or spirit canoe, a motif in sha-manic mythologies the world over for the boat of the dead: "Moving in the Dark like Loaded Boats at Night, though there is no Course, there is Boundlessness."[59] Space, Boundlessness, Tremendousness, and Infin-ity are frequent synonyms for Immortality in Dickinson's oeuvre and so too is the "kind" behind the door. As she wrote to her "little children" the Norcross Cousins: "'Tis not that Dying hurts us so—/ 'Tis living—hurts us more—/ But Dying—is a different way—/ A Kind behind the Door—" (J 335/F 528).

Finally, and perhaps most importantly, Dickinson reported in a let-ter to Elizabeth Holland (as if she were a modern-day parapsychologist, investigating end-of-life-experiences!) that Gib's last words were: "open the Door, they are waiting for me." Dickinson then added in her letter: "*Who* were waiting for him, all we possess we would give to know—Anguish at last opened it, and he ran to the little Grave at his Grandpar-ent's feet—All this and more, though *is* there more?" she asked. "More than Love and Death? Then tell me its name!"[60]

In all of these musings we can find what Dickinson called her "main business" as a poet, which was to comprehend the ultimate: "—My Business is Circumference—"[61] As she wrote in another letter to the Norcross cousins: "An earnest letter is or should be life-warrant or death-warrant, for what is each instant but a gun, harmless because 'unloaded,' but that touched 'goes off'?"[62] Thus we are returned to the *violence* of her own intent to rob others of their complacency. "Vesuvius at Home" is the place of *volcanic vocation*, the violence or wildness from which Dickinson wrote. There were probably minor eruptions that came to her in her childhood and latency years, but the major eruption, her "Earthquake Style" and "lips that never lie— / Whose hissing Corals part—and shut— / And Cities—ooze away—" on "this side Naples—"

---

59 *L*, III, p. 801.
60 *L*, III, p. 803.
61 *L*, II, p. 411.
62 *L,* III, p. 670.

(J 601/F 517) is a style she perfected at around the age of thirty, and only came much later to say in 1885, a year before she died:

> Go thy great way!
> The Stars thou meetst
> Are even as Thyself—
> For what are Stars but Asterisks
> To point a human Life?   J 1638/F 1673

Here, Dickinson's goal is clearly in sight: the way of stars led her to her stardom in the integrity of a human life. As we shall see, Dickinson was a master of the technique of shamanic ecstasy. This was her calling, her vocation: to give assurance to the world, through the voice of one who *knows* that we needn't fear death. We would be wise therefore, to take instruction from Dickinson as a mistress of Spiritual Democracy dressed all in white, which as we've seen is a symbol for death and spiritual transformation. At the age of twenty-eight, she wrote "Ah! dainty—dainty Death! Ah! Democratic Death!…Say, is he everywhere? Where shall I hide my things?"[63]

This book shows a *way* through Dickinson's life, relationships, and art that elucidates for students of psychology, theology, literature, and shamanism the basic pattern of the shaman's call, upon which her *destiny* was patterned. What she disseminates to us through her oeuvre is nothing short of a new myth, as "Bride" to a grieving nation, caught in the conflict of Civil War. As she wrote to Higginson: "When much in the Woods as a little Girl, I was told that the Snake would bite me, that I might pick a poisonous flower, or Goblins kidnap me, but I went along and met no one but Angels, who were far shyer of me, than I could be of them, so I hav'nt the confidence in fraud which many exercise."[64] And about publication, Emily said to Higginson, on June 7, 1862, after he told her to delay publishing: "I smile when you suggest that I delay 'to publish'—that being foreign to my thought, as Firmament to Fin—If fame belonged to me, I could not escape her—if she did not, the longest day would pass me on the chase—and the approbation of my Dog, would forsake me—then. My Barefoot Rank is better—You think my

---

63 *L*, II, p. 321.
64 *L*, II, p. 415.

gait 'spasmodic'—I am in danger—Sir—You think me 'uncontrolled'—
I have no Tribunal…The Sailor cannot see the North—but knows the
Needle can—."[65]

What was she talking about here? We have already seen the connection between her barefoot rank and her rebellion against patriarchal
authority. Here, she asserts her authority to this rank *consciously*, for she
has forsaken not only her career to publish by this time; she has ceded
her call to wed, as well. She has given up both careers, and these two
losses have led her to *choose* her own destiny and overcome the fractures
of her fate. Interestingly, these two decisions arose during a moment in
time when she renounced Christianity in its limiting sense altogether:

> I'm ceded—I've stopped being Theirs—
> The name They dropped upon my face
> With water, in the country church
> Is finished using, now,
> And They can put it with my Dolls,
> My childhood, and the string of spools,
> I've finished threading—too—
>
> Baptized, before, without the choice,
> But this time, consciously, of Grace—
> Unto supremest name—
> Called to my Full—the Crescent dropped—
> Existence's whole Arc, filled up,
> With one small Diadem.
>
> My second Rank—too small the first—
> Crowned—Crowing—on my Father's breast—
> A half unconscious Queen—
> But this time—Adequate—Erect,
> With Will to choose, or to reject,
> And I choose, just a Crown—   J 508/F 353

Dickinson had stopped going to Church by this time, so this poem
is obviously not about conventional baptism or confirmation, Christian
rites she no longer found meaning in at all; this poem is about, therefore,

---

65 *L,* II, pp. 408-409.

her experience of being "twice-born" as an American bard. Yet, I believe she means this in an entirely new sense, one that may not be found in the Hebrew-Christian Bible. That new status she calls "Adequate" is superordinate to that from which she has been "ceded." Her new "Second Rank" is the Birth of the Self, in herself, and by way of her vocation in the world soul of humankind. Aware of herself now and this time "Erect," she is "Called" to her "Full" to embody not just the crescent of her existence, but "Existence's whole Arc, filed up, / With one small Diadem." Her second rank is therefore the shaman-poets' *exuberance* at the transformative powers of her art. She has consciously chosen "just a Crown—" and her "Crowing" as a "half unconscious Queen—" leads to her great pride in herself, for she has solved the riddle of her life in time, which is to attain the diamond body. "Crowing" on her "Father's breast—," with "Will to choose, or reject" whatever title she may bestow she has married God and the Goddess, "Her sweet Weight on my Heart a Night" (J 518/F 611).

These poems find their spiritual orientation well beyond the dogma of traditional Christianity and chart a new way ahead to comprehend the transformations and symbols of her creative energies as an artist. But there are also many Christian roots, of the more arcane sort, such as in "Nicodemus'" central "Mystery" (J 140/F 90) of rebirth: "But how shall finished Creatures / A function fresh obtain? / Old Nicodemus' Phantom / Confronting us again!" (J 1274/F 1218). The mystery of Nicodemus was the question of how a man can enter into his mother's womb a second time and be born, to which Christ answered only via water and spirit can such a second birth be fully realized. In "I'm ceded" Dickinson uses a political trope ("ceded") to cast doubt on the conventional notion of the only way to the new Jerusalem being strictly through a symbolic rebirth through the mother's body, to include a rebirth in imagination on her father's breast, and to assume thereby a marriage "Crown" that encompass' a fuller bi-erotic "whole" that includes All. Thus, her "Barefoot Rank" that she proclaims to Higginson, himself a minister, was an act of "Crowing" and Crowning that signaled her acceptance of her own authority as a sovereign poet whose style was not to be tampered with. "A Woman White to Be" in fact *is* what she became for herself, her family and friends, and for the world: a mediator between life, death, and a pointer to the way of spiritual transformation.

3

FATE AND DESTINY

Fate and destiny are notions that have appeared across the centuries in the myths and philosophies of all nations. Arthur Schopenhauer dignified them for philosophy, and they are central to the practice of psychotherapy today. For instance, each time a patient struggles with something that keeps happening, transformation takes place when she or he can learn from that experience and *take charge* of what becomes of her or his life. In so doing, such a patient's fate can indeed be transformed. One does not typically think of these variables—fate and destiny—as pressing issues for Emily Dickinson; however, as we've seen, she was a poet who overcame her second-class status as a single woman to achieve total independence and liberty as a writer, while still suffering the stigma of unmarried life in her father's house in Amherst.

Emily is sometimes claimed as an ancestor of modern-day feminists because she embraced the American spirit of personal *empowerment* as a woman at around the same time of the first feminist gathering in the United States at Seneca Falls in 1848. In her own time, Dickinson had little choice but to accept the way of financial dependence upon her family, but she learned to claim her freedom in the widest sense possible through her poetry.

Powerful, fierce, and transformative, she speaks for herself as someone who not only surpassed her father Edward and brother Austin in intellectual prowess, but mocks her own status in the family from a place of supreme dignity. She wrote ironically, we saw in "I'm ceded," that she crowed proudly on her father's breast. Similarly, she never surrendered in any relationship to a man that might have forced her to relinquish the sovereign power of her Wife's Voice, even though she fell in love with more than one man in her lifetime.

Even more telling, she never sacrificed her bi-erotic vision of loving both men and women passionately, which suggests that she loved both sexes *equally*. As we'll see, her psyche became victorious over fate, through the invincibility of the relatedness and compassion she brought to her art.

Nevertheless, she was a woman of her times, and it is obvious that in the domain of marriage, Dickinson failed to fulfill her heart's desire. She suffered the stings of the arrows of love that is the fate of many humans, whether married or unmarried, on a material plane; yet, on a spiritual plane, she was free, and transcendent. The Christian Church was all-powerful in her immediate community and at times she turned to "Jesus Christ of Nazareth" for inspiration and love. But her image of Jesus is not the traditional view of the historical man who walked the streets of Galilee. It is far deeper and far higher; deep as the fiery crust of the earth and vast as the sky. "At least—to pray—is left—is left— / Oh Jesus—in the Air— / I know not which thy chamber is— / I'm knocking—everywhere—/ Thou settest Earthquake in the South— / And Maelstrom, in the Sea— / Say, Jesus Christ of Nazareth— / Hast thou no Arm for Me?" (J 502/F 377).

She imagines wedlock with Christ during moments of her deepest anguish. Yet her truest lover was not, however, this immediate Divinity, but the entire Cosmos, a realm beyond names and forms that is not limited to male or female avatars of its supreme and unnamable magnificence.

In this way, she was able to change her fate as an unmarried woman to a destiny that enabled her to speak up for all humans. Accepting that she had been called to be a different kind of woman from other women in her generation, she took her charge to vocalize the "simple News" of Nature, news of the immortality of the whole Universe:

> This is my letter to the World
> That never wrote to Me—
> The simple News that Nature told—
> With tender Majesty   J 441/F 519

Such overcoming of fate by someone with an unmarried and unpublished life, through the inner good fortune to know about God through His writings in Nature, is as much a Greek idea, as any other. It's part of the perennial philosophy that became in the 19ᵗʰ century an American prerogative to call upon. Walt Whitman called it Religious Democracy. Dickinson needed many people around her, young and old, male and female to inspire her.[66] As a writer of poetry and letters, Dickinson arrived at a linguistic method whereby she could hold the opposites between fate and destiny in a beautiful way and what she learns from her relationships she dispenses to us in her writings for purposes of our own personal and cultural transformation.

Let us begin to tease out some of the shades of meaning Dickinson herself formed between these two concepts—fate and destiny—by looking first at a few of her poems and then at some of her letters.

> Superiority to Fate
> Is difficult to gain
> 'Tis not conferred of Any
> But possible to earn
>
> A pittance at a time
> Until to Her surprise
> The Soul with strict economy
> Subsist till Paradise.   J 1081/F1043

The way I read this poem is that the Soul, which can obviously become bogged down and depressed by bad fortune in love (its fate) may, with surprise, embrace the good luck of having been given a chance to look inward to the immense richness that inheres in *emotional experience itself.*

In fact, the dimension of the American Soul Dickinson enters into is so rich with gold and gems, inner light and love, that she can register an abundance of spiritual energy that is released simply by affirming the validity of her inner world and its royal unity, even when outer fulfillment has denied her, materially in matrimony. Becoming a poet *is* her

---

66 See Endnote G.

solution, and it allows her a full and richly satisfying inner life and a meaningful life in social and familial friendships.

On the other hand, even a destiny as grand as the one Dickinson envisioned to herself cannot ever erase the fate that occasioned it. The Fates are great teachers! There were three major blows of fate in Dickinson's life that we'll take a close look at in some detail in this chapter: 1) All of the men she fell in love with either died abruptly, or were married, meaning her dreams for marriage were forever frustrated in her lifetime by a perpetual "no" from the universe. 2) Only seven of her poems were published before her untimely death in 1886. 3) Some of her loves were almost certainly directed toward members of her own gender at a time when this was strictly taboo. Such outer frustrations were all transcended by Dickinson in her art, where she claimed the spiritual freedom and liberty that enabled her to embrace the men and women she needed, and give voice to the *secret of her fame.*

What she previously had experienced as a "pittance" of superiority could thus become a true spiritual "gain" from the Self through her writing. Her Soul could then distribute such "earned" superiority having achieved oneness across the many categories of her life. This abundance of opportunity for spiritual realization and Awe was not conferred by anyone on the outside, but was a genuine triumph over fate. The destiny she earned she could declare, along with her male contemporaries, Emerson, Whitman, and Melville, as an assertion of the independence of the American Self. Superiority to Fate is the introvert's embrace of spiritual independence. It is an intoxicant, as in "I taste a liquor never brewed" (J 214) as well as a psychological attitude towards personal suffering. She delights in Ecstasy in a way that indicates she knows about inflation even better than Whitman or Melville do. She is the most psychologically Self-aware of these three.

How did such a transformation of her fate to be so different than her contemporaries come about in Emily Dickinson's lifetime so that she could accept her *destiny* as a shamanic post-Christian American poet—any of which terms would have done many another New England woman in?

To answer this question, it is important to grasp the religious background she was born into. Dickinson's ancestors were fervent Puritans, who had shared in the dreams of a New Jerusalem in New England. Emily's first new world ancestor, Nathaniel Dickinson, had crossed the Atlantic in 1630 with no less a figure than John Winthrop during the Great Migration. This paternal ancestor became the governor of the Massachusetts Bay Colony, just as Dickinson would one day govern the commonwealth of her own Soul.

Emily's paternal grandfather, Samuel Fowler Dickinson, had graduated from Dartmouth and built Amherst's first brick house in 1813, and undoubtedly it was he who played the greatest influence on her sense of the importance of developing a spiritual identity as the happiest prerogative of being an American. Following teachings in vogue at Yale University, where Emily's father would go to college, Samuel had become a Trinitarian deacon of the West Church of Amherst. Trinitarian thought followed the theology of the 18th century Puritan pastor, Jonathan Edwards, the most important Christian intellectual of the American colonies, and Samuel Dickinson took it as his main task to promote this uniquely American brand of religious education at Amherst Academy, where Emily later attended elementary and middle school. Samuel Dickinson was also one of the founding fathers of Amherst College, a more doctrinaire school that defined itself, along with Yale, Williams, and Dartmouth, as resolutely Trinitarian, eschewing the schisms that had formed with the arrival of the liberal Bostonian Unitarians at Harvard. (This latter group would claim Emerson and Edward Everett Hale in the course of the 19th century).

From family documents, it is crystal clear that Samuel Fowler Dickinson was not a reformer, as Jonathan Edwards had been. His granddaughter, Emily, would become in time and in a real spiritual sense, in her own private way, anything but a religious zealot. Nevertheless, his love of education at Amherst extended across many branches of knowledge: history, philosophy, literature, languages, mathematics, art, sciences, etc. Having a broad educational base in his day was seen by university administrators as a way of consolidating institutional power, which corresponded to the dawn of the modern attitude in Europe following the defeat of Napoleon in 1815, to effect biblical doctrine and thus to quell any doubts about the need to believe rather literally in Jesus Christ. For Samuel Dickinson, this meant He was Father, Son, and Holy Ghost in one Trinitarian dogma, not needing any new "fourth" identity of the divine feminine to be able to redeem mankind. As a woman, Emily would offer *herself as that fourth*, saying "I do not respect 'doctrines,'" something that would have been inconceivable for Samuel. The only question for him was which creed would play the leading role in defining the direction of religious life in the young nation, and he was determined to make it Trinitarianism, a dogma from which Emily ceded.

Emily Dickinson's father, Edward Dickinson, however, hardly dared dissent. He graduated from Trinitarian Yale with a law degree and returning to his childhood home in Amherst, opened a law office. In 1835 he became treasurer of Amherst College, where he carried on the community tradition of his father, with the important exception that he never proselytized for the Trinitarian Church to which he belonged. This was an important and great affirmation of all American's right to choose rather than be dictated to where religion is concerned. Spreading the Word of Scripture, in a nation that sixty years earlier had proclaimed in its political documents that no image of God save "Nature's God" would be established in its Declaration, was a typical American contradiction. It was one Edward Dickinson certainly recognized and that Emily would in turn defy, by defining her own quite different spiritual standpoint in a courageously outspoken way within her poetry. This is not unrelated to the other contradiction that so undermined the United States pretension to being a land where "all men are created equal"— slavery! That plague had yet to be eradicated by the insistence on racial equality that Lincoln underscored, but it is out of a similar struggle for real *democratic spiritual freedom,* among other things for women, that Dickinson found her true calling.

Dickinson's ability to chart out a path for both feminine and shamanic spirituality as a route to *true* spiritual freedom did not emerge in the same moment as the Civil War by accident. It was part of what Whitman recognized and celebrated in Lincoln in 1865, the need to keep on struggling in the American nation for political and legal rights for *all* people.

Fortunately for Emily, who was five years old at the time her father Edward became treasurer of Amherst College, in 1835, Edward did not share in *his* father Samuel Fowler Dickinson's messianic mission to convert all heathens to Christianity, and all Christians to a more truly Trinitarian Christianity. Rather, Edward thought that schools like Amherst, on the model of Yale and Harvard, should advance the American value of the Freedom of Religion.

Emily, therefore, was free to introduce a feminine fourth, a way to wholeness, into the masculine trinity and open up Christianity to a radically altered shamanistic version of faith that could include both sexuality and a *feeling* for the dead, the very values Freud and Jung were able to advance for the 20th century. She was really I believe that far ahead of her times.

At Amherst, Edward maintained a questioning attitude towards his father's faith. This questioning of theological values was taken up by his independent daughter, Emily, who like Whitman, refused to succumb to the all-too-frequent American fate of being swept up, unthinkingly, into a religious movement, whether Trinitarian, Calvinist, Methodist, Mormon, or Unitarian.

What Emily felt called to do in her lifetime was much more than to bridge the polarities of Unitarians and Trinitarians, in her own way. Rather, her ambition was more truly transcendent than that. She would not allow her Soul to become simply a convert to ecstatic Christianity. Instead, she attempted in her poetry a genuine marriage of spirituality and science. North America, to her mind, was a nation where ecstasy could function to unlock the secrets of Nature itself, and she as its prophet, a "Bride" not of Christ, but of the Universe. Her "God" would therefore never fully be named. Emily Dickinson became perhaps the first poet to be completely free of all historical God-images in an age where, as William James would later write, "'Science' in many minds is genuinely taking the place of a religion."[67]

> A great Hope fell
> You heard no noise
> The Ruin was within

---

67 William James, *William James: Writings 1902-1910*, p. 58.

Oh cunning wreck that told no tale
And let no Witness in   J 1123/F 1187

But before she could write this, she needed to get a good lesson in science and natural theology that was not hard for her to come by. While she was at Mount Holyoke Female Seminary there was someone at nearby Amherst College to give her a head start in this endeavor. This was the professor of natural theology there who became the first president of the new College: Edward Hitchcock. Hitchcock was as convinced about the finality of Christianity as Emily's grandfather, Samuel Fowler, had been. But he was far less dogmatic than Emily's grandfather. Hitchcock, to be sure, was like many Americans of that time a proselytizer, but his vision extended to the Cosmos as Humboldt had defined it for his generation.

Hitchcock founded the American Association of Geologists in 1840 and served as its first president; it is important to add that he was internationally active in discussing Humboldt's spiritually relevant scientific vision, whose influence was felt widely in the United States and Europe. Hitchcock had a direct influence, moreover, on the head teacher at Mount Holyoke, Mary Lyon, who was Hitchcock's especial protégé.

Miss Lyon's main mission in education and life in her New England circle was to make young women at Holyoke Seminary into "Brides of Christ." Her goal to save Emily Dickinson's soul would be resisted by "inner voices" of Emily's *destiny*, however. Emily's aim would be, like Whitman's, to transform religious institutional understandings into a personal relation to the boundless Universe.

Following the "Great Awakening," the religious revival that had been ushered in by Jonathan Edwards' teachings at Yale, a new science of religion had emerged as an "Argument from Design," bridging Christianity and Deism, i.e., the structure of God's world revealed by scientists like Newton and Humboldt. An 1802 work by William Paley, *Natural Theology*, which Emily avidly read at Mount Holyoke, laid out the implications.

Edwardsianism looked to the natural world for practical evidence of the resurrection of the soul. Coincident with this "Argument from

Design," Alexander von Humboldt found studying languages and cultures of indigenous tribes in Central and South America and Mexico a clearly spiritual pattern that was not incompatible with Christianity and in fact explained why the Spanish had so little difficulty converting the indigenous people to Catholicism. In other words, people are naturally theological.

Natural Theology was a subject that was dear to Edward Hitchcock. For Hitchcock and his colleagues at Amherst College the world and its secret "Design" could only be revealed to a person through perceptions of a "golden link" that exists throughout all Nature, and this ability to perceive God's great chain of being was something he felt called to proclaim as a theologian and teacher.

Natural theology appealed to Emily Dickinson because of its respect for the *aesthetic properties of Mother Nature*, which form the pattern of integrity and it elegies that so evidently exist throughout the universe for anyone with an eye or ear for beauty to attest. According to Hitchcock, this "Design" pattern could only be seen through an acquired grace, via the Christian faith, whereas for Emily, with her nature-aesthetic attitude, all one had to do to behold the miracle of God's glory was to glance at one's own garden, with its ever-transforming wondrous plants shimmering with verdant power. (It should be said that a New England garden was particularly suitable to such an interpretation, since the seasons are so sharply defined in that part of the world).

The spiritual fact of rebirth, metamorphosis, and ultimately resurrection of the soul after death, could then be made manifest as in a garden's plants through certain emblems, signs, or analogies, which could be detected once one had a Christian *aesthetic conscience* to perceive them.

It was Dickinson's task to make such alchemy transparent. One of her favorite symbols was Hitchcock's preferred metaphor for change: the caterpillar's metamorphosis into a butterfly. (We will take a close look later at some of her most beautiful poems about Butterflies.) In this miracle of metamorphosis, obvious to any garden keepers, the butterflies morph into a winged creature of air, and they became one of Emily Dickinson's most beloved emblems for spiritual transformation, to which she returns frequently in her art. The ability of the emerging butterfly to shed its cocoon and fly to its instinctively perceived sign stimulus—the flower—and migrate on wings of air over vast distances became the basis of her heartfelt confidence in her transcendence, assurance that her poetry could soar above the indifference to it of her contemporaries.

Dickinson imbibed Humboldt's cosmic vision directly from Hitchcock's teachings. She appears to have heard his remarkable 1848 lecture on the Book of Revelations at Amherst College on two consecutive occasions.[68] It was not long after Emily began her first semester at Mount Holyoke, in the fall of 1847 and just before her eighteenth birthday, that Edward Hitchcock gave the first of these, his famous sermon on Revelations 21, which was to become Dickinson's chosen chapter in the whole King James Version of the Bible.

Emily was present at this seminal sermon's delivery and it was one of those special moments in her lifetime. Hitchcock spoke of the building of the great city of pure gold (Revelation 21: 18) in a way that touched Dickinson directly. "I love this Seminary & all the teachers," Dickinson wrote to Abiah Root in Amherst at the age of eighteen.[69] Later, she wrote, before her final semester ended: "I have not yet given up the claims of Christ." She refers to this claim further as "my fate":

> I tremble when I think how soon the weeks and days of this term will all have been spent, and my fate will be sealed, perhaps. I have neglected the *one thing needful* when all were obtaining it, and I may never, never again pass through such a season as was granted us last winter. Abiah, you may be surprised to hear me speak as I do, knowing that I express no interest in the all-important subject, but I am not happy, and I regret that last term, when that golden opportunity was mine, that I did not give up and become a Christian. It is not now too late, so my friends tell me, so my offended conscience whispers, but it is hard for me to give up the world.[70]

---

68 Cynthia G. Wolff, *Emily Dickinson*, p. 560.
69 *L,* I, p. 59.
70 *L,* I, p. 67.

With this whispering of her *Nature-worshiping conscience*, Emily's fate was sealed. Hers was a spiritual vision that included not only good, but evil also, since both were evident in the operations of nature. She could never accept the Trinitarian point of view without her own metamorphosis of it into something entirely new, in effect adding to it a *fourth*, transcendently transformative element, the eternal femininity of Nature. If change in the masculine religious notions of her day was to happen in her culture, a woman was needed to lead America towards a more egalitarian vista. A feminine conscience would have to triumph, become victorious over fate. This was the way past convention that James Madison said was so necessary to democracy in the generation just prior to Dickinson's.[71]

When the storm of the Great Revival was blowing its religious fervor through Amherst, Emily Dickinson was somewhat differently stirred than most of her contemporaries. She knew that to completely realize the proffered redemption she had to accept the fall as well as the Savior from the proffering. This meant she had to heed not just the call of Christ, but that of the Serpent in the garden as well: her "Snake" would be the eventual result.

At first, she began to write poems in secret and to pronounce faithful syllables that were not merely "good." Her aim was to uncover a Design-pattern, not of the Bible, but from the depths of Mother Nature. (One wonders why her father Edward decided to withdraw Emily from the Mount Holyoke Female Seminary?)

She had already realized, by the time she was twenty, that it was *her destiny* to allow the Satanic voice inside her consciousness to be heard by others as well. It too, she saw, was part of God's kingdom, part of the "vivid ore" of the soul to be refined by a post-Christian alchemy.

---

71 James Madison argued persuasively that "the civil rights of none shall be abridged on account of religious belief, nor shall any national religion be established, nor shall the full and equal rights of conscience in any manner be infringed." Madison might best be described as a Deist, for he could defend the Constitutional government by appealing to its progenitor as "God," who he described as "the supreme lawgiver of the universe." Derek H. Davis, *Religion and the Continental Congress 1774-1776*, p. 208.

Dickinson appears to have begun to realize the loneliness of her spiritual position when she wrote to her dear friend, Jane Humphrey, from Mount Holyoke, on April 3, 1848: "Christ is calling everyone here, all my companions have answered, even my darling Vinnie believes she loves, and trusts him, and I am standing alone in rebellion, and growing very careless."[72] This seeming reluctance was on account of the chthonic and feminine aspects of herself she could not simply suppress. The so-called evil in herself was equivalent to a goodness that she was called to embrace to fully become herself.

At first, of course, Emily saw herself merely as one of the unconvinced ones who had remained unconverted by Hitchcock's disciple, Mary Lyon. She wrote similarly, to her closest friend Abiah Root about her resistance to accepting the hand of the "Bridegroom" wooing her and all the young girls at Holyoke as a Suitor, to eternally Wed Him: "*I* am one of the lingering *bad* ones, and so *I* slink away, and pause, and ponder…and do work without knowing why—not surely for *this* brief world, and more sure it is not for Heaven—and I ask what this message *means* that they ask for so eagerly…will you *try* to tell me about it?"[73]

But there was more to her fallen state than any rude refusal of redemption here. It is clear from this letter that what Emily was pondering at this pivotal time in history was the *meaning* of spiritual marriage as a phenomenon of great significance in the evolution of humanity, outside the limited horizons of the Christian message of betrothal to a Lord of Heaven and His Kingdom and Glory. What she would cherish most was His, or Her invincible *Power*.

Hitchcock had already given Emily a key to solve the mystery of a wedding outside the conventional sense, when he brought together Revelations 21 and Emily's beloved geology in a single sermon, which she pondered over deeply. She was already imagining herself as a destined new "Bride" for the nation.

In a phenomenological way, the vocation she saw assigned to herself in this role involved exploration, experimentation, and experience. She was being called to do work not for this transitory world alone, but

---

72 *L*, I, p. 94.
73 *L*, I, p. 98.

also for the spiritual world of the dead and for eternity, a shamanic task requiring a mythopoetic journey into Night.

In May of 1848, at a time of rebellion in Europe, she felt her own American spirit of rebellion surface. Her fierce libertarianism became stronger than ever and her rampart in the Self became indomitable, impenetrable to the droves of "obedient" girls, like those around her flocking to Mary Lyon as sheep to their Shepherd.

As the "Bridegroom" continued to try and woo her, she did not relent and chose instead the path of one of the very few disobedient "bad" ones. In this sense, she became a rebel for *Liberty*, a poetess of democracy, who listens to the voice of evil, as well as good, in order to realize the fullest freedoms of the soul: "I have come '*to* and *fro,* and walking up and down' the same place that Satan hailed from, where God asked him where he'd been, but not to illustrate further I tell you [Abiah] I have been dreaming, dreaming, a *golden* dream, with eyes all the while wide open."[74]

In the fall of 1847, Emily, we've seen, had twice heard Hitchcock's famous sermon on Revelations 21, which describes the New Jerusalem as a city of pure gold, implying the alchemical process required to get there. This is also the chapter of the Christian Bible, which so directly spoke to C.G. Jung a century later, as he records near the end of his masterwork, *Answer to Job.* This vision of Heaven could no longer be contained by the conventional image she had heard her parents incant as a child, "Our Father who art in Heaven." Dickinson's "Zenith" included an image of Night, which she refers to tenderly as Her, with a capital H; a lover few if any spiritual patriarchies have ever tolerated.

In the actual America of Dickinson's dawning maturity, on January 24, 1848 gold had been discovered by John W. Marshall, a foreman working for Sacramento pioneer John Sutter, at Sutter's Mill in Coloma, California. By March of 1848, newspaper publisher Samuel Brannan had announced in the streets of San Francisco: "Gold! Gold! Gold from the American River!"

Dickinson is sure to have heard the newspaper shout from across the continent at Mount Holyoke. So, when she said to Abiah Root that

---

74 *L,* I, p. 99.

she'd been "dreaming, dreaming, a *golden* dream, with eyes all the while wide open," she meant what she said. Her eyes had been opened by the simultaneous co-discovery of gold in the Far West. Among the three leading East Coast poet-shamans, Whitman, Melville, and Dickinson, I would say Dickinson was the one who took the notion of a new alchemy most geologically, as Humboldt and Hitchcock would have wanted. Like Humboldt, she went West in imagination to find the furthest degree of development of spiritual ideas grounded in the majesty and mystery of what lay hidden in the earth. Where Whitman and Melville had also relied on the voice of Satan to compensate the sanitized images of God, Dickinson summoned the Goddess in so vivifying a way that her new Suitor had become as often a woman as a man. Satan had indeed tempted her to find her own "power" and pride two months before the first women rights meeting at Seneca Falls Convention in July 1848. From the beginning of her realization of her poetic vocation she was a ferocious fighter for Liberty. This is the same year, furthermore, that Lucretia Mott, a Quaker famous for her oratorical ability, was gathering her notes together for her speech at the historical Seneca Falls Convention.

Of the scant *seven* of Dickinson's poems that were published in her lifetime, her sixth, "The Snake," shows her embracing her destiny as feminist in whom the satanic voice was not demonized but equalized as a part of nature. Once "A narrow Fellow in the Grass" (J 986/F 1096) was released for publication in the press, her instinctive protection of it in the name of the Goddess Liberty became immediately self-evident. Dickinson's biographers, scholars and literary critics refer to "The Snake" often as the single verse she agonized over the longest. She also complained about it loudest after her sister-in-law, Susan Gilbert, published it with the help of their mutual friend Samuel Bowles, on the front page of the journal he edited: the *Springfield Republican.* The poem went into print on February 14, 1866,[75] which ironically was Valentine's Day!

Dickinson seems to have been in love with Bowles, despite the fact that he was a happily married man. He has sometimes been considered to be one of the two most likely candidates of her mysterious "Master Letters." With altered punctuation and the integrity of her lines seri-

---

75 *S*, p. 6.

ously compromised by the editor, however, Emily rebelled. This is the same year she wrote poem (J 1081/F 1043), "Superiority to Fate," which suggests that her attitude at this time was quite oppositional and defiant. What could not be edited out of her oeuvre was her determination to let evil, the Serpent, her "Snake," and Mother Nature have their place in her evolution as a writer and in *her* garden.

About Bowles' intrusions on "Snake's" unique design, Dickinson complained in March of 1866 to Thomas Wentworth Higginson. Higginson, a radical Abolitionist had taken command of a black regiment in South Carolina in the fall of 1862. He was a Unitarian minister to whom she had turned to for help in getting her poetry published when their correspondence began. One letter to him, after "Snake" had been published in the *Springfield Republican* magazine, begins: "Lest you meet my Snake and suppose I deceive it was robbed of me—defeated too of the third line by the punctuation. The third and fourth were one—I had told you I did not print—I feared you might think me ostensible."[76]

What Dickinson means in this rather oblique communication of her distress by the third and fourth lines being one is that she was entirely in earnest in the way she wrote and punctuated the original poem. The rhythmic pattern she had released in that way was for her *part of the poems elegiac integrity*. (And she thought he could read that intent even though the poem was terribly bowdlerized). In the poem, the One God of the Deists is referred to simply as "Nature's God," confirming Dickinson's belief that her democratic American notion of the Divine was to be found in the natural setting of a still unfolding Cosmos. "The Snake," written at the pinnacle of her art, at the age of thirty-five, made its entry into published literature at the same time as its author's entrance into midlife. This was a time of transvaluation of values. The poem was published at the very end of the Civil War, 1865, and its spirit of Liberty from previous conceptions accords with its time. But its science transcends its time, which was already Darwinian in outlook. Dickinson's cosmology was first and foremost a Humboldtian one. As we've seen, Humboldt's vision in *Cosmos* had been transmitted directly to Dickinson via Hitchcock's geology.

---

76 *L*, II, p. 450.

Like a poetic American revolutionary, Dickinson felt called to lead her country out of sectarianism to full democratic freedom from old patriarchies. She may have been the so-called "weaker" sex, but she did not have a weaker Voice for that. It was filled with authentic *Power*. In another letter to Higginson, she wrote famously: "[W]hen I try to organize—my little Force explodes."[77] By "little Force" she means both soul-force and spiritual power as a woman. In "I'm Czar—I'm 'Woman' now—" (J 199/F 225) she claims her rights as a woman to be with a capital W, a person whose animus is equal to that of any Russian King, whether Peter, or an Ivan. She can match them all.

Inequality of women is a fate she endured quietly in her person but triumphed over in her art, which speaks to men and women and the anima in men in a completely democratic way. Her wrestling with masculine authority is not merely a displacement of her own frustrations with men around her, but also with their sexist notions of Divinity. Dickinson's God is not "Our Father," but the "Yourself" in everyone across all nations and continents. Dickinson's art is addressed to the society of the Soul within (J 746/F 783), which is a "Columnar Self" (J 789/F 740), an "Undiscovered Continent" (J 832/F 814), an "indescribable estate," an "undiscovered Gold," an "ecstatic Nation" (J 1351/F 1359), etc. With the word "Nation" she appropriates American nationalism, as well as the budding nationalism of countries like Italy and Germany, to speak to the spirit that she knows can light up the country of the Self in all of us.

No less than Jung's, hers is a spiritual call to individuation, what Jung called "the Christification of the many." She speaks, in Christian terms of the "Impregnable Light" inside all "Human" souls (J 1351/F 1359), which is a celestial metaphor too. In her poem "'Arcturus' is his other name—" she says further: "What once was 'Heaven' / Is '*Zenith*' now—" and "Perhaps the 'Kingdom of Heaven's' changed—" (J 70/F 117), by which she means that the image of the "Father" in the skies, inscribed in the Hebrew-Christian Bible has now been replaced by the Humboldtian notion of Cosmos.

---

77 *L*, I, p. 271.

Wherever we are on the planet, then, all we have to do is look upward towards the Zenith—that, to her mind, is our new "God." For Dickinson, the new Church is simply "Home": "Where Thou art—that—is Home— / Cashmere—or Calvary—the same" (J 725/F 749).

This post-Christian myth of Dickinson's is all-encompassing, so that its essential democracy is transmitted transnationally across many of the world religions. In a single poem (J 725/F 749) she takes on the patriarchal Judeo-Christian-Islamic monotheistic God-notion and includes the big three in a fourth revelation of a theory of truth that includes Hinduism; and by embodying Hestia, Goddess of the hearth, she includes the Greco-Roman religions as well. "I scarce esteem Location's Name—" she says, "So I may Come—" (J 725/F 749). "Faith," she says moreover, is "a Revolution / In Locality" (J 972/F 839). Thus, regardless of the "Location's Name" and in whatever nation of the world the reader might be, the Self is forever present and can be accessed within and worshipped everywhere in Nature. Whether found in "Cashmere" or "Calvary" the "Thou" that appears as a local Divinity is always "the same" or is at least *equal* in degree of transforming power, since all religions are manifestations of an evolving Cosmos welcoming individuals into its developmental pattern.

Zeroing in on a "Locality" in the world that has been rife with religious wars in human history between Hindus and Muslims ("Cashmere"), she says that they are the "same" so that she can "Come" as a promoter of Liberty. The British pacified "Cashmere" in 1846 and installed a Hindu dynasty there when Emily was sixteen. So this fact makes it all the more relevant to the time in which she was living. Moreover, "Calvary" is not just Jesus' site of crucifixion in the poem; it is also our "Home." Similarly, "Cashmere" is not only a historical region in Northwest India and Northeast Pakistan conquered by Muslims in the 14th century, which became part of the Mogul empire after 1587, but a fact that Dickinson is sure to have been aware of through her study of world history, and it too is an equivalent metaphor for "Home." So, wherever one is, that is our place of spiritual victory over the fate of dogmatic religions. That is "Home."

More, in a poem about the "reeling Oriole" that frequently visited her garden in Amherst, she says of him that he is "One of the ones that Midas touched" with gold and she then paints him with a broad international brush as "An Ecstasy in chief—" as "The Jesuit of Orchards," "The splendor of Burmah" and as "Jason" on a quest for the "Golden Fleece." "But then" she adds simply: "I am a rural man / With thoughts that make for Peace—" (J 1466/F 1488). In Dickinson's mind the Oriole is a spiritual democrat. He is equal to all Divinities. This poem shows just how democratic she really is. By Peace, Dickinson means the "Peace" of Spiritual Democracy. As a representative woman, with an inner "rural man" or home-based animus, she is a forerunner of world Peace. If the world's religions were all treated equally on a par with Nature, what impact would this have on global politics, the environmental revolution, and individual well-being on our planet? Could spiritual democracy help resolve longstanding debates on topics such as same-sex marriage, religious tolerance, gender equality, civil liberty, women's rights, and help to encourage world peace? How might we work toward this goal together?

Psychologists must join forces today with theologians, environmentalists, and political leaders to become effective in the march towards spiritual revolution and world change. To be Peacemakers in an age of spiritual democracy, a radical change in mind and heart is needed on ethical, psychological, and relational grounds. Psychology needs religion, science, and politics; it cannot stand alone. All these vocational fields are sisters of the same democratic spirit. When you vocalize the power of spiritual democracy, such as Dickinson does in this poem about the Oriole, you're going to be challenged to communicate words from the core of your heart center. Spiritual democracy is a calling to speak out of the divinity of the Self while remaining empathic during one's moral considerations. Spiritual democracy is an attempt to treat all religious paths as equals with "Nature's God." It is not a system of national preferences and arguments about God based on locality. Spiritual democracy is a way to practice religious tolerance without putting anyone else's religious beliefs or practices down. Spiritual democracy says: When we disagree about God, why argue about it? Let's celebrate the supreme in the other person's standpoint and not judge, as if we know who is right, who is wrong. The impulse to correct an outer attitude towards religion is typically patterned on a power motive. Analyze the power problem and let go the argument. Vocalizing the way of spiritual democracy is a divine calling from the Self in all of us. It exists as a potential in each and every human heart. The aim of spiritual democracy is to enlighten the world with three simple words: Liberty, Compassion, and Equality. American poetry uncovered the roots of spiritual democracy in the religious clauses of our US Constitution, but it added to what the founding fathers left out. Spiritual democracy is the *archetype of all archetypes*, because it includes all religious ideas in an experience of the Cosmic Self within and without, which transcends all possible categories of thought.

In "The Soul Has Bandaged moments—" her "little Force" explodes to "Touch Liberty," "Noon, and Paradise" (J 512/F 360). To touch *Liberty* for Dickinson is to "know no more," a kind of shamanistic ecstasy, where the top of her head is taken off and she experiences perpetual "Eternity" at Zenith: "The soul has moments of Escape— / When bursting all the doors— / She dances like a Bomb, abroad, / And swings upon the Hours" (J 512/F 360). By Bomb she means "Vesuvius" has erupted into an explosion of Light and Ecstasy that has rent all the doors of her "House" wide open and she swings upon the hours in "Liberty."

Her destiny as a post-Christian poet-shaman was not unlike C.G. Jung's in this regard, who chose for the title of a paper he read during his first visit to the United States with Sigmund Freud in 1909: "On the Significance of the Father in the Destiny of the Individual." Amongst the poet-shamans I have surveyed, it is Dickinson, moreover, who most anticipates C.G. Jung's psychology and his myth for our times, only her concept of the shadow goes beyond Jung to include bi-erotic desire in her notions of spiritual marriage. This is of course one of the primary cornerstones of female empowerment, pointing the way to a liberated post-patriarchal society. "To be alive—is Power— / Existence—in itself— / Without a further function" (J 677/F 876) she says pithily, and we can guess that for her to be alive is to be so sexually too.

When she looks into her "Antique Books" for antecedents to her new God-notion the "Themes" that concerned the whole "Literature of Man" including her male competitors, Plato and Sophocles, center on a time in cultural history when "Sappho—was a living Girl—" and extends to when "Beatrice wore / The Gown that Dante—deified—" (J 371/F 569). This is quite a trajectory in human history indeed!

Sappho was for Dickinson a person with exceptional self-consciousness, capable of being a transformer of social norms and gender and sexual stereotypes. Dickinson's fight against sexism led her to challenge the patriarchal God. Power is not found in Puritanism as a synonym for a woman's ability to undergo a Resurrection equal to Christ. But for Dickinson, spiritual equality is a keystone to her human right to tell the truth as a poet. "Power," moreover, is a word Emily had heard in the Lord's Prayer, along with "Kingdom" and "Glory," even as a little girl. "When a little girl," she wrote in 1869, "I remember hearing that remarkable passage ["For thine is the Kingdom, the Power, and the Glory" in the Lord's Prayer] and preferring the 'Power,' not knowing at the time that the 'Kingdom' and 'Glory' were included."[78] Dickinson's Christ, as we've seen, is not the typical image of Jesus taught by the churches of her day. It is a Christ of agony and ecstasy and Resurrection on the Cross, the "Prayer / I knew so perfect—yesterday— / That Scalding One—Sabachthani— / Recited fluent—here—" (J 313/F 283), or, Dickinson's soul set ablaze at a "white heat" during poetic compositions (see Chapter 12).

Her images of Christ are far from strictly devotional of any renderings of the historical Jesus; they are volcanic and include the searing fire of His Crucifying Bliss. Her answer to the problem of world religions is not exactly like Jung's in the final pages of *Answer to Job*, where he says we are to become in the age of the "Holy Ghost, the Third Divine Person" the "Christification of the many."[79] She goes to the root of the Judeo-Christian mythos in her alignment with Jacob, the God-wrestler at Peniel, the "bewildered Gymnast" who "Found he had worsted God" (J 59/F 145).

Jesus, of course, comes out of this God-wrestling lineage in Judeo-Christian history. Yet Dickinson goes further. Where God told Moses that no man shall see Him and live (Exodus 33:20), Dickinson says

---

78 *L*, II, p. 460.
79 Jung, *CW* 11: ¶ 758.

in "Love is like Life—" that "Love is the Fellow of the Resurrection / Scooping up death and chanting 'Live'!" (J 491/F 287). This Judeo-Christian ethic includes the need for a death of the ego (see chapter 11) and to the undemocratic sovereignty of patriarchy.

Writing as a representative woman, Dickinson spoke personally to everyone in an I-Thou dialectic aimed to transform her own and her readers' consciousness into a Consciousness that is Aware. As she wrote to her sister-in-law, Susan Gilbert in 1864: "Cherish Power—dear—Remember that stands in the Bible between the Kingdom and the Glory, because it is wilder than either of them."[80] As a speaker of her own theory of truth, her own personal theology or subjective myth, she speaks directly to "You." Dickinson has transformed the Lord's Prayer in Matthew 6, in a truly remarkable way. She chose Power over the Kingdom and Glory of God, because Power was more "wild" and true to her uninhibited Nature, as shaman-poet who can fill us with sudden Awe. After reading Emily's "Alabaster Chambers," for instance, Susan Gilbert described the poem as "breath taking," and "remarkable as chain lightning that blinds us hot nights in the Southern sky..."[81]

Emily tells Susan in effect to cherish her own power as an unrestrainable feminine wildness in Nature. This statement about power epitomizes Dickinson's poetry at this pivotal point in her oeuvre and its message rings true as a cultural statement to all women during a time of emergence of modern feminism; she is telling Susan, therefore, to throw off the chains of patriarchy. Her prayers were not, moreover, directed to an exclusively Judeo-Christian image of Divinity, but also to Islam. In this sense, she is like Whitman and Jung, a spiritual democrat at heart.[82] As she wrote ironically, in a letter during the fall of 1861, to Samuel Bowles of the *Springfield Republican* literary magazine: "Mr. Bowles. I pray for your sweet health—to "Alla"—every morning."[83]

It is obvious today that the sense of religious "freedom" in Dickinson's overall poetry centers on the theme of equal human rights for

---

80 *L,* II, p. 631.

81 *S,* p. 201.

82 S. Herrmann, "Colloquy with the Inner Friend: Jung's Religious Feeling for Islam," *Jung Journal: Culture and Psyche,* Vol. 3, No. 4, pp. 123-132.

83 *L* II, p. 34.

everyone. This freedom helped her overcome the slings and arrows of her fate and rise to a truly *post-heroic destiny*. Spiritual Democracy was Dickinson's central path to Ecstasy and to *healing*. For Dickinson, such healing was always shamanistic, that is, Nature-oriented and equalizing. Her healing from love's hurts was always an affair with Mother Nature and it was *She*, finally, that led her to become superior to Fate.

4

ACKNOWLEDGING HIM A MAN

In Jung's view, fate and destiny are intertwined as great natural powers of the collective psyche and to view the former (fate) as exclusively negative and the latter (destiny) as strictly positive would create an all-too opti-mistic view of life that omits the shadow and darkness and human evil from our purview.[84] The so-called negative divinities (pagan ones Emily honored) are aspects of the Self too, and they are always vying for hege-mony in society, family, and nations through religious channels. This is true particularly in theological wars, so that by repressing them in our own character, social or national, we lose their fateful and forceful pow-ers as daemons. In this chapter, we will continue with our explorations into the question of how Dickinson overcame her fate and arrived at her poetic destiny by focusing on her creative *animus* and turning to Jung's reflections on the concept of two destinies.

Jung speaks of "fear of fate,"[85] and "power of fate,"[86] and time as a universal "symbol of fate."[87] Fate is something to be feared because it has tremendous explosive "force" behind it and it can erupt at any time. Fate weds us to temporality and limitation regarding the inevitably of our finiteness and infirmity. On the other hand, fate is nothing to be feared; it is a *force* to be stood up to and endured with equanimity and inner strength; an energy field of Nature.

---

84 Herrmann, "Melville's Vision of Evil," *The San Francisco Jung Institute Library Journal*, Vol. 22, No. 3.

85 Jung, *CW* 5: ¶ 165.

86 Jung, *CW* 5: ¶ 102, footnote 51.

87 Jung, *CW* 5: ¶ 426.

To endure Fate's arrows can be transformative and ennobling of one's moral character. We all live and die. There is no way out of the eternal fate of life and death. Yet, as Emily had learned from Hitchcock, death can be transcended in this lifetime; like the butterfly's metamorphosis, resurrection according to her is a *reality*, here on this plane, God's life and secret design can in time ennoble us if we are modest.

In the following poem, Fate turns violent arrows on Emily's creative animus, yet, he does not succumb to their inner or outer blows of misfortune. He (whoever He was), rises to their requirement and becomes a man. Listen:

> Fate slew Him, but He did not drop—
> She felled—He did not fall—
> Impaled Him on Her fiercest stakes—
> He neutralized them all—
>
> She stung Him—sapped His firm Advance—
> But when Her Worst was done
> And He—unmoved regarded Her—
> Acknowledged Him a Man.   J 1031/F 1084

This is her creative animus speaking. Dickinson did not struggle against fate. She recognized its superior power as a strengthening force in her personality through writing. This was no mad woman in an attic, stuck in a father or a mother complex; not at all. This is the Voice of the Medicine Woman, the mature Emily Dickinson speaking to us of a fate overcome.

If we are to follow her, we too might be summoned by her art to experience Fate's fiercest stakes. Why did He not fall? Because her creative animus had already died on the cross of Dickinson's personal and transpersonal destiny, yet, unlike Christ, He did not drop. Fate initiated her creative animus into full manhood, wounding Him mortally, but He was not felled because He *returned to this life in a Resurrected state*. Through her shaman's wound, Emily survived and became a wounded healer, one who listens to the wisdom of the superior personality, the universal Self within.

One of her most frequent metaphors for such a universal wisdom-figure is the poet who is superior to the sun, a pun on the word "Son": "I reckon—when I count at all— / First—Poets—Then the Sun— / Then Summer—Then the Heaven of God— / And then—the List is done—" (J 569/F 533).

In this regard, Jung sees the sun as a "symbolical expression of human fate;" where, during the hero's battle for deliverance in life, the ego passes from "the domestic hearth" to his or her "destined heights"[88] to achieve a victory of consciousness through the soul's rising at life's zenith, which represents one's triumphs at the full career of midlife, followed by a bittersweet setting of sun.

Fate is this way: it humbles us and makes us modest before the mystery of the All. But the traditional model Jung used in his 1912 book, *Symbols of Transformation,* to depict this process, does not coincide in exact detail with the experiences of Dickinson.

Unlike Whitman, who was hailed by Emerson at the beginning of his career, in a famous letter in 1855, Emily Dickinson had virtually no career to crow about, and she seldom left the domestic hearth, nor did she ever receive an iota of public acclaim that would have *confirmed her destiny in space and time.* Her career was never fully celebrated and her destiny was not mirrored for its native brilliance and radiance. As a result, her rebellion became all the more forceful in the zone of her vocation, hidden from most of the public, except for the few fortunate ones to whom she wrote her letters or shared her poems.

When we look at the earliest poems included in *The Complete Poems* it is interesting to note that 1851 was a pivotal year for her. In this year, Dickinson wrote: "I climb the 'Hill of Science,' / I 'view the landscape o'er;' / Such transcendental prospect, / I n'er beheld before!" (J 3/F 2). At first glance one might imagine that she was a post-transcendentalist poet in the Emerson tradition, but I think she goes much deeper to promote an *embodied spirituality of the earth* as a progressive representative of human rights and women's freedom.

One of the persons who helped her achieve such transcendental vista was her first tutor, Ben Franklin Newton, who was Dickinson's clos-

---

88 Jung, *CW* 5: ¶ 553.

est male friend as she was just beginning to compose poetry. After she was withdrawn by her father Edward from Mount Holyoke, she studied privately with Newton, who was a law student in her father's firm from 1847 to 1849. Newton had given Emily a copy of Emerson's *Essays* in 1850 and she is certain to have read "The Poet," where the "Hill of Science" is referred to as "Chimborazo," an obvious reference to Humboldt's *Cosmos*.

Humboldt in his *Cosmos* had hailed the discoveries of Columbus as having opened the way to an enlarged view of the world and Emily in 1851 not only identified with Columbus but stated with audacity: "It was the brave Columbus, / A sailing o'er the tide, / Who notified the nations / Of where I would reside!" (J 3/F 2).

She takes her hat in this poem and runs as an immortal heroine, because her country is calling her to unite the nations of the globe in a movement towards Spiritual Democracy.[89] It would be in error to suggest that Dickinson's fierce rebellion against traditional Christian religion and her possibility of following a humbler path of submission under Mary Lyon's direction on the well-worn path of becoming a "Bride of Christ," in a conventionally religious sense, was an easy act of letting go for Emily. It obviously wasn't so simple and uncomplicated a decision, as is clear in the letter written on May 16, 1848, to Abiah Root, where Emily voiced her missing a "golden opportunity" to become a "Christian": "I am not happy, and I regret the last term, when that golden opportunity was mine, that I did not give up and become a Christian."[90] As we've seen, this letter is pivotal because it provides us with evidence of her ambivalence about the traditional path as a "Bride of Christ" and the submissive role of women in conventional marriage.

Dickinson was not called in the traditional religious sense to marry and assume the role of "mother" and "wife." Her marriage was much broader in amplitude. At this time, however, her sense of a lost "golden opportunity" was palpable. For a time, she appears to have transferred

---

89 Herrmann, "C.G. Jung and Teilhard de Chardin: Peacemakers in an Age of Spiritual Democracy." In *Pierre Teilhard de Chardin and Carl Gustav Jung Side by Side*.

90 *L* I, pp. 66-67.

some of her erotic fantasies onto Ben Newton. Before that, however, her fantasies in adolescence had tended teasingly towards more homoerotic unions with her Amherst girls.

Years before the gold frenzy hit the consciousness of the nation in 1849, Emily had written letters to Jane Humphrey, for instance, between April and May of 1842: "I miss my beloved Jane—I wish you would write to me—I should think more of it than a mine of gold… what good times we used to have jumping in bed when you slept with me"![91]

As Dickinson scholar, Paula Bennett tells us, while Dickinson lived almost her entire life "at home" she spent most of her time in circles of women consisting mostly of her sister Vinnie, Mrs. Holland, the Norcross cousins and her sister-in-law Susan Gilbert Dickinson. Earlier still were her childhood friends, Abiah Root and Jane Humphrey, who we will hear more about later. Emily relied almost constantly upon her relationships with such women for emotional support in her letters. Bennett adds, "Her relationships with them were intense, satisfying," and "in some instances, unequivocally erotic."[92]

It was Ben Newton, however, who first encouraged Emily to write poetry. Dickinson would later use volcano symbolism to give visual shape to her explosive "little Force." Surely, this is a most potent symbol for shamanistic power.

The Judeo-Christian mythos had long been waiting for a woman to assume a role in carrying the works of the Holy Spirit into a new post-Christian dissemination that could open doors for women to find their authentic voices, with equal authority to men. As we'll see, *door* symbolism is penultimate in Dickinson's poems. Her metaphor of the door symbolizes her way into her depths to unite with Liberty.

Dickinson *is* Liberty's Voice. She is an American original. She passes off the torch to women of the present and future by empowering them with her command over language. She breaks the chains of slavery and oppression of women's voices to find freedom and empowerment through a natural language that is unsurpassed for its native brilliance.

---

91 *L* I, 7, pp. 196-197.
92 Paula Bennett, *Emily Dickinson: Woman Poet*, p. 14.

Dickinson made *Libertas* conscious in the nation as a medicine for everyone.

For Columbus to notify the nations where Emily Dickinson would reside suggests that her ambition and sense of destiny as a woman were immense. What might the young Dickinson have meant by this? In "dreams," she writes in this same poem, a new breed of Americans is depicted taking to the Humboldtian "skies." She takes her hat under her arm and runs as an immortal *heroine* towards a future victory, because she feels her country is calling her with a revolutionary trumpet to pronounce its independence.

I believe her "calling" in this early poem was to unite the nations of the world in a myth of liberty, to embrace her countrymen in a cosmic way. On her death bed, she wrote in a letter to a dear friend: "The Savior's only signature to the Letter he wrote to all mankind, was a Stranger and yet took me in." She signed the letter: "America."[93]

"America!" What audacity it must have taken to write this. To sign her name "America" speaks up for her own revolutionary independence of spirit. Like Whitman, she clearly felt she was the Voice of the nation. That Voice was bequeathed not only to her, but to everyone who can claim it for America and the world. As she exclaimed in 1863: "No Prisoner be— / Where *Liberty*— / Himself—abide with Thee" (J 720/F 742). She assigned Liberty with a male gender here, but by this, I take her to mean her creative animus: her power to overcome Fate's fierce arrows and stand up to Her as a liberated person.

In the same year, at the height of the Civil War, she added: "God of the Manacle / As of the Free— / Take not my Liberty / Away from Me—" (J 728/F 754). Like the Statue of Liberty, the colossal neoclassical figure on Liberty Island in the middle of New York harbor in Manhattan, New York City, Dickinson holds up the torch of a new consciousness that is aware of the need for equal rights in all the women of America and the world. The meaning of this torch is of lady "Liberty Enlightening the World." Interestingly, the statue constructed by Frédéric Auguste Bartholdi was given to the people of the United States from the people of France and dedicated on October 28, 1886, the

---

93 *L*, III, p. 882.

same year Dickinson died. The tablet of the law, in Lady Liberty's hand, reads: "American Declaration of Independence, July 4, 1776." Also, it is important to note that a broken chain lies at her feet. So, when she said in 1865, "God of the Manacle / As of the Free— / Take not my Liberty / Away from Me—" she was speaking not only of African American freedom, but of human Freedom in all of its aspects, perhaps especially freedom for women from the chains of suffrage: equal rights for all. Being unchained and sharing *equality* with all people in the land of Liberty was Dickinson's way to claim the name "America" for herself as the forerunner of a new international myth. She saw that Liberty had been compromised by slavery. Yet, all forms of freedom were the first principles that her rebellion was aimed at abolishing: slavery to dogma being the ultimate chain of conscience, as all humans and their myths are created equal.

Lord Baltimore first applied freedom of religion as a system of government in America during the founding of the colony of Maryland, and Dickinson must have been aware of this. The first colonial law by Baltimore led to the establishment of the Maryland Toleration act in 1649, and the Protestant Revolution of 1689 followed this principle forty years later. The inseparable connection between democracy, religious freedom, and other types of freedom became the political basis for our new nation in 1776.

Her poems are aimed to liberate America from its patriarchal dominance towards a more egalitarian spirituality in the name of the Roman Goddess *Libertas*. In "Read—Sweet—how others—strove— / Till we— are stouter" (J 260/F 323), Dickinson's view of what she owes to the dead is captured beautifully, although tragically, in an unmistakable tribute to heretics, mystics and witches who "bore faithful witness" to the Divine, but whose names have long since "Passed out—of Record," and yet, whose faith nevertheless "shone above the fagot" (a bundle of burning sticks). She added that their "Clear strains of Hymn / The River could not drown—." By this she means the "Brave names of Men— / And Celestial Women—" (J 260/F 323). Who these "Celestial Women" she is referring to are, is not altogether clear. Who might they be? Again, they are figures of the Cosmos. More: "As if a Kingdom—cared!" she exclaims angrily, but their names are nevertheless written into her book of life, "Till we—are less afraid—" to hail them as our own sisters and brothers. This poem, like perhaps no other, affirms Emily Dickinson's poetic project as an advocate of Spiritual Democracy.

Her faith in women as bearers of a new message of *cosmic spirituality*, reveals her as an advocate for the earth and Mother Sky, Night, in a more just, equal, and democratic society that places Liberty at its lead. In "Could I but ride indefinite" she compares herself to the "Meadow Bee" and years to "marry whom I may," whether "Buttercups" or one of her male, or female friends; then she exclaims: "What Liberty!" (J 661/F 1056).

Jung speaks of the dream as "a harbinger of fate," "a portent and comforter, messenger of the gods" and "emissary of the unconscious."[94] As a visionary artist,[95] Dickinson sometimes wrote directly out of dream states and her decisive moments are those where she stood up to Fate. Jung adds that there are "fateful decisions" that we each must make in our personal lives and "it is a fundamental error to try and subject our own fate at all costs to our will."[96] Dickinson teaches us that sometimes the only thing we can do is to welcome fate's painful arrows!

The sacrifice of a heroic will to the transpersonal will of the Self is also basic to Jung's approach towards the unconscious. In his view, we must each develop a "religious attitude to fate,"[97] to bow our heads to fate and become thereby her equal. No one is free from fate, as we can see in all life-altering interventions, Jung says, and in "those careers where there has been some violent and destructive intervention of fate."[98] In "Fate slew Him" Emily shows us that she escaped the fate of many modern women whose voices were silenced. "Only a few," Jung says "especially favored by fate escape the great conflict of modern man; the majority [of men and women] are caught in it from sheer necessity."[99] Not only did

---

94 Jung, *CW* 7: ¶ 21.

95 Herrmann, "The Visionary Artist: A Problem for Jungian Literary Criticism." In *The San Francisco Jung Institute Library Journal*, Vol. 16, No. 1.

96 Jung, *CW* 7: ¶ 72.

97 Jung, *CW* 7: ¶ 164.

98 Jung, *CW* 7: ¶ 254.

99 Jung, *CW* 7: ¶ 438.

Dickinson escape fate in her embrace of the Goddess Liberty, she was our first truly modern poet. Dickinson speaks with modernity's Voice.

Gathering up the threads of Jung's comments on fate and destiny, it is important to ask what Dickinson might have to teach us about this recondite problem. Dickinson probably met the Presbyterian Reverend Charles Wadsworth in 1855 during her trip to Philadelphia, where the Declaration of Independence and the Constitution were signed. Wadsworth was one of the leading pulpit orators of his day and a happily married man. Dickinson began corresponding with him sometime after 1855 and their imagined love affair lasted until Wadsworth's death in 1882; unfortunately, their letters have not survived the passage of time.

Wadsworth was interested in "Scientifics," and especially the writings of Louis Agassiz, who was a personal friend of Humboldt's, and who delivered the centennial address on Humboldt in Boston. Agassiz was the first geologist, moreover, to propound the theory of glacier movement in 1838, two years before Hitchcock founded the American Association of Geologists.

These two followers of Humboldt split on views of natural theology and natural science after Charles Darwin drove a wedge into the national debate that would affect the United States on the pernicious issue of race relations. Wadsworth must have transmitted to Dickinson something of Humboldt's cosmic observations, moreover, for in a letter to her friend, Charles Clark, shortly before her death, Emily's grief over the loss of Wadsworth is deep. She asks: "'Going Home,' was he not an Aborigine of the sky?"[100] Here, she obviously meant by "sky" not the Heaven of the Lord's Prayer, but the immense Power of the Cosmos, and by "Aborigine" we take her to mean a kind of shaman-preacher whose calling was to administer a medicine to traditional Christianity. As well as being inspired by Wadsworth, she was also led to be influenced indirectly by an interest in Agassiz, minus his racist belief in Black inferiority, which Higginson, Wadsworth, nor Dickinson ever shared.

Another important figure in the romantic domain of her erotic life was Judge Otis Phillips Lord of Salem, who Dickinson referred to in her letters with such effusions as "My lovely Salem," "my Darling," "My

---

100 *L,* III, p. 901.

Sweet One," and "my Church."[101] In a letter from 1878, furthermore, she writes, one year after the death of Lord's wife: "I confess that I love him—I rejoice that I love him— …the exultation floods me. I cannot find my channel—the Creek turns to Sea—to the thought of thee— … my Darling come oh *be* a patriot now—Love is a patriot now Gave her life its…country Has meaning now—Oh nation of the soul thou hast freedom now."[102] It is remarkable how much these exaltations are about America. She repeats the word *now* three times here, which suggests now is all that is, when she rejoices she loves him. "Creek turns to Sea" at the mere thought of him.

Dickinson models for us the psychological principle of acceptance of fate in the now of creation to endure all life's challenges. By remaining true to love's arrows, she attains the object of her love fully after Lord's wife has died. He courts her for a while but she only plays with him, for her loves are many and she embodies the bi-eroticism of the whole nation as her spiritual Husband.

By finding meaning in her suffering, as a lover of both women and men, Dickinson broke through to the meanings of the national spirit regarding the nature of the Soul and its need for union with the beloved as an embrace with the whole American Self, whether married or unmarried in flesh and spirit. By signing her name "America" Dickinson foresaw bi-erotic freedom in her soul's country long before the nation was ready to embrace it. Her love for men and women was equalizing, like her spirituality of love; her patriotism, moreover, was for universal equality, which is post-Christian in the best sense, in that it affirms fate as identical with the will of God. This equality analytical psychology develops too, as when Jung wrote for example:

> "My fate" means a daemonic will to precisely that fate—a will not necessarily coincident with my own (the ego will). When it is opposed to the ego, it is difficult not to feel a certain "power" in it, whether divine or infernal. The man who submits to his fate calls it the will of God; the man who puts up a hopeless and exhausting fight is more apt to see the devil

---

101 *S*, p. 649.
102 *L*, II, pp. 614-615.

in it. In either event this terminology is not only universally understood but meaningful as well.[103]

In his writings on alchemy, from which the above passage comes, Jung reproduced a remarkable picture from a 16th century manuscript that shows a looming female figure presiding over the three Goddesses of Fate.[104] This picture suggests, to my mind, that fate and destiny are patterned by two interconnected archetypal images, comprised by 1) Three fates and 2) A feminine figure, or towering Goddess of Fortune and destiny, who is superior to Fate, and supersedes them.

This is the Goddess Liberty Dickinson marries *equally* with God in a bi-erotic embrace with the Cosmos that is transcendent finally of all God-images. In her equalizing love for men and women, Dickinson puts forth a bi-erotic spirituality that is simply without precedent in any previous religious dispensations. Her destiny and calling were to overcome her Puritan fate by embracing Fortuna as her equal lover.

If my hypothesis is correct, it might help us understand better what Dickinson and the ancient Chinese sages of the *I Ching* (and especially the sinologist Richard Wilhelm who translated it into German) meant when they spoke of an attitude that is superior to Fate. Wilhelm's translations may indeed be responsible for this specification of one of the line's meanings in this ancient text, for he is sure to have read Schopenhauer, where the concept was first championed for philosophy. As we've seen, changing line number three in Hexagram # 11 of the *Chinese Book of Changes*, states in translation: "As long as man's [woman's] inner nature remains stronger and richer than anything offered by external fortune, as long as he [she] remains superior to fate, fortune will not desert him [her]."

How true this was in the life of Emily Dickinson! The Amherst poet went to the core of the problem in America when she invoked the Greek notion of fate, as being equal to the Christian idea in a way Jung would have applauded. For Dickinson, the fates are God's sisters and the Greeks, after all, have their own religious mythology that rivals the

---

103 Jung, *CW* 12: ¶ 36, footnote 17.
104 Jung, *CW* 12: p. 45, figure 6.

Judeo-Christian myth for its sublimity and simplicity of meanings. Let us ask now: Who were the Fates?

In Greek mythology, the three fates form a *tripartite* image for Fate. Clotho spins the thread of life, Lachesis measures it, and Atropos cuts it. These three aspects of Fate represent aspects of the body's energies in their tripartite nature as soul-powers: 1) development (rising sun); 2) expansion (zenith); and 3) contraction (setting sun). Together they form a trinity of forces that are not always expected. "When trinity appears," writes Jung, "this means that a fateful point has been reached, that something unavoidable will therefore happen."[105] To carry this metaphor a bit further, we might then see that it was unavoidable that the third generation in the Dickinson family line—Emily—would be destined to take Samuel's Trinitarian beliefs to a fateful point of no return, where Trinity would become a reality in the poet-shaman's life, as a Fate she endured and survived. Emily did not believe in the Holy Spirit as the third person of the Trinity, she *became It*, and through her works she delivers a new dispensation of truth that is inclusive of the feminine principle, the body, and evil in one nation, signed "America" under God, which for her is the Cosmos. Only Matthew Fox[106] and Pierre Teilhard de Chardin[107] seem to have grasped the significance of what Emily was getting at when they advanced for theology and contemporary spirituality their notions of a Cosmic Christ.[108]

Anyone with a *destiny* experiences the three aspects of fate side by side. As we've seen, fate can be transcended by a fourth feminine principle superior to Fate. The Chinese sages referred to Her simply as "great good Fortune." Her calling was to illuminate it as something we may earn by running into it: "What Door—What Hour—" she wrote, "Run—run—My Soul! / Illuminate the House!" (J 1492/F 1537).

Dickinson's many references to the Door, reminds me of what James calls the "subliminal door." "Science" wrote William James in his 1902 masterpiece *The Varieties of Religious Experience* "in many minds is gen-

105 Jung, *Children's Dreams: Notes from the Seminar Given in 1936-1940*, p. 115.
106 Matthew Fox, *The Coming of the Cosmic Christ*.
107 Teilhard de Chardin, *Hymn of the Universe*.
108 Herrmann, "Teilhard de Chardin: Cosmic Christ."

uinely taking the place of a religion…If there be higher powers able to impress us, they may get access to us only through the subliminal door…This doorway into the subject seems to me the best one for a science of religions, for it mediates between a number of different points of view."[109] While the Door metaphor was obviously influenced strongly by Christianity at its inception, Dickinson's poetry became increasingly spiritually democratic as her soul continued to run into God and bathe in Its Illuminations. The curious thing about Dickinson, moreover, is that she not only had access to this subliminal doorway in the innermost depths of her psyche, but that she often depicts herself standing or sitting or crouching within it, which suggests that she was writing from within this very Door. She claims that from within the Door (call it subliminal or in a place in her higher Self) she "dealt a word of God" for the healing of the world and left us her "Golden lines" (J 430/F 388).

Her notion of "superiority" is far from Germanic idealism; it is American to the bone, built on Liberty, and the spirit of religious equality. Her love for American Liberty—Religious Freedom—is the independent spirit she fights for and sings praise to. It is her myth and ours.

Fate is what occurs to her ego in time, whether for good or ill; whereas destiny is her life-will, and has to do more with her overcoming of fate through the vehicle of her vocation, which, for Dickinson, was her poetry. Regarding "Superiority to Fate" we mustn't confuse this idea, therefore, with a kind of inflated "Nietzschean" heroic sublimity. The shaman-poet gains access to transcendence over fate by means of ecstatic transport. "Superiority" might at first sound like a new kind of national arrogance, hubris, or pride that the Fates abhor. Yet Dickinson uses the word "superior" in a few poems without any compunctions and it is obvious she is speaking about momentary experiences of transcendence in the creative *now*. For instance: "The Soul's Superior instants / Occur to Her—alone—" (J 306/F 630). This poem suggests that superiority to Fate is rare and occurs only in an instant. It does not last long. Not everyone can experience it. One may only know it through direct experimentation. I think she means it in the sense of the ancient Chinese sages, when they spoke for instance of the "superior man." That is

---

109 W. James, *William James: Writings*, pp. 58, 224.

the "He" she spoke of in the last chapter in "Fate slew Him." He does not drop, because his attitude has become one with the superior man inside herself. Her ability to keep cheerful, regardless of fate is a clear indication of her connection to the superior man, which is of course, her creative muse.

For example, about her decision not to publish, Emily Dickinson wrote modestly: "I smile when you suggest that I delay 'to publish'—… The Sailor cannot see the North—but knows the Needle can—"[110] Even after her attempts to publish met with failure, the "Soul's Superior instants" were enough to sustain Dickinson throughout her lifetime and allowed her to maintain her equanimity as a writer. *It came to her by way of absolute knowledge via the superior man, through a process Jung calls objective cognition.*

Before attempting to look further at Emily Dickinson's meanings on fate and destiny, let's take a look now at Jung's schema of fate and destiny that I have condensed into some basic principles for the field of analytical psychology.

---

110 *L*, II, pp. 408-409.

5

OUTGROWING FATE

In Jung's "Commentary on 'The Secret of the Golden Flower,'" he wrote that he observed now and then how a patient suddenly grew beyond him or herself because of some pursuit of unknown *potentialities* that became of prime importance during the course of an analysis. He learned from examining such patients' lives, that their dreams often contained solutions to problems that at first seemed insoluble. While reflecting on dreams that aided patients in overcoming unsolvable fates, he asked himself if the outgrowing of a patient's neurotic symptoms might in fact have been the normal thing in the self-regulating system, and getting stuck or mired the pathological thing. Getting over a neurosis, or bad fate, for Jung, was the simplest way the psyche leads patients to a natural *cure*. He hypothesized further that everyone must possess at least a potential to attain higher levels of consciousness with help of favorable, or "fortuitous" circumstances. Such life-altering changes, he noted, corresponded to concomitant changes in one's conscious attitude towards fate, which can alter a person's destiny-pattern:

> When I examined the course of development in patients who quietly, and as if unconsciously, outgrew themselves, I saw that their fates had something in common. The new thing came to them from obscure possibilities either outside or inside themselves; they accepted it and grew with its help.[111]

Jung learned a great deal from the study of Chinese philosophy about fate and destiny. While he was reflecting on the meanings of a

---

111 Jung, *CW* 13: ¶ 18.

more obscure Chinese text than the *I Ching* (the *Hui Ming Ching*), Jung had asked himself: "What did these people do in order to bring about this development and set themselves free? As far as I could see," Jung answered, "they did nothing (*wu wei*) but let things happen."[112] As a physician in search of solutions to problems of neurotic suffering, Jung came to see that the calling to vocation, the way to transform fate, is patterned by *fateful dispositions* that originally incline a person to pursue a certain professional course:

> The more one sees of human fate and the more one examines the secret springs of action, the more one is impressed by the strength of unconscious motives and by the limitations of free choice. The doctor knows—or at least he should know—that he did not choose his career by chance; and the psychotherapist in particular should clearly understand that psychic infections, however superfluous they may seem to him, are in fact the predestined concomitants of his work, and thus fully in accord with the instinctive disposition of his own life.[113]

The more I've looked into the secret springs of action in Emily Dickinson's life, the clearer it's become to me that the way she got out of her psychological difficulties and outgrew her fate was to simply follow the way of her animal helpers, her spirit guides into the unconscious, most notably "Snake," "Blue Bird," "Hummingbird," and the little "Green tree People," or frogs. In what lies ahead, we'll turn to her poem "A narrow Fellow in the Grass" to see how she was led from what could have been a bad fate to a beautiful *destiny* by boldly following its lead. First let us see what Jung said about the snake as a symbol for fate.

In Jung's *Seminars on Dream Analysis,* he speaks of the snake as a piece of our instinctive psychology, a tremendous power and inexorable thing we cannot make compromises with: "It [snake] is like a fate that cannot be twisted."[114] Later, in the same seminar, Jung speaks of a "feeling of fate" and those who become so modest in their conscious atti-

---

112 Jung, *CW* 13: ¶ 20.
113 Jung, *CW* 16: ¶ 365.
114 Jung, *Dream Analysis: Notes of the Seminar Given in 1928-1930*, pp. 326-327.

tudes that they accept fate willingly and without struggling hopelessly against the life-will, and follow it instinctively as "a sort of guidance."[115] The Universal "Will" Jung writes, which "creates life and being on all levels, and which modulates" one's fate, "in harmony" with "synchronous parallels" also prepares and arranges "future events in the form of Fate or Providence."[116] Dickinson sees Providence as not always so kind for the "Little One predestined / To the Native Land" (J 1021/F 1032).

It is important to keep in mind, therefore, when reading the chapters ahead that what looks like a conscious choice of Dickinson's personal will to forego publication and go her own way, four years before "Snake" was rudely tampered with, was probably a choice that was made over her head, and her creative animus may have had only a little to say about the matter. As her Fate or Providence would have it, 40 packets of her poems ("fascicles" as they were so-called) were found in her desk drawer by her younger sister, Lavinia, or Vinnie, after her death. Lavinia was left in full charge of all her worldly belongings. Over eight hundred of her poems were bound and sewn neatly together in these forty fascicles (a number symbolical of her wholeness!) for posthumous publication. Through remarkable synchronicities, her poems were edited and published after she died by Higginson and by Mabel Loomis Todd.

In 1955, Thomas H. Johnson came out with the first full edition of her poems and the fascicles were more mindfully restored by Ralph W. Franklin in 1981. One of the most interesting analyses of the fascicles, I think, was *Emily Dickinson's Fascicles: Method and Meaning,* published in 1995 by Dorothy Huff Oberhaus. No doubt, some of the most interesting and exciting books published on Dickinson were written by women. What is clear from my overview of the Oberhaus text is that between 1858 and 1864, a period of eight years, Dickinson engaged in a form of self-publication that was preparatory for some kind of a planned career as poet. That she imagined having a career is unmistakable, according to the available facts. In other words, her ego had desired it. To be sure she imagined success and at least some modest measure of fame in her lifetime. During this eight-year period, she made copies of more than

---

115 Jung, *Dream Analysis,* pp. 617-618.
116 Jung, *CW* 8: ¶ 828.

eight hundred of her poems, assembled them carefully together in forty booklets, and bound them together with string in the form of a literary collection. What interests me most about these "books" is Oberhaus' examination of the fortieth fascicle, in light of the Christian "poetry of meditation" in Dickinson's library, such as Thomas á Kempis' *The Imitation of Christ*.

Another significant find made by Oberhaus was the remarkable coincidence that Dickinson cut out the words of God in the Book of Job in her Bible, along with the first two verses of Revelation's twenty-first chapter, which was of central import to F-40.[117]

The fact that Emily cut out these two sections of her Bible, suggests that she was preoccupied with them deeply, as central to her oeuvre, which as I've said, was essentially post-Christian. These two chapters, Job and Revelations, form, not incidentally, the very core of Jung's musings in his masterpiece, *Answer to Job*. So, the issues she takes on actually anticipate Jung in his attempts to transform the Judeo-Christian God-image through an inclusion of the feminine principle and the shadow into the Godhead.

At every moment of Emily's life, fate gave her an opportunity to turn defeat and death into victory. To be victorious over fate was the aim of her full spiritual realization, and in the domain of mortality, Emily Dickinson was fearless. She rode fearlessly in death's carriage, as a shaman-poet, whose main functions were, as we've seen, to mediate between the two worlds, the living and the dead, and to provide a medicine to those who would listen.

We can see her preoccupation to what we all owe to the dead as early as 1855, during her trip to Mt. Vernon, with Lavinia, Vinnie (her sister) for short. She told Mrs. Holland in a letter how after reaching the tomb of General George Washington, she and Vinnie walked hand in hand "within the door—raised the latch he lifted when he last went home— thank the Ones in Light that he's since passed in through a brighter wicket!"[118] She was preoccupied here with Washington's spirit having passed through the door into the brighter gate (horizons of Eternity)

---

117 Dorothy Oberhaus, *Emily Dickinson's Fascicles: Method & Meaning*, p. 14.
118 *L*, II, p. 319.

thanks to the "Ones in Light." Thus, she sees Washington's spirit having passed into immortality.

All her life Emily was fascinated with the question of what happens to the soul of the deceased after death. In this letter, she was concerned with the notion of what she owed to her country in a nation of many nations founded upon religious Liberty. Her aim was to disseminate the Light she lit as a poet to America and the world. To accomplish what she achieved she must have made friends with the three Fates and been blessed by the Goddess of good fortune and luck. "Luck is not chance— / It's Toil— / Fortune's expensive smile / Is earned— / The Father of the Mine / Is that old-fashioned Coin / We spurned—" (J 1350/F 1360).

In fairytales, three female figures are always spinners of fate, such as the three Norns: Urth, Verthandi, and Skuld. The first two are kindly and gracious weavers of life; the third, however, the darker one, places a curse on their gifts.[119] Archetypes have a fate-like feeling to them, a *feeling for destiny*. It is felt in our bodies and our bones. It cannot be resisted against. If we struggle against Fate, it can make us ill, or kill us through fateful accidents.

It is the Medicine Woman, the ancient one, the fierce listener, who summoned Dickinson to her greatest shamanistic art to overcome her fears of Fate. Dickinson's fate was teleological: her fate had a goal, her fate was goal-directed; her life had a plan, a Design that was predestined.

My hypothesis in this book, as I said above, is that there is a fourth element that transcends the three fates, an *archetype of destiny* and this is what takes when the vocational summons becomes active in Dickinson. Destiny becomes her Voice as a transnational poet; she speaks with destiny's authority, she vocalizes Her truths. As an archetype, destiny is, therefore, a supraordinate totality that subsumes and supersedes the three fates.

How this may happen in a life, how fate can be overcome, or transcended, is a mystery. Manifesting one's destiny-pattern, its action-potentials, is a central problem of human life. We all must struggle with it. Like all archetypes, the Self contains a destiny-imprint. When Emily wrote to Higginson, for instance, that her "barefoot rank" was better

---

119 Erich Neumann, *The Great Mother*, p. 228.

than a life of one who sacrifices one's vocation for the sake of a career, she meant that her decision to follow the way of her totem animal— Snake—was her life's very challenge. His twisting path was the most sacred way she could travel, even if she had to travel it alone. As a Medicine Woman, she followed fate's twisting path. She seems to have been aware of her destiny since her early childhood. In his 1909 essay "The Significance of the Father in the Destiny of the Individual," Jung wrote:

> The child is guided by the power of the parents as by a higher destiny…The parental influence, dating from the early infantile period, is repressed and sinks into the unconscious, but is not eliminated; by invisible threads it directs the apparently individual workings of the maturing mind. Like everything that has fallen into the unconscious, the infantile situation still sends up dim, premonitory feelings, feelings of being secretly guided by otherworldly influences.[120]

One of the ways that such feelings were embodied by Dickinson was through the startling emergence of lightning as an objective reality.

Lightning: The Bolt She would not Exchange for all the Rest of Life

For Dickinson, the lightning she saw and thunder she heard reverberating through her whole being at the age of two, while strolling in Monson with her maternal aunt, Lavinia, can be said to have formed into a *destiny-imprint*, a portrait of the destiny-pattern out of an early experience evoked deep inside of her and simultaneously outside, in the field of Nature. This startling event stayed with her in memory for a lifetime. The experience left her with powerful *feelings* that were experienced as transcendent of the field of time, and were, therefore, reverberations of something cosmic, timeless, and eternal.

As the story goes, after the birth of her younger sister, Lavinia, Dickinson's maternal aunt took Emily at age two years three months for an extended stay at Monson. Halfway to aunt Lavinia's home, Lavinia and the future poet were suddenly stopped in their tracks by a fierce

---

120 Jung, *CW* 4: ¶ 739.

thunderstorm, which shot down lightning arrows from a dark cloud overhead. When little Emily saw the lightning flash before her eyes, she called it "*the fire*" and implored, with sudden fright to her aunt: "Do take me to my mother." Lavinia is said to have kindly soothed the child and gently covered her head with a cloak[121] yet, the memory impression of this event imprinted itself on her mind forever.

Perhaps this was her first impression of "Nature's God," "Awe," or the God/Goddess of immense instinctual and spiritual Power. Lightning is a common symbol amongst Native American shamans for the electrifying power of the Great Spirit.

Many of her most illuminating metaphors are addressed to the transformation of her child psyche on the verge of midlife with *healing* metaphors that quicken her mind. For instance, about 1873, she wrote an eight-line quatrain describing what she thinks of poetry and love, and the childhood memory imprint is easily recognizable:

> To pile like Thunder to its close
> Then crumble grand away
> While Everything created hid
> This—would be Poetry—
>
> Or Love—the two coeval come
> We both and neither prove—
> Experience either and consume—
> For None see God and live—   J 1247/F 1353

Jung hypothesized that the archetype of destiny is a natural intelligence that is millions of years old and is inherited with the brain structure. Emily's "Snake" and "Lightning" poems are prime symbols for this. "The inhuman quality that the snake represents," writes Jung "is linked up with the lower centers of the brain and the spinal system" and "these are snake powers."[122] So, too, with secret *destinies* hidden in the snake brain.

When we dive deeply into Jung's writing on fate, we are led invariably to the archetype of destiny. Destiny is indefinable. It is perhaps the

---

121 *S*, p. 323.
122 Jung, *Dream Analysis*, p. 327.

central mystery of human life. Once crucified by that awful stroke at her "Being's Centre—" (J 553/F 670), Emily moved from the umbilical point of Gethsemane to the great Round of the cosmic Wheel, the whole Circuit of Consciousness. She was led during such numinous moments to recite the words of the Lord and Savior, "Sabachthani" and "Crucify / Defeat whets Victory" (J 313/F 283).

Yet the metaphor she uses for such a sacrifice of her ego on the cross of her destiny was also shaped by national imagery that was indigenous at its national roots. Here's a powerful example: "He fumbles at your Soul /...Deals— One—imperial—Thunderbolt / That scalps your naked Soul—" (J 315/F 477). To be scalped by "Lightning" was the surest sign that a poem rang true for Dickinson. After that awful scalping occurred, at around the age of thirty, she put down her simple wardrobe, put on her white dress, and started for Eternity. In so doing the Lightning hit her again and again from the transcendent dimension, as she piled on like thunder to her stupendous close.

Mircea Eliade says in this regard that "the role of lightning in designating the shaman is important; it shows the celestial origin of shamanic powers." He states further that "lightning is sometimes portrayed on the shaman's costume."[123] In a poem written in 1883, Dickinson tells us, moreover, that her head was "scalped" by "Doom's Electric Moccasin" (J 1593/F 1618), the divine "Bolt" she would not exchange "For all the rest of Life—":

> The farthest Thunder that I heard
> Was nearer than the Sky
> And rumbles still, through torrid Noons
> Have lain their missiles by—
> The Lightning that preceded it
> Struck no one but myself—
> But I would not exchange the Bolt
> For all the rest of Life—   J 1581/F 1665

In a private conversation, later recorded by Higginson, furthermore, Dickinson stated famously: "If I read a book [and] it makes my whole body so cold no fire can ever warm me I know *that* is poetry. If I feel

123 Eliade, *Shamanism*, p. 19.

physically as if the top of my head were taken off, I know *that* is poetry…
Is there any other way?" she asked him to consider.[124] When I speak of
the archetype of destiny as it pertains to Emily Dickinson, then, I'll be
speaking in a circumambulatory way of her convergence towards a center of her *shamanistic personality*: snake, center, Gethsemane, crucifix,
sun, boundlessness, sky, Vesuvius, lightning Bolt, Awe, etc. These are all
synonyms for her white election or spiritual marriage with the Cosmos.

> A nearness to Tremendousness—
> An Agony procures—
> Affliction ranges Boundlessness—
> Vicinity to Laws   J 963/F 824

She is at one with the crucified Christ here. Her death through spiritual marriage with the universal wheel has led her to a second state: A
Oneness with the whole Cosmos. This aspect of her poetic personality
has an apparent design inborn within it, an individual destination: *des-
tinatus*, the goal, the aim of the individuation process. Fate and destiny
are paths fraught with risky perils. But if a person has faith in their fate-
like destiny, and follows it to the end, without thought of profit, or a
successful career, one might if one is lucky attain in the end the goal of
one's vocation, nonetheless, or as Dickinson simply says: "Dropped—my
fate—a timid Pebble— / In thy bolder Sea—" (J 966/F 827). By "Sea"
she means the Cosmic Ocean of bliss, or the divine "Ether." "Dropped
into the Ether Acre— / Wearing the Sod Gown—" (J 665/F 286).

The Convergence Point of the Two Destinies

In Jung's 1916 paper "Adaptation, Individuation, Collectivity" he uses
the German word *Bestimmungen,* which translates as "destinies," or "des-
tinations," to describe a convergence point of inner and outer factors
involved in the co-creation of an indissoluble unity of fate and destiny
in life. The destiny-factor holds a key for Jung to the way of individuation: "Individuation and collectivity are a pair of opposites, two divergent destinies."[125]

---

124 *S*, p. 566.
125 Jung, *CW* 18: ¶ 1099.

One needs to be adapted to both, Jung says. Finding a place of convergence, a path between the opposites, requires flexibility in inner and outer adaptation. This is what Dickinson gets at when she writes: "Each Life Converges to some Center— / Expressed—or still— / Exists in every Human Nature / A Goal—" (J 680/F 724). Expressed vocationally, the Self is the point where we are all the *same* as regards to universal human rights, the point of equality with Nature and Spiritual Democracy. The convergence point is where the two divergent destinies meet in the pivot of one's calling. In this regard, Jung says that if we can develop that "function" that he calls "transcendent" the disharmony between the two destinies may lead to "further stages of transformation for the sake of their own development" and we may move towards *higher stages of conscious differentiation*. Such stages of conscious transformation are only attained by individuals who are "destined to it from the beginning, i.e., who have a capacity and an urge for higher differentiation,"[126] and they "are arranged in a quaternion when they represent the totality."[127] By quaternity, Jung means realization of the Self arises from demands of adaptation to inner and outer reality during the course of individuation, a synthesis of the pairs of opposites, through which two destinies, or *bestimmungen* are brought together into a fourth unitary reality.

In Dickinson's art, she repeatedly shows that all animal species have destinies too, even the little green tree people, frogs, who sometimes through violent interventions of fate are blasted by the searing heat of a thunderbolt. "Nature—sometimes sears a Scalping— / Sometimes— scalps—a Tree— / Her Green People recollect it / When they do not die—" (J 314/F 457). Thus, for Dickinson lightning is an archetypal image for fate that comes from her first encounter with its immense electrical power at the age of two. This archetype of the lightning continued to play an important role in her poetry until her final years. "Perhaps—who knows?" Jung wrote about the archetypes in general, "these eternal images are what men mean by fate."[128]

---

126 Jung, *CW* 7: ⁋ 198.
127 Jung, *CW* 14: ⁋ 261.
128 Jung, *CW* 7: ⁋ 183.

"From the beginning I had a sense of destiny," Jung writes in his autobiography "as though my life was assigned to me by fate and had to be fulfilled."[129] So too with Dickinson: "It was given to me by the Gods— / When I was a little Girl— /…Rich! 'Twas Myself—was rich— / To take the name of Gold— / And Gold to own—in solid Bars—" (J 454/ F 455).

Jung and Dickinson both take a positive view towards fate, particularly if the arrows of fate strike early in one's vocational journey with decisive blows, at the age of thirty, or so.[130] *Destinare* means to make fast. Looking back at her transformation, at age thirty, Dickinson writes with *amor fati,* love of her fate: "I've got an arrow here. / Loving the hand that sent it / I the dart revere. / Fell they will say, in 'skirmish' / Vanquished, my soul will know / But by a simple arrow / Sped by an archer's bow" (J 1729/F 56).

The Destiny Field

The *destiny-field* is a numinous energy field of the Cosmos that courses through the souls and bodies of every human life and its aim is to wake up the divine energies in each and every one of us through a calling to live by. Destiny is a *vocation*, a transpersonal calling from a superior intelligence in the Universe. Where transpersonal feelings of destiny come from is a theological as well as a psychological question, yet, whether the feelings of destiny come from God, the unconscious, the Self, the Goddess (Fortuna), Fate, the ancestors, stars or planets, animal-powers, or Nature, it is often heralded by "big dreams" that are well-known amongst the indigenous societies of the world. We can get glimpses of the destiny-field in dreamtime. Shamanic cultures know that if "a child has such a dream," then, as Jung says, the village elders will insist "that sure enough that child has a great destiny."[131] We see this in a Dickinson poem where the Self appears to the poetess in a dream as a snake "ringed with power—" (J 1670/F 1742). As Jung says further, in a 1930 seminar

---

129 Jung, *Memories, Dreams, Reflections*, p. 48. (*MDR* refers throughout this publication to C G. Jung's *Memories, Dreams, Reflections*.)
130 Jung, *The Visions Seminars*, 2 Volumes, 1: 1.
131 Jung, *The Vision Seminars*, 1: 22.

on dream interpretation: "there are no mistakes in fate. Fate is greater than we are."[132] Jung's attitude towards fate is a lot like Dickinson's. Fearlessness is fate's antidote.

The Overcoming of Fear

Fear is perhaps the greatest obstacle fate puts on our path and Dickinson was faced with many fears bordering on panic in her lifetime. This was a fate arising from psychological complexes. If one gives way to the fear of fate, psychic life stagnates and one may fall into a bad depression, suicidal despair, panic, rage, or an anxiety disorder.

On the other hand, "If we normal people examine our lives" we may "perceive how a mighty hand guides us without fail to our destiny, and not always is this hand a kindly one."[133] How beautifully true this was in the life of Dickinson! She suffered terribly at the hands of mentors, editors, family and friends, who failed to appreciate her greatest works of art and her love. This fate she experienced as an agony of crucifixion. Yet, she picked up her cross with dignity, and lifted up her head with integrity. She said straightaway and unflinchingly: "I like a look of Agony, / Because I know it's true—" (J 241/F 339). Despite her agonies and temporary fears, her infantile situation continued to send up "premonitory feelings," as Jung said above "feelings of being secretly guided by otherworldly influences."[134]

Instead of a career, she chose her barefoot rank. Fate could not mar her. Dickinson learned how to overcome her fears of life by sitting in meditation on the source of her immense power, "Vesuvius at Home." Vesuvius is an active volcano on Italy's West Coast overlooking the city of Naples. It is most famous for destruction in AD 70 of the Roman cities of Pompeii and Herculaneum. For Dickinson, it was the archetypal source of her explosive power within. To look down at the fiery rocks below into the burning center of her being, was a metaphor she created. Sitting on her volcano at home gave Dickinson tremendous medicine-power.

---

132 Jung, *The Vision Seminars*, 1: 145.
133 Jung, *CW* 4: ¶ 727.
134 Jung, *CW* 4: ¶ 739.

In his *Red Book*, Jung too described his experience of becoming smelted anew with the fiery magma of his primordial beginnings: "The scene of the mystery play is a deep place like the crater of a volcano. My deep interior is a volcano that pushes out the fiery-molten mass of the unformed and the undifferentiated."[135] In Jung's paper delivered for the Terry Lectures at Yale University in 1937, he noted further: "As a matter of fact, we are constantly living on the edge of a volcano, and there is, so far as we know, no way of protecting ourselves from a possible outburst that will destroy everybody within reach."[136]

After his near-fatal heart attack, Jung came "to understand how important it is to affirm one's own destiny. In this way we forge an ego" he said "that does not break down whenever incomprehensible things happen; an ego that endures, that endures the truth, and is capable of coping with the world and with fate. Then, to experience defeat is also to experience victory."[137]

The destiny of the Self is a psychic power. It can enlighten a person; it can also destroy one. Destiny is a cross we each must bear consciously if we are not to collapse under its burden. In Jung's view, we are the "makers of fate, the makers of our lives."[138] "Fate is crossing you ever day," Jung adds. "We ourselves are doing just the things we don't want to do. And who is doing it?" he asks. "Well," he answers, "that is the other being, and if you follow it up—if you carefully examine what that being means that is crossing your line—you will see something."[139]

Superiority to Fate

"Some keep the Sabbath going to Church—" Dickinson wrote, "I keep it, staying at Home—" (J 324/F 236). Spiritual experiences are what she needed. *This* was her place of superiority to Fate, a detached meditative space where she attained her "Center" and medicine power.

---

135 Jung, *The Red Book*, p. 247.
136 Jung, *CW* 11: ¶ 25.
137 Jung, *MDR*, p. 297.
138 Jung, *Nietzsche's Zarathustra: Notes of the Seminars Given in 1934-1939*, pp. 2, 942.
139 Jung, *Nietzsche's Zarathustra*, pp. 2, 919.

As the Israeli analyst, Erich Neumann tells us, the Goddesses of fate the world over are all spinstresses; he adds that the three Goddesses represent the "three temporal stages of all growth (beginning-middle-end, birth-life-death, past-present-future)."[140]

In my view, the *archetype of destiny*, which includes the three fates, is patterned by four female figures. It is made up by a quaternary structure of Gods or Goddesses conjoined as One. In Roman mythology, the fourth is the Goddess of destiny as Fortuna, she who supersedes the three fates. In her spiritual character, she embodies the transformative power to bestow protective powers of destiny on any individual by virtue of her quaternary nature as a Self-figure. In a medieval Italian manuscript, for instance, Fortuna was depicted wearing a four-pointed King's crown. In her left hand, she held a triune scepter, in her right hand, a peacock, her symbol for Immortality. As a symbol of triumph over the three temporal stages of growth, Fortuna is victorious over death. She stands in a square cart, with four wheels, drawn by four lions, which pull her royally ahead in a majestic regal gown.[141]

Destiny is, therefore, an operative principle patterned by the Gods and Goddesses of good fortune: good mothers and benign fathers of destiny. To be chosen by the destiny archetype is a blessing and a curse, an agony and ecstasy. The three fates operate within the Self's destiny-field and for this reason they must not be vexed. For they are the Self's agents.

As a Goddess of compassion, Fortuna is sister to Sophia, the Virgin Mother, Kwan-Yin, Tara, Parvati, Shakti, Changing Woman, the divine Mother of the Universe, and Night. She asks one thing of us: *love our fate*. In this context, Jung writes beautifully: "Behind the neurotic perversion is concealed his vocation, his destiny: the growth of personality, the full realization of the life-will that is born with the individual. It is the man without *amor fati* who is neurotic; he, truly, has missed his vocation."[142] To be sure, Emily did not miss her calling. She gave voice to it unequivocally with unsurpassed beauty.

---

140 Neumann, *The Great Mother*, p. 228.
141 Neumann, *The Great Mother*, p. 129.
142 Jung, *CW* 17: ¶ 313.

When the call to vocation takes, Neumann calls it a "time of fate": "Beyond the normal threefold time of our conscious mind there seems to be a 'time of fate,' in which the personality is determined by archetypal structures of a general or individual nature."[143] Dickinson entered this time of fate between 1858-1860 and by 1862, she had arrived at the place her destiny had in store for her, the place of the "Poet—.../ Himself—to Him—a Fortune— / Exterior—to Time—" (J 448/F 446). By "Fortune" she is referring to the Goddess Fortuna.

In "A Spider sewed at Night" (J 1138/F 1163) Dickinson penetrated, moreover, to the background of the threefold time of fate to the *fourfold* time of her destiny-pattern in space-time; to the timelessness, that is, of the Feminine Godhead itself. She incarnated the archetype of Spider Woman, and became for the world a shaman-poet for her times and ours.

In her lexicon, there are no accidents or errors in her relations with editors, mentors and friends, for all appear to have been ratified in the final reckoning by the divine hand of "Destiny": "Meeting by Accident, / We hovered by design— / As often as a Century / An error so divine / Is ratified by Destiny, / But Destiny is old / And economical of Bliss / As Midas is of Gold—" (J 1548/F 1578).

Spiritual Gold is the alchemical gold of the West that she offers to each reader from her place of destiny: her home in Amherst. In a whimsical letter written to Mrs. Holland, during the election year of 1880, Dickinson wrote about her sister Vinnie that her caretaking function for her family and for Emily was one that extended to the whole Cosmos: "Vinnie is far more hurried than Presidential Candidates—I trust in more distinguished ways, for *they* have only the care of the Union, but Vinnie the Universe—."[144] Here, the accent in her letter is on Vinnie's vocation as opposed to her career, destiny, as her life-pattern, which Vinnie loyally served to the end. Let the Presidential Candidates care for the outer Union! Dickinson's main business was the care of "Circumference." Vinnie's vocation was to care for her sister, Emily, and her family, which was a much broader caretaking function, care of the "Universe."

---

143 Neumann, *The Place of Creation*, p. 45.
144 *L* III, p. 676.

In an 1862 poem, "I saw no Way" Dickinson says further: "I touched the Universe—" (J 378/F 633). To touch the Universe was a destiny and vocation to God indeed, made possible through her love and Art.

6

SPIRITUAL MARRIAGE

In Jung's book *The Psychology of the Transference* he writes that the aim of analytical psychology is to lead people to the *trans-subjective unity of the Self.*[145] As Jung demonstrated empirically, the phenomenon of the transference is a fundamental human experience that is religious at its roots, and it tends to personify itself in *trans-cultural or trans-national* symbolism that is common to all people.

To my mind no poet exemplifies the transcendent nature of spiritual marriage as magnificently as does Emily Dickinson. The goal of Dickinson's art is to describe some aspect of the mystery of spiritual marriage beyond its corporeal aspects and to lead the reader towards an approximation of the crowning of the nuptials, King and Queen, Queen and Queen, as a lived trans-subjective experience of union with the Cosmos.

As we've seen, she tells us what it means when one arrives at the center of one's destiny-pattern and becomes superior to the obstacles of fate. She did this through poetic meditations on the meanings of *marriage* as a transcendent shamanistic experience with simply no antecedents. "At the highest summit of her art," wrote Dickinson scholar Louise Bogan, "Emily Dickinson resembles no one."[146] It was her destiny and her fate to write poetry in her own way, and to love whomever she wanted.

Jung's aim as an empirical scientist was to teach the professional and the lay public the way of the transcendent function as a destiny inside

---

145 Jung, *CW* 16: ¶ 532.
146 Louise Bogan, "A Mystical Poet." In *Emily Dickinson: A Collection of Critical Essays*, p. 141.

of one. This was Dickinson's aspiration too, and her feminine way of conveying the meaning of spiritual marriage is just as all-embracing.

Like Melville and Whitman, Dickinson's metaphors of marriage are trans-cultural, trans-national and mythopoetic in origin and *the trans-subjective union they all embodied is essentially bi-erotic.*

As we'll see, no poet explores the experience of the *coniunctio* more deeply than Dickinson. Her poems are all Spiritually Democratic at their core. Here's a beautiful example: "There is a flower that Bees prefer— / And Butterflies—desire— / To gain the Purple Democrat / The Humming Bird—aspire—" (J 380/F 642). Bees, butterflies, and hummingbirds all seek union with the "Purple Democrat." This is a kind of marriage symbolism imbedded in Nature that her poetry excels in. She was a dweller in the emotional states that accompany such spiritual marriages and she spoke out of such delightful emotions from depths of her lived experience.

She became during such moments of mythopoetic seeing a bride to everyone. Jung used an alchemical text from 1544, the *Rosarium Philosophorum,* to amplify the meaning of the spiritual marriage, as he and his patients, mostly Europeans, but many Americans too, experienced it. His decision to meditate on this text was conditioned by the subjective factor of his personal myth. We all have a personal myth, Jung teaches us, and it is important for us to discover what it is. Jung believed that to help us with this, we need to find our meaning within the context of our national mythologies supplied by great masters of world literature. This is what I am trying to do by focusing so intensely on Dickinson. Since spiritual marriage is an experience with great relevance to the individuation of all people the world over, we must consider images of *coniunctio* that are spiritually democratic at their core. In this domain, Dickinson has so much to offer. It was her destiny to leave us with an answer to what was left out of the Bible as a strictly patriarchal affair that did not take into account the rights of all humans for dignity and liberty.

As Jung wrote in "The Psychology of the Transference" the most direct way to understand a problem experimentally is to contemplate it from a point outside one's own time, or *zeitgeist,* that is, from a point of view in "some past epoch that was concerned with the same problems."[147] So it is my hypothesis that Dickinson can enlighten us on the trans-subjective nature of the democratic *typos* of spiritual marriage in question in this book.

The aim of depth-psychological analysis, according to Jung, rests on the unsurpassable "fourth" stage of the psychotherapeutic work, portrayed in the alchemical *Sapientia*, Wisdom, or Sophia, whose parallels Jung located in the Shulamite of the "Song of Songs."[148] It is precisely this wisdom-factor, the voice of the Divine Feminine, the Goddess, Gaia, that Dickinson gave voice to most eloquently from her Vesuvius heights. She can help us expand our views regarding marriage today by providing us with some practical spiritual insights into a science of the soul.

In *Psychology of the Unconscious* Jung drew parallels between fantasy-thinking, myths, dreams, and the similar thinking of children and he added that in a child's psychic life we may detect re-echoes of the pre-historic.[149] In "The Psychology of the Transference" thirty years later he said that in postulating the "provisional character" of his investigations[150] he did not consider enough the "homosexual forms" of Eros, such as "father-son," or "mother-daughter" incest imagery. For he could not find more than a single reference to homosexuality in his alchemical research.[151] There were, therefore, no sufficient reasons to assure Jung of its importance to a science of the human psyche.

Thus, as the notion of the spiritual marriage pertains to the helping professions nowadays, whether in the fields of psychiatry, psychology, clinical social work, spiritual counseling, or marriage and family therapy, we are inclined to look beyond alchemy, the Bible, and poetries of Europe, moreover, for models. We need to find antecedents wide enough to subsume the possibilities of the bi-erotic marriage for post-

---

147 Jung, *CW* 16: p. 166.

148 Jung, *CW* 16: ¶ 361.

149 Jung, *Psychology of the Unconscious: A Study of the Transformations and Symbolisms of the Libido*, p. 25.

150 Jung, *CW* 16: p. 165.

151 Jung, *CW* 16: ¶ 357.

modern times to aid us in our work today. Dickinson is a great teacher in this regard.

From where we stand today, it is evident that our multiplicity of instincts form a "primal unity," or "primal libido"[152] as Jung says, that tends to converge towards a central goal, a "desexualized primal libido,"[153] as Jung called it that has belonged to humanity as a normal function of reality and adaptation ever since prehistoric times.[154]

Let us listen now to what Dickinson says about the multi-valence of the libido, where Sun, Zenith, Snake, Wife, Husband, Sea, Vesuvius, Stars, Universe, Lightning, Great Spirit, the Goddess, Empress, volcanic force, Wildness ("Wild Nights"), Gold, Crown, Fire, and Melody are all metaphors for her trans-subjective unity in the Self in its bi-erotic nature. I think my readers will agree she is simply breathtaking. Listen:

> Title divine—is mine!
> The Wife—without a Sign!
> Acute Degree—conferred on me—
> Empress of Calvary!
> Royal—all but the Crown!
> Betrothed—without the swoon
> God sends us Women—
> When you—hold—Garnet to Garnet—
> Gold—to Gold—
> Born—Bridalled—Shrouded—
> In a Day—
> Tri Victory
> "My Husband"—women say—
> Stroking the Melody—
> Is *this*—the way?   J 1072/F 194

What the source of psychic energy is will always remain a great mystery, as there is no way to circumscribe it empirically from a purely pragmatic point of view, except by means of circumambulation, a circling around mythological motifs, or poetic metaphors that have heuristic

---

152 Jung, *Psychology of the Unconscious*, p. 134.
153 Jung, *Psychology of the Unconscious*, p. 134.
154 Jung, *Psychology of the Unconscious*, p. 136.

value. If we follow the tracks of Dickinson's libido analogues towards their instinctive-spiritual gradients, in her "higher" and "lower" *coniunctio* symbolisms, we invariably find certain numinous spots of time, pivotal moments, when she entered non-temporal eternity to describe her experiences of "Tri Victory." As we'll see, there was a fourth element that comes through her "Stroking the Melody—" a highly erotic image of the feminine. In this context, Dickinson wrote: "What would the Dower be, / Had I the Art to stun myself / With Bolts of Melody!" (J 505/F 348).

By "Bolts of Melody" we take her to mean the Art of catching emanations of light from the luminous center of her shamanistic personality, aesthetic rhythms that may transport readers momentarily into shamanistic states of consciousness, or ecstasy. But she also suggests that the Bolts of Melody are evoked through stroking, an action that does not leave sex and the body out. This dowry is the gift she bequeaths to us as a "Bride of Awe."

She may have dropped down deeper, through lyrical chant techniques, to an archetypal-developmental source of rhythmic activity,[155] to a *place* in her feminine body and psyche that is essentially matriarchal, shamanistic, and cosmic in its native Ground. "When you—hold—Garnet to Garnet— / Gold—to Gold—" might imply moreover that her "Tri Victory" had led to a marriage quaternion of four marriage rings (red to red, gold to gold). The reader will remember that Emily's paternal grandfather, Samuel Dickinson had become a Trinitarian deacon of the West Church of Amherst after he graduated from Yale, so the Trinity was fresh on Emily's mind and is a frequent symbol for God's grace. Her father too had graduated from Yale. Emily was determined, not unlike Jung, however, to prove that the way of the divine feminine, wholeness of her personality was through a quaternary path. For instance, she wrote in 1863 the following opening lines: "Four Trees—upon a solitary Acre— / Without Design / Or Order, or Apparent Action— / Maintain—" (J 742/F 778).

No spiritual marriage can be attained in its highest emotional forms without the "conscious acknowledgement and acceptance of our fellow-

---

155 Jung, *Psychology of the Unconscious*, p. 141.

ship with those around us," writes Jung. This means that the *coniunctio* has to some extent be projected outwardly, otherwise "there can be no synthesis of the personality,"[156] no real union, or integration with the supra-personal non-ego, or Self. In Jung's view, no spiritualization of Eros towards the fourth and final stage[157] is possible without the company of friends. For it is exceedingly difficult to withdraw our projections without a relationship to a partner. Human relationships are typically tainted with subjectivity and contaminated with emotional projections and spiritual marriage, therefore, remains mostly unrealized by the majority. Spiritual marriage is typically made known by means of a "celestial spouse;" a celestial husband, or wife, that transforms the neophyte's identity, according to Eliade, into an androgynous semi-divine being.[158]

In Dickinson's life, her shamanistic identity took place through the donning of the white wedding dress, which she wore as a "Bride" of the divine "omnipresence" (J 1496/F 1529). In this dress, Emily could manifest the regal state of a Queen betrothed to her beloved Bridegroom, or her Bride; a woman dressed in a "Royal Gown" wearing garnets and gold and victoriously "crowned" by herself as a "Wife" of Liberty. In "The Day that I was crowned," she says the "Grace" she "chose" to wear (J 356/F 613) was gold. She obviously means much more, however, than the conventional reading of grace, as we can read in "The World— stands—solemner—to me— / Since I was wed—to Him" (J 493/F 280). She means by this her marriage to God or the Self.

The circumferential life of the Medicine Woman was one of continual marriage with the Godhead; she returned again and again into its Tremendousness and Boundlessness for replenishment of her personal power and love. Jung explains further that the penultimate stage of *coniunctio* is symbolized by the "falling dew" that portends the divine birth, or descent of heavenly wisdom, the "fire of the Holy Ghost,"[159] a subtle, breath, or spirit-presence of the glorified body or *corpus glori-*

---

156 Jung, *CW* 16: ¶ 444.
157 Jung, *CW* 16: ¶¶ 445, 448.
158 Eliade, *Shamanism*, p. 168.
159 Jung, *CW* 16: ¶ 484.

ficationis.[160] The ultimate stage of alchemy comes to the adept when he receives the "crown of victory" through a trans-subjective union that is no longer projected into subjective preoccupations. By this Jung means the spiritual marriage is achieved only through objective cognition.[161] He equates the crown of victory, further, with the "cabalistic *Kether* (corona), the marriage Bride, or Shekinah (the Divine Presence),"[162] and adds that the "higher coitus" is a transmundane affair occurring in the psychic non-ego, "a hieros gamos of the gods and not a mere love affair between mortals."[163]

Dickinson says: "A dew sufficed itself— / And satisfied a Leaf / And felt 'how vast a destiny'— / 'How trivial is Life!'" (J 1437/F 1372). When she was in possession of the inner crown of victory, symbolized by gold, life was never trivial. This led her to states of supreme Happiness. "How happy is the little stone / That rambles in the Road alone, / And doesn't care about Careers" (J 1510/F 1570) she wrote.

The ecstasy she asserts in this poem is made known in Jung's words, as "an *experience of feeling.*"[164] In her simple way, Dickinson conformed to the *archetype of the shaman who is married to her spirit helpers, and through their help becomes the whole experience of her inner wedding, as Jung also realized in 1944.* She died and opened herself up to an embrace with the Self, as her ultimate lover.

How the *coniunctio* is achieved in life is perhaps the greatest mystery at our being's center. How did this dowerless young woman who was not mothered as she said become the matron of American poetry by 1862? Whatever her experiences of love were, she is never selfish with what she was given. She offers it freely to us. The "word of Gold" she directs towards "every Creature" she meets. This is her life's aim, for she says that she has "Dowered—all the World" with "Dew," and "Golden lines—" (J 430/F 388). This "Dowerless Girl" who was mothered by the Cosmos arrived at an image of spiritual betrothal that was truly equal-

---

160 Jung, *CW* 16: ¶ 486.
161 Jung, *CW* 16: ¶ 496.
162 Jung, *CW* 16: ¶ 497.
163 Jung, *CW* 16: ¶ 500.
164 Jung, *CW* 16: ¶ 531.

izing and remarkably contemporaneous with current trends in analytical psychology. "I am ashamed—I hide—" she said with modesty,

> What right have I—to be a Bride—
> So late a Dowerless Girl—
> Nowhere to hide my dazzled Face—
> No one to teach me that new Grace—
> Not introduce—my Soul—
>
> Bring Me my best Pride—
> No more ashamed—
> No more to hide—
> Meek—let it be—too proud—for Pride—
> Baptized—this Day—A Bride—   J 473/F 705

Wherever we meet one of Emily Dickinson's marriage poems, we can be sure she is in earnest. She was no extrovert; she remained true, like many shamans do, to her solitary introverted nature. She did not waver from the truth of her "hidden" personality. She wrote on "superior soil" (J 325/F 328) the meaning of her life and vocation, illuminating, instructing, seeking to transform us at every stroke of her pen. As a woman, she was writing a feminist critique of our most widely read religious texts, the Old and New Testaments, and she means what she says. She calls for social justice and insists we listen to the voice of Woman. She is every bit as much a God-wrestler as Melville and Whitman were. As she wrote in a letter: "My Country is Truth…I like Truth—it is a free Democracy."[165] The "Country" of "Truth" is her land of "a free Democracy" in which all men and women are created as equals, and where we all have a voice in a governance of participatory liberties because of our freedom of speech.

For Dickinson, the same-sex *coniunctio* was no apprentice piece to individuation. It was central to her experience of Spiritual Democracy in an evolving world, her love for the "Purple Democrat." Her *union of sames* was of great significance for the evolution of the world in transit towards a socio-political-spiritual democracy for the spiritual liberation

---

165 Richard Sewall, *The Lyman Letters: New Light on Emily Dickinson and Her Family*, p. 71.

of all people. This is something Dickinson conveyed beautifully through her feminine depths of Eros and *feeling*. She says: "I can't tell you—but you feel it—" (J 65/F 164). This is key: By reading her we come to feel it. She can't tell us what Ecstasy is, but when we read her closely, and deeply, we *feel* it. We feel her; she touches us with her love. The truth can be told; but it needs to be told slant.

Dickinson's marriage imagery is exquisitely personal, because all her melodious metaphors are incarnated as her essential voice, her vocalized *feminine experiences as an embodied woman*.[166] Dickinson's voice, the mature "Voice of the 'Wife,'"[167] rests on a broad granitic base and her grounding in the female body was inspired, as we saw, by her equal love for science and religion. Letting go her career as poet did indeed hurt her; but poetry healed the hurt. It was her medicine. "We—tell a Hurt—to cool it—"[168] she says. In this sense, she is a *healer* for our times.

As regards to her belief or faith in God, she said, in no uncertain terms: "I know that He exists" (J 338/F 365). This is Spiritual Democracy: an equality with everything that leads us to an experience of absolute knowledge. She came to this knowledge experientially: through her lived experiences in the company of women and men, whom she loved dearly. Through her tropes, we can see her footsteps leading to what we now know and feel to be the better union of equality between women and men, free of sexism and homophobia, and attuned to equal rights for all human beings. Such freedoms were anticipated by Dickinson: "Garlands for Queens, may be— / Laurels—for rare degree / Of soul or sword. / Ah—but remembering me— / Ah—but remembering thee— / Nature in chivalry— / Nature in charity— / Nature in equity— / The Rose ordained! (J 34/F 10).

In another amazing poem, she wrote: "New Horizons—they embellish— / Fronting Us—with Night." (J 972/F 839). By Night she means Awe: The Divine Masculine and Divine Feminine, which she spiritually married.

---

166 Communication from Lori Goldrich.
167 Cynthia Griffin Wolff, *Emily Dickinson,* p. 200.
168 *S*, p. 341.

7

AN INQUIRY INTO THE SIGNIFICANCE
OF SHAMANIC INFLUENCE

As Emily wrote to Higginson in 1862: "I had no Monarch in my life, and cannot rule myself, and when I try to organize—my little Force explodes—and leaves me bare and charred."[169] As we saw, this is a clear reference to Volcano symbolism as a metaphor for the Self. It is a principle in her psyche that cannot be ruled. As a poet of Nature, her ego learned to serve It. The emergent power of the Volcano recurs repeatedly in Dickinson's poetry as a symbol for the force of her personality and creative power, which was wild, and could not be subdued. No Monarch could subdue It. Thus, it is fitting that Dickinson's place of contemplation and home was a Volcano in her mind, from which she beheld the beauty of all life, animate and inanimate, in the Infinite depths of her ecstatic imagination in harmony with Nature. "He," the "Infinite" is "not a man," she says further, for "he foundeth, with his Arm" the magnificent "Himmaleh" (J 350/F 352).

Dickinson wrote in the second stanza of her Chimborazo poem:

> Love—thou art deep—
> I cannot cross thee—
> But, were there Two
> Instead of One—
> Rower, and Yacht—some sovereign Summer—
> Who knows—but we'd reach the Sun?

---

169 *L*, II, p. 414.

Love—thou art Veiled
A few—behold thee
Smile—and alter—and prattle—and die—
Bliss—were an Oddity—without thee—
Nicknamed by God—
Eternity—   J 453/F 452

In this chapter, we will look at the transmission of shamanic knowledge from medicine-powers that were dear to Dickinson: Butterfly, Bee,
and Hummingbird. The intelligence of Nature is an age-old concept,
perhaps as old as human consciousness itself. Carriers of shamanic
knowledge in pre-civilized cultures knew how to harmonize themselves
with this ancient intelligence and to keep their tribes in alignment with
it. Shamans are people who, through experiences of self-wounding, open
him or herself up to animal, bird, reptile, amphibian, insect, plant, and
mineral levels of experience. The shaman has access to levels of reality
in the world soul that are necessary for our sustenance. Such individuals find ways to atone with the souls of the deceased that can be found
in specific regions and to help the living remember the wisdom of the
ancestors. The transmission of shamanic knowledge is brought about
through various techniques. One of these techniques is poetry. In this
domain of art, Dickinson has no rivals. Dickinson is in a special category of her own when it comes to the articulation of her own unique
vision of Spiritual Democracy because she is by far the most scientific
of her shamanic-minded contemporaries. She is a poetic botanist, ento-
mologist, and ornithologist all-in-one.

Butterflies, Bees, and Hummingbirds are symbols in her art for
spirits of the earth; they are necessary in the maintenance of Spiritual
Democracy, and it is the shaman-poet's job not only to engage with
them in imagination, but to become temporarily identified with their
powers. We endanger species of butterflies, bees, and birds by destroying
forests and marshes and fields and plants and flowers. The symbols of
the hummingbird, bee, and butterfly are age-old archetypes of an intelligence in Nature we must listen to if we are to survive. Albert Einstein
is rumored to have said that, "If the bee disappears from the surface of
the earth, man would have no more than four years to live." Honey bees
are responsible for the pollination of countless crops of fruits and veg-

etables worldwide. Insecticides and global warming increases the growth rates of invasive killers, such as mites, viruses, and fungi that in recent years have contributed to an alarming collapse rate of bee colonies. As a shaman-poet Dickinson not only worshiped bees, she became them! "Because the Bee may blameless hum / For Thee a Bee do I become" (J 869/F 909). By "Thee" she means the Divinity of Nature. She even went so far as to write her own new version of the Lord's Prayer:

> In the name of the Bee—
> And of the Butterfly—
> And of the Breeze—Amen!   J 18/F21

This poem shows just how pantheistic her spirituality in point of fact is and how much her theology is a medicine of Spiritual Democracy. She replaces the Father and Son and Holy Spirit with living symbols of nature. This makes her a poet of the highest spiritual order. In Dickinson's poems about such creatures, we hear her songs flow from a fountain of knowledge and joy and love that is transmitting wisdom from the Medicine Woman archetype within her, for the good of our very own survival.

We know from archaeological records that the vocation of the Medicine Woman is at least 70,000 years old. When I speak of Emily Dickinson as a Medicine Woman in this book, therefore, I'm speaking of her ability to tap into an archaic *archetype of sacred medicine* within herself; to activate an image of healing, an instinct-type, or pattern of behavior within all humans. In so doing, she offers her poetry to the whole world. The *typos* upon which her verses are patterned is an innate channeling design to manufacture holy medicine through Art. Dickinson's poems offer readers a medicament through her immense artistic productivity. Through silence, suffering, and solitude, she taps into the curative energies of the Medicine Woman *typos* and becomes thereby Its Voice. Overcoming the malaise in her patriarchal 19th century American culture enables her to transform her own dislocated states of mind, body, and soul and to produce a panacea for her nation, humans, Nature, and God. Her poems are enduring imprints of the Medicine Woman archetype, or impulse to redeem, within all of us. Amongst a list of Dickinson's consecrated medicine-animals are Snake, Butterfly, Bee, and

Hummingbird; she also summons powers to medicate through Volcanoes, Flowers, Herbs, and Home.

Medicine of compassion is transmitted to her from wounds and Diadems and transparent *Crystals*: "Burden—borne so far triumphant— / None suspect me of the crown, / For I wear the 'Thorns' till *Sunset*—/ Then—my Diadem put on" (J 1737). In the final analysis, her calling to cure comes from her being betrothed spiritually to the meek "Fellow" that was Crucified and "Lives" through Woe and Lovingkindness: "Love is the Fellow of the Resurrection / Scooping up the Dust and chanting 'Live!'" (J 491).

Magic crystals and power-chanting words, such as "Ecstasy," "Love," and "Live!", enable her to give body and soul-energy and Eros to her lyrical lines of a beautifully transmuting kind. Sometimes it is not crystals, her Diadem, Resurrection-chants, or hopeful Feathered-people, but Snake and Lightning Bolt that give her medicine-power to heal with.

The Medicine Woman imprint is acausal and like all archetypes, it may constellate synchronicities. It may cross our paths at the most unexpected moments; sometimes in the utmost meaningful and miraculous of ways. By tapping into the immense supremacy of this protection principle, Dickinson allows the Divine Feminine Voice—the female speech of the Earth-and-Sky-Goddes—to sound through her. Her poetry can influence us also, if we are open to her healing influences. She is a Medicine Woman, a dispenser of a new American myth for our times.

It is transmitted to her during shamanic states of mind as a form of absolute knowledge that aims at disseminating earth-wisdom on a transpersonal and trans-temporal plane of existence that is meant to sustain our Spiritual Democracy, our sense of equality with everything that is. In a complimentary way, she transmutes her soul into a butterfly as well, which enables her to see across vast distances through shamanic flight.

To be sure, Awe was a cocoon in which she lived in her garden, or took incubation in at home. "Cocoon above! Cocoon below! /…The Universe to know!" (J 129/F 142). By "Cocoon above!" I take her to mean the Circumference of the whole Cosmos. By "Cocoon below!" I think she means the individual soul and its individual depths of untrammeled freedom, liberty destined for all races of the globe, all nationalities, all individuals.

What she is describing in the poem is the first and second births that we are *all* meant to experience in life as *spiritual democrats* on this green earth: "An hour in Chrysalis to pass, / Then gay above receding grass / A Butterfly to go!" (J 129/F 142). In "Cocoon above!" we can see an astounding realization of what she must have understood from reading Hitchcock's *Religious Lectures* (1850) and *The Religion of Geology* (1851), where "The Scientist of Faith" had referred to the metamorphosis of butterflies as a miracle of nature that confirmed to his mind that "*All* science…is of God and from God."[170] For Dickinson, the whole notion of God, as an all-male Trinity, was in the process of being radically changed from one that excludes the feminine to one that includes her in the entire Universe in a single breath of human life. Breath was for Emily a symbol of a change in nature from a triune God-image to a quaternary one, such as in "Three times—we parted—Breath—and I—" (J 598/F 514). This poem is made up of sixteen lines, comprised by four quatrains. In the fourth quatrain, she ends with these stunning lines: "The sunrise kissed my Chrysalis— / And I stood up—and lived—" (J 598/F 514). Thus, from three to four there is only one integer, and that is She. The "I" that lived during her fourth breath is the instinct of Self-realization, Immortality, Resurrection of "a Particle—of Space's / Vast Society—" (J 679/F 773).

Dickinson's poetry, therefore, is a spirituality of science, nature and the Cosmos, or what Thomas Jefferson inscribed into the Declaration of Independence in 1776 as an expression of "Nature's God." All nature shares in the grandeur of Liberty; humans with bees, butterflies with hummingbirds, trees with flowers; we all share in the universal design of the God-in-Nature, as do, for instance, the purple flower for which bees have a preference and that butterflies yearn for, Dickinson's beloved hummingbird's desire: "The Purple Democrat" (J 380/F 642).

Her greatest poem pitting herself against the dangers of domesticity, motherhood, and traditional marriage as opposed to the life of freedom

---

170 *S*, p. 355.

she chose for herself are emblazoned in tones of tragedy, when contemplating the fate of her own mother:

> She rose to His Requirement—dropt
> The Playthings of Her Life
> To take the honorable Work
> Of Woman, and of Wife—
>
> If ought She missed in Her new Day,
> Of Amplitude, or Awe—
> Or first Prospective—Or the Gold
> In using, wear away,
>
> It lay unmentioned—as the Sea
> Develop Pearl, and Weed,
> But only to Himself—be known
> The Fathoms they abide—   J 732/F 857

As Paula Bennett says about this remarkable poem, it is a compassionate and angry lament about "the fate of women who (like her mother) buries her talent (her 'Gold') in a domestic life."[171] The work of woman and of wife is an honorable vocation she said, yet one must not sacrifice one's link to the creative principle and Muse in the process. In this sense, the Hummingbird was one of Emily's totem aviators: a transporter to the wheel of Ecstasy. So too were flowers, and bees, and butterflies. "Within my Garden, rides a Bird / Upon a single Wheel—" (J 500/F 1582).

Amplitude exists in all God's creatures. As a potential experience in every human heart, body, and mind, we can all gain access to it. It is the Awe and Amplitude the Butterfly knows within her: unity with the Self and the All: Sun, Stars, Moon, Volcanic peaks and migratory paths across southern to northern continents, finally to touch home base in the "Purple" and "Gold" of the favorite flowers in her Garden.

"She rose to His Requirement" is a poem about the risks women like her mother faced in achieving the tasks of their individuations. What her mother kept was the "Moth" part of the house. Emily kept the Butterfly part, the self-aware soul and spirit that soared and sipped

---

171 P. Bennett, *Emily Dickinson: Woman Poet*, p. 11.

the flower of life and flew shaman-like towards the Sun. As she wrote to Judge Otis P. Lord: "I don't keep the Moth part of the House—I keep the Butterfly part."[172] The butterfly part was her way to marry Awe. The Butterfly part was her calling to vocation, Bliss, and her desire for Joy. No metaphor in Dickinson's cannon depicts such joys better than do the tropes of bees, butterflies, or hummingbirds.

In surveying Dickinson's views of the Cosmos and the myths she created, we must not hesitate to turn to religious and theological questions she raised about the nature of the Deity—or Self. Her point of unification in her poetry is captured in the metaphor of America as a second Eden. Here are a couple more examples from Dickinson:

> Come slowly—Eden!
> Lips unused to Thee—
> Bashful—sip thy Jessamines—
> As the fainting Bee—
>
> Reaching late his flower,
> Round her chamber hums—
> Counts his nectars—
> Enters—and is lost in Balms.　　　J 211/F 205

And here is another:

> All the letters I can write
> Are not fair as this—
> Syllables of Velvet—
> Sentences of Plush,
> Depths of Ruby, undrained,
> Hid, Lip, for Thee—
> Play it were a Humming Bird—
> And just sipped—me—　　　J 334/F 380

Emily sent the latter poem to her cousin, Eudocia (Converse) Flynt. The delight she appears to have *felt* in sending it, enclosed with a flower, moreover, is probably the unfulfilled delight of erotic desire, yet, it appears to have been completely spiritualized through art. She asks Eudocia to sip *her* "Syllables of Velvet." The "Lip" of the poet-shaman

---

172 *L*, III, p. 924.

invites the lips of her cousin to sip her poem. In playful droughts, she teasingly ends with "Play it were a Hummingbird— / And just sipped— me—" These supreme metaphors are reflective of her *democratic spiritualization* of the archetype of Self into a universal medicine.

What she tapped into in these poems is the primordial image of the Medicine Woman who administers a balm of bi-erotic love, to whomever is called, to be healed by her words. When I speak of the shamanic archetype that was activated in Dickinson's poetry, I am referring to an instinct of activity that is ancient and was very active within her. This is the archetype of Spiritual Democracy.

In discussing the concept of Spiritual Democracy, it is important to point out that it is first and foremost an *archetype*: an empirically verifiable datum of experience that exists as a potentiality of Self-realization in all cultures, ethnicities, and religious groups across the globe. It is an instinct of a certain kind of spiritual activity that is democratic at its core. It tends to encourage the principle of universal equality and lives transnationally in the perpetual "Now." Its roots are archaic and cosmic and can be found in the practices and visionary products of shamanism and modern psychology worldwide. As an image of instinct, a pattern of behavior for a certain kind of trans-conscious perception, it is centered on world peace through a harmonization with Mother Nature. It can take on a number of symbolic representations and may be portrayed mythopoetically in the lives of artists, political leaders, environmentalists, religious leaders, and national poets, such as Dickinson. Many of the greatest ideas in religions, philosophies, and ethics go back to this archetype. And as with all archetypes, which reach a consensus of opinion in the collective thinking of the human race, its dimensions and scope in space and time are transgressive and trans-temporal. As an archetype of Nature, it is filled with a hidden and unknown numinosity of meaning.

The aim of Jungian analysis, not unlike the goal of Emily Dickinson's art, might best be described as the approach to the archetypal "nucleus" of the personality. Once this center of wholeness is reached, it can unlock the floodgates of Mother Nature towards a transcendent experience of Ecstasy, which is the essence of the Self's innermost being and awareness. Often its goal has a national purpose, namely to make the national myths by which a nation lives conscious for the generality. The archetype of Spiritual Democracy can be known by the effects it produces.

Just as there are ethnic and racial and gender complexes[173] in every country, so too are there national archetypes that continue to influence each of us and that can become a channel of healing for an entire culture. One of these archetypes is the archetype of the Peacemaker and it is the shaman-poets who become its greatest spiritual representatives.

One of the best proofs for the influence of archetypes on a nation is provided by the phenomena Jung called synchronicity. I've had the good fortune to have witnessed some of the most remarkable coincidences as a Jungian child psychotherapist. Such marginal phenomena have simply presented themselves to me as I was engrossed in my studies in American poetry. The insights I've gained through the careful observation of such "chance" events have come mostly from my work with children, whose dreams, sand tray productions, and spontaneous fantasies have often been quite illuminating. Jung hypothesized that "synchronistic phenomena can be evoked by putting the subject into an unconscious state (trance)."[174] Techniques can be utilized that may bring about synchronicity and one of the most direct methods is through shamanic poetry.

Thus, in discussing the archetype of Spiritual Democracy, as it pertains to the work of Emily Dickinson, I have chosen to turn to the wisdom of a six-to-seven-year-old girl, therefore, to demonstrate how a child may tap into national myths in latency. What interests me here is her symbolizing function as a parallel to Dickinson's poems about butterflies and the Cosmos. "Cocoon above! Cocoon below! /…The Universe to know!" Children are in touch with the archaic mind in a way that can help demonstrate how the archetype of the butterfly works at an elementary level and cuts across all national boundaries and racial distinctions.

---

173   See Endnote H.
174   Jung, *CW* 8: p. 232.

I would like to provide my example of the spontaneous emergence of the archetype of Spiritual Democracy in the case material of a six-year-old girl patient of mine who I have called "Clare."[175] About a central dream in the early part of our work, Clare reported as follows, several months after her sixth birthday: "*I turned into an inch worm. Then I went on a train. After that I traveled on a postman's shoe. Then, I found a place to live. I turned into a caterpillar; then I turned into a beautiful Butterfly. My wings had green and yellow and pink and blue colors. I flew to Jupiter!*" As I was reflecting on Clare's dream, I couldn't help but remember a review I had written of Jungian analyst Murray Stein's marvelous book *Transformation: Emergence of the Self*,[176] wherein the now Zürich-based author describes how transformations take place in people passing through periods of deep structural change during midlife, such as Dickinson was when she wrote her chrysalis, cocoon, and butterfly poems. Interestingly, the primary clinical example Stein used in that book to illustrate his idea of the *transformative image*[177] comes from the case of a butterfly woman, whose dreams formed the empirical foundation for *Transformation*. In her transformed state, this woman's dream-body morphed into a beautiful butterfly, which is to say, she became momentarily fused with an image of the Divine, Great Mother, Psyche, or the Self.

Clare told me further that "*God is a beautiful woman with red, orange, yellow, and blue hair who paints the sky.*" Thus, this image of the Divine Feminine was portrayed her in her dreams and drawings as a cosmic artist, a beautiful Goddess who paints the sky. Although she mentioned that the hair of the painting-Goddess consisted of four basic colors from the color spectrum (Red, Orange, Yellow, and Blue), what the Goddess painted was the Sky: the infinite blueness of the visible heavens. So, here, I thought, was an image of Spiritual Democracy in its cosmic unity! Later in our sessions, this same young girl came into my office joyously telling me that she was speaking with the Goddess again. She

---

175 Herrmann, "The Case of Clare: The Emergence of the Self in a Six-Year-Old Girl," *Journal of Sandplay Therapy*, Vol. 18, No. 2, pp. 111-132.

176 Murray Stein, *Transformation: Emergence of the Self.*

177 Herrmann, "Murray Stein: The Transformative Image," *The San Francisco Jung Institute Library Journal*, Vol. 17, No. 1.

said: "*There is only One God. God appears in a lot of places!*" Who could argue with this? Later she told me: "*I think God has a Rainbow Eye and I am the Eye of God!*" The best word for such thoughts may be autochthonous.

If we hypothesize that there is a luminosity in the unconscious that is superconscious, therefore, then the Eye of God (or Sky-Goddess) may be understood as a prism, through which she can paint the stars. Thus, I believe it is an authentic emblem of Spiritual Democracy. Her statement provides empirical evidence for the existence of a consciousness that is aware of Itself in the American psyche concerning the archetype of Spiritual Democracy. Her thoughts and images remind me of Emily Dickinson's poetry. What my six-year-old girl patient was experiencing was a momentary breakthrough of a luminosity emanating from the transcendent Ground of all being. The Eye of God can be found in Egypt, India, Israel, Indigenous America, and in most all other cultures of the world. It is a universal thought-form, therefore, an image with a strong feeling-tone. I never thought a little child would say: "*I am the Eye of God!*"

Another fascinating example of the transformations we've been considering in Dickinson's life was a drawing Clare did with colored pencils in my office. In the top left corner of her picture was an illustration of what Clare called the "*shadowy girl who died.*" I interpret the shadow of this girl's soul as Clare's chrysalis self that she had to slough off: the girl in the picture appeared to have left her dead body behind, and out of this ghostly figure, four smaller spirits appeared to have arisen and were descending around a "seventh" butterfly. This seventh butterfly had four yellow dots on the tips of its wings, and it appeared to be emerging out of the dead girl's body at the level of her heart. Through her symbolic death, it seemed as though she were sloughing off the *pupal* skin of her heart, the way the snake sheds its skin, a butterfly leaves its chrysalis behind, or the moon, Luna, throws off her shadow. The shadowy girl who died might represent a shadow of Clare's former self, a neurotic part of her nascent personality that died during her psychotherapy process. The dead girl and five ghostly figures might correspond to the six years she was leaving behind. She was six and one half at this point in her treatment, nearing seven. In the picture a scene of her metamorphosis, with the themes of death and rebirth, are explicitly depicted. The 7th yellow-winged butterfly reveals the miracle of transformation. I believe this drawing provides an x-ray picture into what the Self-in-transformation might look like in its nascent form during latency, as a preparation for changes in adolescence, early adulthood, and midlife metamorphosis.

As I've said above, the image of Spiritual Democracy can take on a number of different forms in the fantasy products of children. It can be portrayed in the lives of poets, artists, political activists, environmentalists, and religious leaders as well. Its roots are archaic and may be traced to the practices of archaic shamanism. The likelihood of Spiritual Democracy ever becoming dead, as a mere sign, with only historical significance, is improbable. I believe it will remain vital so long as the human species survives. Spiritual Democracy, in this sense, is not a faith; it is not a religion; nor will it ever be. It is outside religion; outside psychology; outside theology; outside politics. It is a *spiritual attitude*, transcendent of all creeds, pure and simple. The simplest teachings of what Spiritual Democracy really means is that, it does not need a long winded theological treatise to prove it. Poets, artists, scientists, and children are a testament to its very existence as an idea of metamorphosis. Perhaps the best symbol for a transformational image in the human psyche is the emergence of the butterfly from its cocoon portrayed by Dickinson.

In Dickinson's poetry, she establishes a primitive relationship with a number of diverse object-images carrying great soul-force (i.e., stones, gems, sun, stars, quartz crystal, Night, mountain, lightning, universe, volcanoes, snakes, bees, butterflies, hummingbird, etc.). How Dickinson tapped into such a deep source of artistic power to generate some of the greatest lyrical lines ever written is a question that is as much spiritual as it is psychological and scientific. A possible answer to my question might be found, I believe, in the marriage or union in her poems between science and Nature.

Dickinson had direct access to the shamanic archetype as a source of great artistic power.[178] If we can understand the mystery of how Dickinson tapped into this energy-source, we might be able to catch a glimpse of her method.

> I stepped from Plank to Plank
> A slow and cautious way
> The Stars about my Head I felt
> About my Feet the Sea.
>
> I knew not but the next
> Would be my final inch—
> This gave me that precious Gait
> Some call Experience.   J 875/F 926

While there are many poems and letters in Dickinson's oeuvre that support my hypothesis about the bi-erotic base of her marriage symbolism, perhaps the best source of empirical data was vouchsafed to her through a dream.

> Her sweet Weight on my Heart a Night
> Had scarcely deigned to lie—
> When, stirring, for Belief's delight,
> My Bride had slipped away—
>
> If 'twas a Dream—made solid—just
> The Heaven to confirm—
> Or if Myself were dreamed of Her—
> The power to presume—
>
> With Him remain—who unto Me—
> Gave—even as to All—
> A Fiction superseding Faith—
> By so much—as 'twas real—   J 518/F 611

If one discovers how to tap into such a nuclear energy-source as she in fact says she *touched*, a revolving wheel of the Universe at the center of

---

178 Herrmann, "A Conversation with William Everson: Shamanism, American Poetry, And the Vision Quest," *The San Francisco Jung Institute Library Journal,* Vol. 24, No. 4.

her shamanistic personality, we may be able to show that her medicine is a universal balm intended for everyone:

> I saw no Way—The Heavens were stitched—
> I felt the Columns close—
> The Earth reversed her Hemispheres—
> I touched the Universe—
>
> And back it slid—and I alone—
> A Speck upon a Ball—
> Went out upon Circumference—
> Beyond the Dip of Bell—   J 378/ F 633

In Jung's view, to reduce the psyche's explosive power to sexuality or even the personal complexes would be limiting, as psychic energy is situated on a much broader instinctive foundation than sex alone. On this point, Jung disagreed with Freud that sex was the source of the libido. Dickinson's "Columnar Self" sits on a "Granitic Base" (J 789) that transcends all categories of thought and her "little Force" sometimes erupts in emotional imagery that is impersonal and universal in scope.

To be sure, the "still—Volcano—Life— /…The lips that never lie— (J 601/F 517) is a symbol for the Goddess, as much as Night is. In her "Dream," Night covered her as a "Bride." Writing was for Emily a *therapy*, a "talking cure," a *balm* for soothing the pain. Dickinson refers to healing and wholeness of the Divine as the "All":

> Unto the Whole—how add?
> Has "All" a further Realm—
> Or Utmost an Ulterior?
> Oh, subsidy of Balm!   J 1341/F 1370

The word "subsidy of Balm" suggests the idea of monetary assistance granted by a government, or perhaps, at least payment for her poems; yet it is *balm* that is her true subsidy. The balm (a word for a kind of ointment, palliative, or *medicine*) may be Dickinson's best metaphor for the experience of spiritual marriage to the All that appears to have healed her during her "Seven years of troth" (J 1737/F 267). These seven years are roughly the time period when she was composing and sewing her forty fascicles together for self-publication.

The "New Horizons" had by this time come to her through "the Stupendous Vision / Of His diameters—" (J 802/F 858), diameters that is, of an infinite Universe. When the Church Bells stopped ringing for Emily, she began to hear "The Positive—Bells" of "Circumference— / The Ultimate—of Wheels" (J 633/F 601). "Circumference" was also the main business of "F-40's meditator."[179]

As Cynthia Griffin Wolff has indicated, moreover, at least six of her poems are "explicit recastings of the moment when Jacob struggled with the Lord."[180] To these six poems, for instance, "Rearrange a 'Wife's' affection!" (J 1737/F 267), is a probable seventh, because it contains a reference to an excruciating experience of "dislocation" to her brain; not to her hip, as in Jacob's famous struggle.

The first reference to her brain is in an 1861 poem "I felt a Funeral in my Brian" (J 280/F 340); the second in 1864, "I felt a Cleavage in my Mind" (J 937/F 867 b); and the third, a late poem from an unknown date, "Rearrange a 'Wife's' Affection! / When they dislocate my brain!" (J 1737/F 267). All three of these poems show a deep connection Dickinson made between her crucifying experience of death at midlife, and her attempt to heal herself through writing. She was clearly writing in the biblical tradition with an aim to transform the Judeo-Christian God-image. In 1862, for instance, she wrote:

> It always felt to me—a wrong
> To that Old Moses—done—
> To let him see—the Canaan—
> Without the entering—
>
> The fault—was doubtless Israel's—
> Myself—had banned the Tribes—
> And ushered Grand Old Moses
> In Pentateuchal Robes   J 597/F 521

Writing as a "Housewife" in "Pentateuchal Robes," Dickinson was a lover of Nature, and the Canaan she entered was "Home." Gathering flowers and observing the splendor of bees, butterflies, and humming-

---

179 D.H. Oberhaus, *Emily Dickinson's Fascicles*, p. 37.
180 Wolff, *Emily Dickinson*, p. 145.

birds, flitting like lightning from one flower to the next in her garden, was one of her most beloved activities. Interestingly, Mabel Loomis Todd, the mistress of her brother Austin, sent portraits of Indian Pipes, otherwise known as ghost plants, or corpse plants, to her in September of 1882. In her modesty, Dickinson wrote back: "I cannot make an Indian Pipe but please accept a Humming Bird."[181]

The Hummingbird was by this time a totem animal for her and a symbol for her vocation, for the ruby-throated Hummer (*Archilochus Colubris*), which she writes about so eloquently in "A Route of Evanescence" (J 1463/F 1489) is the sole breeding variant of the spectacular species that is indigenous to the Eastern region of North America. As an animal power, Hummingbird carried a spiritual significance for her as an animal ancestor. With its emerald-green back and crown and its iridescent, brilliant ruby red gorget (throat), the male species is said in particular to glitter like a jewel in sunlight. Its "magical" qualities of flight, moreover, become particularly meaningful when we view it in the context of Emily's shamanistic cannon, and how it may have come to her indigenously by way of ancestral *influence*.

She was a pantheist and post-Hebrew and post-Christian poet par excellence, for she saw God in all natural things. She did not place herself above Nature, but in many ways envisioned herself to be an equal with the earth; she acknowledged in one of her late poems that her whole poetic oeuvre was "Superfluous" beside the "Bird" (J 1655/F 1739), just as plaudits would have seemed superfluous next to "Fame of Myself" (J 713/F 481). This goes to show how shamanistic she really was.

In a mysterious way, Birds had a special meaning for her as soul-images or soul-animals. Butterflies too carried deep meaning for her as symbols for the soul in flight. Here is one example: "Delight is as the flight— / …The Rainbow's way— / …Flung colored, after Rain, / … And I, for glee, / Took Rainbows, as the common way, /…And so with Butterflies— /…And Dower latitudes far on—" (J 257/F 317).

To Dower us with Rainbows and Butterflies suggests she is at one with Noah's covenant from God, with God within herself, the God in Nature. While her modesty is everywhere apparent in her relationship

---

181 *L*, III, p. 740.

to Nature, there are a few instances when she places herself not only on par with Nature's God, but as *superior to both God and Nature*. During such moments of transcendence, she arrives at the source of her purpose and aim of her myth simply to *sing*. "I reckon—" she wrote boldly, in 1862 "when I count at all— / First—Poets—Then the Sun— / Then Summer—Then the Heaven of God— / And then—the List is done—" (J 569/F 533). Wow!

I might cite numerous instances to lend support to my hypothesis that she was a poet-shaman of Spiritual Democracy, but let me stop here. What we have briefly outlined is a postulate that her active vision-ing methods were in some mysterious ways shaped by her childhood memories of being in the presence of Awe in Nature. This reverence for the awesome beauty of nature grew out of her emotional experiences, which were sometimes traumatic. Her use of mythopoetic motifs, such as volcano symbolism, had a *healing* effect on her soul or psyche. All of these natural forces within herself and outside of her were part and par-cel of the shamanic influences that changed her and of her continuing ability to *influence* us.

It was out of her fate and suffering as a girl that she was able to make direct unmediated contact with powerful forces of the natural world that ultimately transformed her. She dowered us with what is essen-tially a new covenant as a Medicine Woman of Nature's infinite riches. Archaic man knew how to activate shamanic structures and potencies in the human psyche, Andreas Lommel says. Yet above all, he knew how to *cure mental disorders through aesthetic productivity*.[182] This is as much evident in shamanic burials of women, as of men. The oldest known archeological site that lends weight to this hypothesis is located in the Zagros Mountains of Northern Iraq, at Shanidar, two hundred and fifty miles north of Baghdad, at a burial cave of a medicine man or shaman. His body was laid to rest with two women and an infant, with a bouquet of *seven* different types of medicinal herbs as a bed for the shaman to lie on.[183] He was buried next to the two women, who may have been

---

182 Andreas Lommel, *The World of the Early Hunters*, p. 13.
183 Cited in Joseph Campbell, *Historical Atlas of World Mythology Vol. 1: The Way of the Animal Powers*, p. 53.

his wives, and the infant. This burial points to a probability of an older lineage of shamanism, extending back to the antiquity of the vocation of Medicine Women. Women were typically gatherers of sacred medicines and knew how to administer them. The burial could be seventy thousand years old, making it forty thousand years older than the caves of Southern France and Northern Spain. The other interesting feature about this Medicine Woman burial is that they were laid to rest next to a male shaman of some kind. This is the bi-erotic archetype that Dickinson was in touch with directly.

Clearly, she tapped into the archetype and made liberal use of it to cure herself. This fact alone makes her a shaman. Yet as I see it, her aim was transnational. She wished to heal the world that was suffering from a misreading of the Bible. She was intent to bring the Divine Mother back and to bless us with healing powers.

What we need today is a theology that can put her in the right spiritual context, such as Oberhaus does in *Emily Dickinson's Fascicles: Method and Meaning.* It's obvious to Oberhaus that so many of her poems of agony are like St. Theresa of Avila's writings, poems of Ecstasy. Emily was a mystic, for whom religion was alive only through experiment and experience. She was an avid reader of the 1857 edition of Thomas á Kempis' *Imitation of Christ,* a copy of which has survived and can be viewed in the Beinecke Library at Yale University, and is inscribed during the centennial of the United States in 1876 "To Emily with love" from Sue. Yet, for Emily, it was not the imitation of Christ that she was modeling in her poetry. She became her own spiritual Awakener. She did not imitate Jesus, she became Herself. She was *Her*! And her domain of consciousness was a Self-awareness that exists throughout the entire Cosmos. This, finally, was her "Faith."

8

JUNGIAN THEMES IN DICKINSON'S POETRY

Jung's "myth of meaning" was to create as much consciousness as possible by giving unselfishly to others what he had learned about the symbolic life through direct personal *experience*. By teaching others to live a "symbolic life" Jung opened up a channel for people to live out that innate urge of existence, or instinct of individuation. This is the same urge that may have moved Emily Dickinson to declare: "I do not know the man so bold / He dare in lonely Place / That awful Consciousness / Deliberately face—" (J 1323/F 1325). To face Consciousness deliberately, to become Self-aware, may in fact be the central aim of human life.

What do shamanism and analytical psychology have in common with the field of American poetry? One aim of Dickinson's art was to take readers on a psychic voyage to the Beyond through states of active visioning and feeling that are acutely aware. Her poems are an attempt to lead readers into shamanistic states of mind. As well as being a shaman of her tribe, Dickinson is also a visionary seer and Medicine Woman and during her trance-states she often writes in ecstatic verses. Her metaphors are arranged in grand symbolical images that depict a transformation process in her soul, a metamorphosis of consciousness that can be mind-altering for the reader. "From Cocoon forth a Butterfly" she writes, "As Lady from her Door / Emerged—a Summer Afternoon— / …In purposeless Circumference—" (J 354/F 610).

From center to Circumference she flies towards the summits of human consciousness. Like Snake and Hummingbird, Butterfly, too, is a symbol for her shamanistic personality. The winged-Lady dressed in

Royal Gown emerges from her "Door" on a "Summer Afternoon," which is to say at the Zenith of her life, in full glory. The analogy between Butterflies coming out from their cocoons, and Dickinson's emergence as a poet-shaman has much to do with her transformation *into* an animal spirit. Entomology became a metaphor for the miracle of psychological transformation and it also connotes her spiritual marriage: putting on the "Butterfly's Assumption Gown" (J 1244/F 1329).

The "Gown," like her white dress, is a wedding symbol. How these metaphors relate to shamanism and analytical psychology was made clear to me through a dream I had in the spring of 1997.

> *I find myself on a University Campus, listening to some spectacular violin music by the classical Italian composer, Vivaldi, like the summer section of his Four Seasons. As I walk on the Campus grounds, I see a flowering bush, where I find a beautiful Butterfly with multi-colored wings, and as I study its singular markings, I suddenly think of Emily Dickinson's poems about butterflies before I wake up.*

The University Campus is a place where my work with the poet-shaman, William Everson, began in 1980 at UC Santa Cruz.[184] The multi-colored butterfly (the colors of the rainbow) has relevance to my writing on Emily Dickinson. I had already completed my first draft of an essay on Dickinson in the winter of 1995. What is most interesting to note now, however, twenty-one years later, is the transition from seeing the Butterfly while listening to the summer section of Vivaldi's Four Seasons and my call to write poetry. "First—Poets—Then the Sun— / Then Summer—" (J 569/F 533), she said.

As I put her butterfly poems together for this chapter, side by side, I began to see that all of them speak of the mystery of her psychological transformation. The butterfly's "spangled journeys to the peak / Of some perceiveless thing—" is what she calls the "more essential thing" (J 1627/F 1650). By "more essential thing" I take her to mean her destiny. Poetry was seen by her as a means to heal the collective malaise of the mid-nineteenth century. Listen again:

---

184 Herrmann, *William Everson: The Shaman's Call, Expanded Edition.*

We thirst at first—'tis Nature's Act—
And later—when we die—
A little Water supplicate—
Of fingers going by—

It intimates the finer want—
Whose adequate supply
Is the Great Water in the West—
Termed Immortality—   J 726/F 750

Writing from "A Quartz contentment, like a stone—" (J 341/F 372), she "conjectured a colossal destiny for herself"[185] says Dickinson scholar Cynthia Wolff. This was true. Probably the most shamanistic of all of her poems is her poem "Snake."

The Call of the Snake

In 1865, Emily wrote "A narrow Fellow in the Grass," a poem about a snake she had seen in childhood and whose sudden notice took her breath away:

Yet when a Boy, and Barefoot—
I more than once at Noon
Have passed, I thought, a Whip lash
Unbraiding in the Sun
When stooping to secure it
It wrinkled and was gone—

Several of Nature's People
I know, and they know me—
I feel for them a transport
Of cordiality—

But never met this Fellow
Attended, or alone
Without a tighter breathing
And Zero at the Bone—   J 986/F 1096

---

185 Wolff, *Emily Dickinson*, p. 13.

What Jung says about dream interpretation might as well be applied to Emily Dickinson's most shamanistic poems, such as "Snake," for she is writing out of the same depths that dreams come from and her linguistic-creations are symbolically laden with metaphorical meanings, making them a rich resource for the generation of theories with regards to how words can be used in depth psychotherapy to assist a patient in the process of transforming the personality. Shortly before his death, in June 1961, Jung completed an eloquent essay composed in fluent English called "Symbols and the Interpretation of Dreams" where he gives a concise theory of how to interpret dreams properly.

Dreams can only be understood, writes Jung, when we are "able to learn the language of the patient" and "we must pay particular attention to the language of dreams that we consider to be symbolic." The dream-language the analyst is most concerned in deciphering arises from one's "original nature" and "peculiar thinking;"[186] and "the study of this language," he adds "is almost a science in itself."[187]

Dickinson is without doubt as dazzling in her intuitions as she is in her feeling-toned cognitions. Her poems reveal her own original *dream language*. This is true particularly when she speaks of the powers of her Snake. Early letters to her friends are of special interest in this regard. When she was writing to some *"Amherst girls"* for instance, from her year at Mount Holyoke,[188] the "snake powers" made their first appearance in her writings and summoned her towards the path of her creative destiny at the age of seventeen. Her love for snakes come through most clearly in these early letters and they give us some hints about who the "Boy" who walked "Barefoot" actually was. Comprehending this connection is important in our attempt to understand her because as we have already seen in her letter to Higginson, upon declaring her decision to forego publication she wrote that, "my barefoot rank is better." "The inhuman quality that the snake represents" says Jung "is linked up with the lower centers of the brain and the spinal system" and "these are snake powers."[189] Thus, from a Jungian angle, what the snake represents

---

186 Jung, *CW* 18: ❡ 518.
187 Jung, *CW* 18: ❡ 521.
188 *S*, p. 368.
189 Jung, *Seminar on Dream Analysis*, p. 327.

is the instinctive wisdom in her reptilian brain, the part that knew what her right vocation was and over which there could be no bowdlerization.

The first evidence of the call to shamanic vocation in Emily Dickinson's art can be found in a series of letters written to her dear friends Abiah Root and Jane Humphrey in 1850, when she was nineteen years old. These letters are fascinating because they show us clearly her playfulness and childlike spirit and the delight she took in the emotion of surprise. Before we consider a few of these letters, let us first look at an even earlier letter to Jane. In this letter, dated May 12, 1842, Emily was only eleven years old:

> I miss you more and more every day, in my study in play at home indeed every where I miss my beloved Jane—I wish you would write to me—I should think more of it than of a mine of gold.[190]

In this letter, she is already showing us what she *values* more than a mine of gold: her love-friendships with girls. In 1846, moreover, after Abiah Root's conversion as a "Bride of Christ" under Mary Lyon's persuasive direction, Emily said she "shed many a tear" and yet she also felt "perfect happiness" because she felt "an heir of heaven as of a delightful dream." Delight came as a heavenly dream when "the Evil one" bid her "wake & again return to the world & its pleasures."[191]

Later, Emily informs us further that while her friends were all "flocking to the ark of safety" she was beginning to delve deeper and deeper into the secret recesses of her creative imagination.[192] Her decision to heed the summons of her vocation and go her own separate way from the rest of her Amherst friends was not necessarily a conscious choice; in her separation from her group of "pretty & fine scholars"[193] at Mount Holyoke, she was following the dictates of her inner voice—her calling. It is a misunderstanding to assume that a girl of seventeen knows consciously what her destiny is and can be certain of her path ahead.

---

190 *L*, I, p. 196.
191 *L*, 1, pp. 30-33.
192 *S*, 1, p. 383.
193 *S*, 1, p. 368.

What the letters show is the fact that unconscious motivations played the larger role in her vocational decision-making.

Something else was pulling her, in other words, to return to her life in Amherst: the magnet of her vocation. There was something pulling her from the North: a loadstone of her destiny. This was not a variable of what can be considered from a traditional Christian standpoint as her goodness or "right" conscience. It came, rather, from the dark, from the feminine, from her instinctive power. "What the inner voice whispers to us is generally something negative, if not actually evil," says Jung. He continues:

> This must be so, first because we are usually not as unconscious of our virtues as of our vices, and then because we suffer less from the good than the bad in us. The inner voice... makes us conscious of the evil from which the whole community is suffering, whether it be the nation or the whole human race...The inner voice brings the evil before us in a very convincing way in order to make us succumb. If we do not partially succumb, nothing of this apparent evil enters into us, and no regeneration or healing can take place...But if we can succumb only in part, and if by self-assertion the ego can save itself from being completely swallowed, then it can assimilate the voice, and we realize that the evil was, after all, only a semblance of evil, but in reality a bringer of healing and illumination. In fact, the inner voice is a "Lucifer" in the strictest and most unequivocal sense of the word, and it faces people with ultimate moral decisions without which they can never achieve full consciousness and become personalities.[194]

We have to reflect on the psychological meaning of what the inner voice that was whispering into Dickinson's ear in 1846-1850. Was the inner voice merely persona, or was it trying to make conscious in her from seventeen to twenty-something more objective? What was the evil from which her whole community was suffering, whether in the United States, or the whole world? I think it is obvious today that the evil in our democracy had much to do with the inequality of women and the

---

194 Jung, *CW* 17: ¶ 319.

emergence of the women's rights movement that was "in the air" when Emily entered Mount Holyoke, in September of 1847. Seventy years had passed since our patriots had fought to free the nation from tyranny. Yet, were the truths that we hold to be most self-evident as men really that all men and women are created equal?

Let us turn now to Emily's 1850 letter to Abiah Root, to see how she dealt at nineteen, with the shadow and evil that her poetry would invincibly illuminate. In this letter, the shadow appears in the metaphor of her snake powers.

> Now my dear friend, let me tell you that these last thoughts are fictions—vain imaginations to lead astray foolish young women. They are flowers of speech, they both *make,* and *tell* deliberate falsehoods, avoid them as the snake, and turn aside as from the *Bottle* snake, and I don't *think* you will be harmed…Honestly tho', a snake bite is a serious mater, and there can't be too much said, or done about it. The big serpent bites deepest, and we get so accustomed to its bites that we don't mind about them. "Verily I say unto you fear *him.*" Won't you read some work upon snakes—I have a real anxiety for you! *I* love those little green ones that slide around by your shoes in the grass—and make it rustle with their elbows— they are rather my favorites on the whole, but I wouldn't influence you for the world! There is an air of misanthropy about the striped snake that will commend itself at once to your taste, there is no monotony about it—but we will more of this again.[195]

"I wouldn't *influence* you for the world!" she says ironically. In this spirited and playful letter, we can see the "evil voices" that began to lisp in her ear were none other than the voice of Lucifer, the light bringer. She had no choice at this point but to follow the call of her Snake if she was to become one of the most eloquent voices for women's rights and for human and environmental rights in the nation. Most people do not take this course. It is a shaman's path, the way of a Medicine Woman, one who is struck internally by Lightning and follows the way of the

---

195 *L*, I, pp. 86-90.

dream. "Whenever a snake appears" in dreams or unconscious fantasy, writes Jung "it symbolizes a piece of instinctive psychology in ourselves that is simply inaccessible, something of tremendous power, a thing that is inexorable and that we cannot make compromises with."[196]

While we cannot know for certain that the voices she heard from age 17-20 were other than metaphorical, I am assuming that when Emily said "Evil voices lisp in my ear" she was referring to actual voices she *heard* within herself emanating from the national unconscious in the form of her calling, even though she describes them ironically as "thoughts," "fictions," "vain imaginations," "flowers of speech." For a shaman-poet, the inner voice, whether perceived as internal or external, personal or collective, is experienced as *real*. This is not a manic phase of a bipolar illness that was arising in her. It was a bipolar complex that was active as a splitting phenomenon in the entire nation.[197] She was taking careful note of the numinous voices that were crossing her path and were calling her from within to take an inward journey towards full conscious Self-realization, empowerment, and Bliss.

In another letter, written the same year, 1850, Emily decided to take leave from Abiah in imagination and set out for the open sea. After "dreaming a *golden* dream," she tells her: "The shore is safer, Abiah, but I love to buffet the sea."[198] The sea is the commonest symbol for the collective unconscious. Enclosed in the mantle of her vocation she had little conscious choice now but to yield to the hidden dangers of embarking from the shores of safety. In a further letter to Jane Humphrey, she writes shockingly: "The path of duty looks very ugly indeed—and the place where *I* want to go more amiable—a great deal—it is much easier to do wrong than right—so much pleasanter to be evil than good, I don't wonder that good angels weep—and bad ones sing songs."[199] The psychological sophistication in this letter written when she was merely twenty is mind boggling indeed. It is filled with wit and profound wis-

---

196 Jung, *Seminar on Dream Analysis*, p. 326.
197 For a discussion about this concept in analytical psychology see my paper "Emergence of the Bipolar Cultural Complex in Walt Whitman," *The Journal of Analytical Psychology*, Vol. 52, No. 4, pp. 463-478.
198 *L*, I, pp. 102-105.
199 *L*, I, pp. 81-85.

dom. By this time, she had without any doubt, become a poet-shaman, as the snake powers were speaking eloquently through her. She had stepped away from the path of duty because as she said in the following year "My country calleth me" (J 3/F 2).

"Since the shadow, in itself, is unconscious for most people" writes Jung, "the snake would correspond to what is totally unconscious and incapable of becoming conscious, but which, as the collective unconscious and instinct, seems to possess a peculiar wisdom of its own and a knowledge that is often felt to be supernatural. This is the treasure which the snake (or dragon) guards, and also the reason why the snake signifies evil and darkness on one hand and wisdom on the other. Its unrelatedness, coldness, and dangerousness expresses the instinctuality that rides roughshod over all moral and any other human wishes and considerations and is therefore just as terrifying and fascinating in its effects as the sudden glance of a poisonous snake."[200]

To be sure, she was undergoing a reversal of her religious values, yet it was not her conscious mind that moved her to choose her path as shaman-poet as much as the shadow that was riding roughshod over her moral standards. The Christian teachings of her family and culture were being sloughed away, like a snake sheds its skin. This pivotal time in her life and the nation corresponds to what Jung refers to as the stage of the integration of the shadow, which became a real moral problem for her and for US citizens generally after the first women's rights convention in Wesleyan Chapel on July 19 and 20, 1848. The women who passionately poured out their feelings of discontent at those meetings were clearly starting a revolution in the political conscience of America, and yet the inalienable rights of women needed a shaman-poet to help guide the movement of democracy in a spiritual direction. It is during this time that Dickinson was becoming a Medicine Woman as she was beginning to shamanize in private through her verses. "Primitive medicine-men [medicine-women]" writes Jung "have their sake spirits, and Aesculapius, the tutelary patron of physicians, has for his emblem the Serpent of Epidaurus."[201] The same is true, I believe, of Emily Dickinson. She

---

200 Jung, *CW* 9.2: ¶ 370.
201 Jung, *CW* 17: ¶ 300.

had her own ethic to follow, her own vocation, her calling to sing songs. This is the solitary path she was obliged to follow if she was to emerge as a national and international leader.

As literary historian Cynthia Griffin Wolff has pointed out, one of the things Emily Dickinson was attempting to escape from at this time, by visiting her family in Amherst during her first year at Mount Holyoke, was the institutional "Jesus" that was courting young women and encouraging them to offer themselves up as "Brides of Christ," to their "Bridegroom."[202] This theological idea had its origins in Europe, going all the way back to the medieval period, yet, it was a notion that no longer served Dickinson, as a path to wholeness, because it left the feminine and evil out of her psychobiological communications.

By listening to the voice of Lucifer, Dickinson was being called to bring forth some of the missing elements of the Judeo-Christian God-image, and her individuation is instructive to all women today. Dickinson followed the call of the Snake towards the denouncement of the path of duty for the sake of her denouement as a "Wife" of "Awe." This meant she had to suffer the fate of being unmarried, while proclaiming the pain of being a birth-giver, one who births new truths through powerful words. She had to embark from the shores of safety at the seminary at Holyoke for the wide-open seas of the objective psyche, where her destiny was to be found. It needs to be remembered that women had no property rights at this time, and were not allowed to vote. Most occupations were closed to women and they were not allowed to enter professions such as medicine and law. Nor were they allowed to participate in the affairs of the church. "What is it, in the end," Jung asked, "that induces a man [or woman] to go his [her] own way and to rise out of the unconscious identity with the mass as out of a swathing mist?" He answers:

> Not necessity, for necessity comes to many, and they all take
> refuge in convention. Not moral decision, for nine times out
> of ten we decide for convention likewise. What is it, then,
> that inexorably tips the scales in favor of the *extra-ordinary*? It
> is what is commonly called *vocation*: an irrational factor that

---

202 Wolff, *Emily Dickinson*, p. 103.

destines a man to emancipate himself from the herd and from its well-worn paths. True personality is always a vocation and puts its trust in it as in God, despite its being, as the ordinary man would say, only a personal feeling. But vocation acts like a law of God from which there is no escape. The fact that many a man who goes his own way ends in ruin means nothing to the one who has a vocation. He *must* obey his own law, as if it were a daemon whispering to him of new and wonderful paths. Anyone with a vocation hears the voice of the inner man: he is *called.* That is why the legends say that he possesses a private daemon who counsels him and whose mandates he must obey.[203]

Medicine-women have their snake spirits too. I believe Dickinson is one of the most powerful of them. When she said to her friend, Abiah Root, at the age of nineteen, for instance that she "loves" the "little green ones" that slide around her "shoes in the grass," or when she spoke of her "love of the sea," of "danger," and of an abhorrence of following the path of "duty," she was obeying an inborn law—the call of her Snake—which made its appearance in the form of "Evil voices" lisping in her ear. This mandate from the Self (Snake) to put conventional Christianity and the mass of women and men aside and go her "own way" led to a certain degree of exile from her New England community, to a condition of enforced isolation, which nearly cost Dickinson her sanity. Yet, this was the risk she had to take. Her love for "danger" and awareness of the "bitter wrecks" in pleasanter waters, was enough to convince her that she had to risk the adventure into the Other World (Beyond), if she was to secure the herb of immortality for her Amherst community; for herself, her family, for all women, and the surrounding World. This is not to single Dickinson out as somehow better than any of the courageous women who were massing together during the women's rights conventions that were meeting regularly in crowds from 1850 to the inception of the Civil War. As she herself would state ironically "I'm Nobody! Who are you?" (J 288/F 260).

"From the standpoint of the way of duty," writes Joseph Campbell "anyone in exile from the community is a nothing. From the other

203 Jung, *CW* 17: pp. 175-176.

point of view, however, this exile is the first step of the quest. Each carries within himself the all; therefore it may be sought and discovered within."[204] And so it would be with this heroine of American letters, that the life-affirming energies of the cosmos would transport her to a region of the psyche that would confirm her sense of identity and vocation, clothing her in a poetic mantle that would appear, to the conventionally-conditioned eyes of her contemporaries as peculiarly appealing, yet at the same time threatening to their very way of existence, women and men alike. In her next letter to Jane written in April, 1850, Emily wrote even more daringly:

> I have dared to do strange things—bold things, and have asked no advice from any—I have heeded beautiful tempters, yet do not think I am wrong…and life has had an aim, and the world has been too precious for your poor—and striving sister! The winter was all one dream, and the spring has not yet waked me, I would *always* sleep, and dream, and it never should turn to morning, so long as night is so blessed. What do you weave from all these threads, for I know you hav'nt been idle the while I've been speaking to you, bring it nearer the window, and I will see, it's all wrong unless it has one gold thread in it, a long, big shining fiber which hides the others—and which will fade away into Heaven while you hold it, and from there come back to me.[205]

This is an extraordinary letter; she is embellishing mythological ideas with her intuitive and emotional understandings here, tapping into the implicit knowledge lodged deeply in her lower brain stem, or reptilian brain, and right cerebral hemisphere, the domain that opened her mind to the larger unitary sphere of the Cosmos. At the time these letters were written to Abiah and Jane (at ages 19-20), Emily was beginning to write poetry in secret, and was feeling minor irritations from her involvements with the Amherst Sewing Society of which she was an active member. Sewing began to take on metaphorical significance for her with regards the frustrations women were also feeling of having to

---

204 J. Campbell, *The Hero with a Thousand Faces*, p. 385.
205 *L*, I, pp. 93-96.

accomplish dutiful domestic handiwork, and against which she began to define herself, and to forcefully rebel. A poem from 1862 reads as follows: "Don't put up my Thread & Needle— I'll begin to Sew / When the Birds begin to whistle— / Better Stitches—so— / …I'll do seams— a Queen's endeavor / Would not blush to own" (J 617/F 681).

Fate and destiny are inseparable from one another in Dickinson's poetry and letters, for they are part and parcel of a single unitary archetype, yet, in this letter, Dickinson takes the notions of fate further than her readings in classical Greek mythology might possibly have led her to comprehend. By penetrating to the very core of the American psyche, she shows us the central archetype of order, the Self that patterned her destiny as a poet-shaman.

Emily had found a way to a mine within herself—songs and melodies that were more precious than any male college or university could buy her, even more precious than gold! A major transformation was occurring in her Soul. This metamorphosis could not have taken place in complete isolation from her community of friends. In his commentaries on the letters we have been examining, Richard Sewall informs us, for instance, that it was through Emily's relationships with "trusted friends like Abiah and Jane" that she developed a "powerful new protective weapon of metaphor" to shield her from the projections and judgments of others. The letters to Jane in particular, he notes, contain a theme, which would become central to her life and work: the "theme of the joy of a new dispensation."[206]

In another letter to Abiah, the tenor of her rebellion for women's empowerment becomes invective: "I have come from '*to* and *fro,* and walking up and down' the same place that Satan hailed from, when God asked him where he'd been, but not to illustrate further I tell you I have been dreaming, dreaming a *golden* dream, with eyes all the while wide open."[207] What the "*golden* dream" was we do not know, but whatever it was, it is a *dream of destiny*, for gold, as in alchemy, is the spiritual aim of the poet's art.

---

206 *S*, p. 396.
207 *L*, I, p. 99.

These letters were first attempts at active visioning through free verse, or vocalism, yet, she was still dreaming, dreaming a wonderful dream. In a valentine to an Amherst student, Emily said, "I am Judith the heroine of the Apocrypha, and you the orator of Ephesus. That's what they call a metaphor in our country. Don't be afraid of it, sir, it won't bite!"[208] Here, she appears to have been bringing in the metaphor of her Snake again. For Dickinson, the "narrow fellow in the grass" was one of "Nature's Peoples," a Thou not an It; a fellow citizen of the earth. However, it is probable that she meant by "bite" her dog, for the valentine ends with: "If it was my dog *Carlo* now! The Dog is the noblest work of Art, sir. I may safely say the noblest—his mistress's rights he doth defend—"[209] We have heard of Emily's dog before, in relation to fame: "If fame belonged to me, I could not escape her—if she did not, the longest day would pass me on the chase—and the approbation of my Dog, would forsake me—then. My barefoot rank is better." Approbation is another word for approval, acceptance, or agreement. What she was saying in this letter I think is that while Higginson did not approve of her poems just the way they were, her dog, Carlo, really did. When she gave her reasons for "'shunning Men and Women'" she replied further: "they talk of Hallowed things, aloud—and embarrass my Dog—"[210]

More than any other animal, dogs have accompanied humans in their evolving quest for individuation. Dogs, such as Carlo for Emily, have evolved to become uniquely attuned to human behaviors, tone of voice, and emotions. In addition to her Snake, therefore, which was an internal symbol for the Self and far more primitive, we also need to consider the significance of Carlo in her life; Carlo as an outer companion, who kept her constant company.

Who was Carlo? Carlo was given to Emily by her father Edward as a Newfoundland puppy in the fall of 1849, when she was nineteen years old; Carlo was possibly a Lesser Newfoundland. In her letter to Higginson from April 25, 1862, she wrote about him: "You ask my Companions Hills—Sir—and the Sundown—and a Dog—large as myself,

---

208 *L*, I, p. 92.
209 *L*, I, pp. 91-93.
210 *L*, II, p. 415.

that my Father bought me—They are better than Beings—because they know—but do not tell—"[211]

Much has been written about the importance of Carlo in Emily's life. Dickinson named him after a dog in the novel *Jane Eyre*. He accompanied her on many long walks through the woods and fields of Amherst. Carlo appears to have provided the poetess with great psychological comfort over her most productive years. He died at about the age of 16, in January of 1866. In one poem from 1862, she wrote: "I started Early—Took my Dog—" (J 520/F 656). We'll hear more about Carlo later.

---

[211] *L*, II, pp. 404-405.

9

THE BI-EROTIC IMAGINATION

Between 1850 (when Dickinson wrote the letters we reviewed in the last chapter) and 1859, when she first began to come into her own power as a poet of supreme literary stature, she battled through the shadow projections of her local Christian (i.e., Puritan & Trinitarian) culture through a semiconscious identification with the Snake-symbol as her totem animal. By aligning herself with the shadow and evil that most people never make conscious in their lives, she became thereby, a *mediatrix* between the sacred and the profane. My aim in this chapter will be to show how she overcame her emotional and psychological difficulties to arrive (at the age of thirty to thirty-two, when she was writing up to a poem per day!) at a full realization of the Self, the center of her conscious and unconscious personality. By following her animal helpers, the tutors of humanity, and heeding her call to follow the way of a shaman, she was led to a transformation of consciousness.

In order to understand just how revolutionary Dickinson really was in her day, we have to grasp the meaning of neurosis. We all suffer from neurosis now and then. No one can escape this condition in the "noise" of modern society. A working definition, therefore, might be for psychology as follows: *a neurosis is a state of mind that comes about whenever a person is out of touch with her true vocation.* Insofar as Dickinson was attuned to the melodies of her calling, then, she was operating as a healer for her tribe and in this sense, she was acting in her sacred role as a Medicine Woman, who offers healing to her culture. When she was out of connection to her authentic voice, her vocation, on the other hand, she was like much of the nation, in a neurotic condition that was in need of a cure.

As Jung wrote,

> the "neurosis is just a defense against the objective, inner activity of the psyche, or an attempt, somewhat dearly paid for, to escape from the inner voice and hence from the vocation. For this 'growth' is the objective activity of the psyche, which, independently of conscious volition, is trying to speak to the conscious mind through the inner voice and lead him towards wholeness."[212]

As we've seen, Dickinson emerged during a pivotal moment in the history of North America, just before Seneca Falls. Her calling went dormant for a number of years when a few poems and breakthroughs found their way into drafts and journal entries until just before the outbreak of the Civil War, when a miraculous transformation of consciousness occurred in her. Fortunately, Dickinson had the courage to face her fears consciously and heroically, and she was able, through a mastery of art, to clarify her inner conflicts and to arrive at a style of poetry that stands in an area of uniqueness that has been unsurpassed by any other poet-writing in America. Dickinson saw clearly that the path of traditional Christianity and patriarchal democracy would only lead her to shipwreck; the only way left for her was to follow the way of her snake-powers: her totem animals. She was eradicating her emotional difficulties by giving way to "beautiful tempters," and turning the tables on the moral values of her local culture. In fact, she tells us in a letter to Higginson that it was in childhood that her fear of the Snake was instilled in her, both by her parents and by religious elders.

There are really two ways a person can resolve such emotional problems as Emily suffered from, and as Jung has shown, both are necessary for individuation to become complete. The first way is through reductive analysis; where everything is traced back to emotional complexes, traumas,[213] and causal disturbances from early childhood; while the

---

212 Jung, *CW* 17: ¶ 313.
213 Herrmann, "Donald Kalsched: The Inner World of Trauma," *The San Francisco Jung Institute Library Journal*, Vol. 19, No. 2

second way is *symbolic, visionary, and emotional*—or, in Emily's terms: *imaginal, fictive, metaphoric*. For Dickinson, who was born in 1830, the only path of healing open to her was shamanistic.

With no suitable shaman-mentors at her side, Emily chose to strike out on her own towards the unknown. Between 1850 and 1858, she was in search for a technique of ecstatic vocalism to revolutionize the world. In a chat with her sixteen-year-old cousin, Louise Norcross, Emily is reported to have said: "It's a great thing to be 'great,' Loo, and you and I might tug for a life, and never accomplish it, but no one can stop our looking on, and you know some cannot sing, but the orchard is full of birds, and we all can listen. What if we learn, ourselves, some day! Who indeed knows?"[214]

To sing like the birds was her greatest aspiration in life, to free up the stop in her voice, by which the Animal Powers could sound through into melody, form, and image—to liberate, that is, the shamanic energies of her mind and imbue it with the transformative power of the English language. That was a task worthy of her art. She had already learned—through active visioning—how to free up her "spontaneity" in her early letters to Abiah and Jane. In 1853, she wrote, moreover: "I have a Bird in spring / Which for myself doth sing—" (J 5/F 4).

It was her first "tutor" and "closest friend," Benjamin Franklin Newton—a law student in her father's office, from 1847 to 1849, that first encouraged Emily Dickinson to "sing" exquisitely (i.e., to write shamanistic poetry). In a letter to Mr. Hale, the young Dickinson tells us, moreover, after Ben Newton's tragic death, that it was Benjamin who taught her: "what was most grand and beautiful in nature, and that sublimer lesson, a faith in things unseen, and a life again, nobler, and much more blessed—"[215]

"Newton's greatest distinction," Sewall says "is that among all of her early friends, male or female, he seems to be the only one who understood her poetic promise."[216] In her third letter to Higginson, Emily wrote the following lines about Newton, as a mentor figure: "My dying

---

214 *L*, II, p. 345.
215 *L*, I, pp. 282-83.
216 *S*, p. 403.

Tutor told me that he would like to live till I had been a poet, but Death was much of Mob as I could master—then—"[217] According to Sewall, Newton's premature "death cut off" Emily's "promising hope for literary guidance and encouragement," and as she later told Higginson famously: "for several years my Lexicon—was my only companion."[218] This comment shows us just how solitary she was.

In her mid-twenties, following the death of Newton, Emily began to withdraw into the depths of her solitude and seek out alone the sources of her disquiet. A few poems trickled out onto the page during this dark period of psychic disorientation and critics hardly cite these poems. Four years later, in 1859, however, her withdrawal appears to have become almost complete, and we can begin to see at this time a sudden change in her relationship to the inner voice and the sudden emergence of her poetic vocation, which shows that the powers of her destiny were indeed at hand. It was a time of great inner and outer growth and expansion in the emerging powers of her art.

At this time, she referred to her sister-in-law, Susan Gilbert, and to her brother, Austin, ironically as "my crowd." Suddenly then, about 1858, she began to assemble her collected poems into the grouping of packets or "fascicles" containing a number of folded sheets, carefully sewn together at the seams, as if she intended to prepare them for publication. In a letter to Susan she sent the poem, "Safe in their Alabaster Chambers," which Susan found "breath taking," "remarkable as chain lightning that blinds us hot nights in the Southern sky..."[219] I don't believe Susan was exaggerating. Listen:

> Safe in their Alabaster Chambers—
> Untouched by Morning—
> And untouched by Noon—
> Lie the meek members of the Resurrection—
> Rafter of Satin—and Roof of Stone!   J 216/F 124

In Chapter 13, we'll see that the "meek members of the Resurrection" anticipate her own Resurrection, in soul and spirit. In response

---

217 *L*, II, p. 408.
218 *L*, II, p. 408.
219 *S*, p. 201.

to Susan's letter, Emily wrote: "Your praise is good—to me—because I *know* it *knows*—and *suppose* it *means*—Could I make you and Austin—proud—sometime—a great way off—'twould give me taller feet'—"[220]

From these lines, it is clear that Emily viewed Susan as a sort of mentor-friend-figure, who she loved and adored, just as she loved Benjamin Newton for the praise and encouragement he gave her. To gain "taller feet" suggests moreover her future arrival at "Doom's Electric Moccasin" (J 1593/F 1618): the divine "Bolt" she says she would not exchange for anything (J 1581/F 1665).

Moreover, the homoerotic elements in her relationship with Susan filled her with a secret thrill, which Sewall says stemmed from Susan's capacity to infuse her mind with "impregnable syllables."[221] In 1877, she summed up her relationship to Susan thus:

> To own a Susan of my own
> Is of itself a Bliss—
> Whatever Realm I forfeit, Lord,
> Continue me in this!   J 1401/ F 1436

This relatively late poem written after the storm of her affections had calmed down substantially, shows us precisely how much energy and power she derived from her *union of sames* with Sue, an emotional love affair between two friends. That Emily loved Sue deeply is obvious. Yet a fracture occurred in the friendship, a rupture in relationship, that later injured her and that she felt was beyond repair. "Now I knew I lost her— / Now that she was gone— / But remoteness traveled / On her face and Tongue… / But Love's transmigration— / Somehow this had come—" (J 1219/F 1274). While Susan was an inspiration for Emily and an object of her love, she also fell in love, after Newton's death, with two other men. The first was Charles Wadsworth, a poet in his youth, who became a Presbyterian minister and lived in Philadelphia. The second was Samuel Bowles, a Unitarian editor, who lived in Springfield. Like Sue, both men were married. Two of the Master Letters in particular are filled with passionate, childlike abandon, and breathtaking love.

---

220 *S*, p. 201.
221 *L*, III, p. 707.

Who the Master was, has never been convincingly determined. According to Sewall, thirty-five of Dickinson's letters were sent to Bowles, and "nearly fifty poems were written to him (some to his wife)—she was deeply in love with him for several years and never ceased loving him, at a distance, for the rest of her life."[222] This equal love for women and men is what I'm calling bierotic. But the preponderance of evidence leans in the direction of heterosexual Eros when it comes to romantic love.

The exact nature of the love Emily and Bowles shared has not been conserved, except in her poems and letters, as some critics have speculated, and because he was editor of the *Springfield Republican* where Emily had hoped to publish, Bowles was at the center of her "turbulent emotional disturbance" during the 1860 period.[223]

The answer to the mystery of who the Master really was, (whether Wadsworth or Bowles) will probably never be solved, although many have attempted to make a choice for the Master's identity final. As Albert J. Gelpi asserted, "Wadsworth would seem the unquestionable choice for Master."[224] However, arguments will continue to exist as to who the man actually was, if indeed he was an external figure. Unless new documentary information surfaces that is more definite psychologically, biographers and literary critics and interested readers will continue to weigh in on either side, as there is convincing evidence to support several possibilities.

The fact of the matter, regardless of what historians might have to say, is that she loved several men but never equally. While only one may have been the Master, the Muse that emerged in her was fully aroused in the intersubjective field between several of her loves. Whether an in-depth psychological analysis can help us solve the problem of the Master Letters has yet to be seen. Like everyone who has attempted to wrestle with such questions, I will try and give an answer in this chapter in my own way as a Jungian.

---

222 *S*, p. 473.

223 S, p. 477.

224 Albert J. Gelpi, cited in Habegger, *My Wars are Laid Away in Books*, p. 421.

In a letter to Bowles, Dickinson professed her "Love" and asked, "Would you—ask le[ss] for your *Queen*—M[r] Bowles?"[225] Passages like this one have led biographers and literary critics to speculate that Dickinson's references to wishing that she were in the "Queen's place," in other words, the place of "wife," are literal indications of her desire to be his lover. Such metaphorical similes have been taken as indications that she wanted to supplant either Bowles' wife's position in marriage, or replace Wadsworth's wife. Such attempts to concretize the *coniunctio* imagery, the spiritual marriage, however, miss the interpersonal nature of the process involved in attaining it internally, as an inner psychological event, transcendent of the field of temporality and time. As Jung has shown, the spiritual marriage can only occur through a withdrawal of projections onto love objects on the outside.

At first glance the reference to her being Bowles' *Queen* might seem to support the possibility that he was the transformative man in question, the Master who liberated her mature voice from the childhood innocence that enveloped her. A poem sent to Bowles in another letter might seem to clinch the matter for those who are looking for a definite answer. "'Why do I love' You, Sir? /...The Lightning—never asked an Eye /...The Sunrise—Sir—compelleth Me— / Because He's Sunrise— and I see— / Therefore—Then— / I love Thee—" (J 480/F 459). We might speculate that this speaks to both her literal longing for romantic love and a symbolic yearning for transcendence.

While Lightning symbolism was originally introduced by Sue in her praise of "Safe in their Alabaster Chambers" it would appear that Bowles may have been the lover who evoked the Lightning in her, the Bolts of Melody, in an electrical energy field between them. At this time, erotic currents that are enlivening were clearly flowing through Dickinson's poetry. It is here, therefore, in the *bi-erotic field*—between her love for Susan, her love for Wadsworth, and her love for Bowles—that we find the emergence of the metaphor of the Queen, one of the central images for the *coniunctio* in alchemy. Further evidence for the possibility that Bowles was Master, is provided by another letter sent to Mrs. Mary Bowles after the tragic death of her husband: "He is without doubt

---

225 *L*, II, p. 393.

with my father," Emily wrote.[226] In another letter to Mary Bowles, Emily added, "I spoke to him once of his Gem chapter [Revelation XXI], and the beautiful eyes rose out of reach of mine, in some hallowed fathom."[227] Thus, this passage shows that Bowles had shared a similar appreciation for the chapter of the Bible Emily loved most since she had heard Hitchcock introduce it.

During the time Dickinson was in love with Susan, Wadsworth, and Bowles, we witness a remarkable transformation of archetypal imagery arising from the psychophysiological bi-erotic field between these literary and spiritual folk in transit towards a new *coniunctio* that includes a *union of sames* (Emily-Susan) and union of opposites (Emily-Bowles, Emily-Wadsworth). In each of these transformative relationships, the scissors of Fate fractured her hopes for an outer marriage. Out of this fracture-line, however, she integrated the qualities of King and Queen in her letters and poetry and constellated in herself the basic requirements for her spiritual marriage. In 1859, for instance, she wrote: "I have a King, who does not speak—" (J 103/F 157). The following year, 1860, she cried out in ecstasy: "I met a King this afternoon!" and spoke "Of this Barefoot Estate!" (J 166/F 183).

It is here that we can see the recurrence of the metaphor of the King who has no shoes, the "Boy" who had roamed the grass "barefoot" and had witnessed the snake. This King is a natural man, who in the course of her inner development eventually was crowned.

In another poem, on the eve of the Civil War, she spoke of following her "homesick—homesick feet" to "native lands" in search for the "Mysterious Bard!" who would become her *true* King. The King was not Bowles, nor Wadsworth. The King was an archetype within her. The way to her destined role as Queen lies through "the royal syllable—" and the "unsteady tongue—" that follows the "trance below" and only this King, she says, "Fittest the Crown!" (J 195/F).

Yet how did she crown herself? What led her to declare: "I'm 'wife'— /…I'm 'Woman' now— / …"I'm 'Wife'! Stop there!" (J 199/F 225)? The same year she spoke of her *One Life* being of "so much Conse-

---

226 *L*, III, p. 621.
227 *L*, III, p. 601.

quence!" and stressed that she wore "*my Gem*! / It burns—distinct from all the row— / *Intact—in Diadem*!" (J 270/F 248).

Here we find a mention of the *Gem* chapter (Revelation XXI) again. Emily's interest in gems goes back to her first term at Mount Holyoke, where she heard the sermon by Hitchcock speaking in a "sparkling" voice that was "famous for its sonority."[228] Jung also spoke of this famous chapter of the New Testament in *Answer to Job* as "Bride," or the "new Jerusalem" whose "radiance [was] like a most rare jewel, like jasper, clear as crystal."[229]

In the poetry and letters from this 1860 period, there was also mention of a "second Rank" in "the West—" that "bore her Master's name— / Sufficient Royalty!" (J 336/F 395). She was not speaking of traditional "faith" or "belief" at this time, for now she *knew he was living in Her*: "I live with Him—I see His face— / I go no more away / ...No wedlock—granted Me— / I live with Him— I hear His Voice— / I stand alive—Today— / To witness to the Certainty / Of Immortality—" (J 463/F 698)! The wedlock was not granted to her in a little "w" wife sense, it was given to her by grace in a big "W" Wife sense, by which she means the immensity of the infinite:

> The Day that I was crowned
> Was like the other Days—
> Until the Coronation came—
> And then—'twas Otherwise—
>
> As Carbon in the Coal
> And Carbon in the Gem
> Are One—and yet the former
> Were dull for Diadem—
>
> I rose, and all was plain—
> But when the Day declined
> Myself and It, in Majesty
> Were equally—adorned—

---

228 *S*, p. 347.
229 Jung, *CW* 11: ¶ 726.

> The Grace that I—was chose—
> To Me—surpassed the Crown
> That was the Witness for the Grace—
> 'Twas even that 'twas Mine—   J 356/F 613

Her Marriage symbolism does not discriminate on the basis of sexual orientation and opens the possibility for all forms of love. "Her sweet Weight on my Heart a Night / Had scarcely deigned to lie— / When, stirring, for Belief's delight, / My Bride had slipped away—" (J 518/F 611).

The term bi-erotic means a union transcending gender, for here the "Bride" of Dickinson is clearly female. The marriage symbolism has another face than what has been historically handed down through the Judeo-Christian mythos, and this is the union of the female body with Night, or Belief's Delight. This was a dream made "solid" in Dickinson's body and mind in 1862, after her painful dissolution from her erotic illusion with the Master. This "Fiction superseding Faith" was so powerful when she dreamt it that she actually felt 'twas *real*. She was clearly seeking a new God-image when she wrote:

> The Soul selects her own Society—
> Then—shuts the Door—
> To her divine Majority—
> Present no more—
>
> Unmoved—she notes the Chariots—pausing—
> At her low Gate—
> Unmoved—an Emperor be kneeling
> Upon her Mat—
>
> I've known her—from an ample nation—
> Choose One—
> Then—close the Valves of her attention—
> Like Stone—   J 303/F 409

The Soul's Society that Emily Dickinson selected, at this point in her individuation was the Society of her own Selfhood achieved through the "new Marriage," which was bi-erotic, after the Emperor made his advance upon Her "low Gate—" The "divine Majority" is the "ample nation" of Spiritual Democracy.

To sum up this chapter, what I have postulated here is that Dickinson arrived at a new image of bi-erotic marriage on American soil one hundred and fifty years before there was any movement afoot to inaugurate a democratic policy that makes room for marriages of different sexual and gender combinations in such a way that contains both upper and lower images of the soul's union with Divinity. This was clearly revolutionary for her time and is an indisputable testament to her powers as a poet-shaman to foresee future developments that extended further than the second wave of feminism that erupted in our country during the 1960s, a century after her soul had written at its greatest intensity and heat. In fact, it was not until the 1990s that women activists began to speak out vociferously about the need for women to assume leadership roles in places of religious worship, such as Churches, Synagogues, and Mosques. Of all the women writing in the United States, not one did more to advance our understanding of women's rights to become leaders in international affairs regarding spiritual matters than Dickinson did. Hers is a living legacy of eloquence that our democracy cannot do without. I would not even place her as a leader of what women proudly called a "third wave" of feminism in 1998, the one hundred and fiftieth anniversary of Seneca Falls. I think that she represents a "fourth wave" that we are now seeing, and that in my view, has just begun. My reasons for saying this, is that she takes on not only the issues of equal rights for women and humans, but the rights of reptiles, amphibians, animals, and the environment. That is how progressive I believe she truly is. She gives us a medicine that only a shaman can bring to an ailing culture that is searching for answers. Now let us see how she came to acquire her invincible powers at a little deeper level.

10

THE LIGHTNING SHAMAN AND THE WHITE ELECTION

Being an introverted intuitive thinking type by natural disposition—
"By intuition, Mightiest Things / Assert themselves—" (J 420/F 429),
Dickinson tended, at least for a period of time, to idealize men of letters
(Hitchcock, Newton, Bowles, Wadsworth, Higginson). We have exam-
ined the roots of her vocation and destiny in her early friendships with
the Amherst girls, in her formative friendships with Ben Newton, Susan
Gilbert, and Samuel Bowles. Now, let us examine the roots of her sha-
manic poetry and writing a deeper level. In a letter to Samuel Bowles,
Emily wrote, "The old words are *numb*—"[230]

After her transference of creativity was evoked in her outer relationships, she had tried to treat her emotional suffering with her "fairy
medicine" (J 691/F 272) or "little Balm." By this point, Emily was well
aware of having gained access to a miraculous "medicine" that could
cure not only herself, but others as well. The medicine she had to offer
at this time was metaphoric and mythopoetic at its spiritual roots. In a
letter to the Norcross' written in May of 1863, she spoke of it as a "balsam word."[231] As Sewall says: "she spoke once about the "balsam word"
as having "more power to heal than doctors…and again she offered
[Bowles] the kind of medicine that only she could give."[232] This supports
my hypothesis of her calling as a Medicine Woman.

---

230 *L*, II, p. 395.
231 *L*, II, p. 425.
232 *S*, p. 482.

The problem is, however, that Bowles did not accept her medicine (poetry), nor did Higginson take it, and so it could not reach the audience for which it was intended, namely the nation. What she was seeking was a "marriage" with the Self in a transpersonal sense in her profession; one which Bowles was not prepared to receive.

Dickinson was so far ahead of her times. She must have been crushed when Bowles failed to comprehend her, such as when she wrote him: "Mine—here—in Vision—and in Veto!" (J 528/F 411). As an early visionary of Spiritual Democracy, Dickinson spoke up for equality in a liberated and empowered sense in print. Dickinson then turned during the spring of 1862 to her literary advisor, minister, and editor, Thomas Wentworth Higginson for healing. She seems to have turned to Higginson for help, almost the way a modern person will turn to a psychotherapist today. In a moment of remarkable clarity, she wrote Higginson the following introductory letter: "I had a terror—since September—I could tell to none—and so I sing, as the Boy does by the Burying Ground—because I am afraid— …I went to school—but in your manner of phrase—had no education. When a little Girl, I had a friend, who taught me Immortality—but venturing too near, himself—he never returned—Soon after, my Tutor, died—and for several years, my Lexicon—was my only companion—Then I found one more—but he was not contented I be his scholar—so he left the Land."[233]

Any therapist hearing such an opening introduction during an initial session would be lost for words. What did she mean here? One might, without doubt, need to ask her many questions. Who, for instance, was the "Boy" who sang by the "burying ground?" What was she *afraid* of? Who was the friend who taught her immortality? Who was the tutor who died? And what about the one who was contented that she be his scholar and left the land? How did singing (poetry) help her overcome her fears? What happened in September that evoked her fear? etc.

The reader will remember that Emily's mother had a fear of death bordering on panic. There are three significant losses indicated here moreover: a friend that taught her immortality, who died suddenly in her early childhood; a second tutor (Benjamin Newton) who died early,

---

233 *L*, II, pp. 404-405.

and another man who was content to have her as his scholar, for a short time (Samuel Bowles?) and who left the Land (in his travels).

By this point, Emily had lost her connections with Susan, Wadsworth, and Bowles; she was in trouble emotionally and in a state of anxiety and depression. After her series of outer losses, she regressed to a place of very early fear. There were intimations of death, fears of annihilation, a "terror" that pursued her, a trembling "Boy" by "the burying ground." Like the Boy who walked barefoot and spied the "narrow fellow in the grass" in her poem "Snake," this was her youthful masculine principle, her creative spirit, or animus, in its *puer aeternus* aspect. Emily tells us, moreover, that it was a compelling "fear" that had led her to "sing" (i.e., to write poetry). Who was the Boy by the burying ground? What significance did he play in the development of her remarkable literary oeuvre? We have already heard a few words about him.

Literary critics have speculated that Emily Dickinson's "terror" at this time in her life had to do with a possible fear of mental illness, or insanity. Her first letter about "insanity" comes in fact from a letter written to Sue in 1852, where she wrote: "in thinking of those I love, my reason is all gone from me, and I do fear sometimes that I must make a hospital for the hopelessly insane."[234] On an experiential level, we have to remember that she sensed that God no longer seemed to care about her life and fate. Her destiny was uncertain and this loss of faith in the traditional image of God contributed to her anxiety. "Of Course—I prayed—/ And did God Care?" (J 376/F 581) she asked while reflecting back on her journey.

As we've seen, the failure of the traditional Father in Heaven to listen to her was likened to an excruciating crucifixion. The sacrifice opened her up to a different kind of prayer than one might be used to hearing in a Church. The "Prayer / I knew so perfect—yesterday— / That Scalding One—Sabachthani— / Recited fluent—here—" (J 313/F 283). "Lama sabachthani" ("Why hast thou forsaken me?") were Jesus' last words of anguish on the Cross!

Dickinson's mature prayer was a cry of having been betrayed by God on the cross of her own destiny at a time in history when women's

---

234 *L*, I, p. 182.

voices were being silenced by patriarchal prejudice. After the first wave of feminism emerged in this country, in fact, some male newspaper editors reacted to the Seneca Falls Convention with a backlash of criticism and Dickinson is sure to have informed herself in this regard. But she was not only fighting for equality in work or education or economics. Her fight was in the religious domain. Turning away from the prayer her parents had taught her about a Father in Heaven, she turned to the Divine Feminine for comfort, to the "Madonna, dim, to whom all feet come" and "knowest every Woe—" but "can'st thou do / The Grace next to it—heal?" (J 918/F 981) she asked. Her aim was to heal herself and others. She was clearly seeking a way to heal the world too by invoking the powers of the Mother. She wrote in the spring of 1861:

> I shall know why—when Time is over—
> And I have ceased to wonder why—
> Christ will explain each separate anguish
> In the fair schoolroom of the sky—
>
> He will tell me what "Peter" promised—
> And I—for wonder at his woe—
> I shall forget the drop of Anguish
> That scalds me now—that scalds me now!   J 193/F 215

She was *feeling* crucified because she had no way to publish her own book of homespun wisdom. No poet surpasses Dickinson in natural intelligence. "'Twas a Divine Insanity—" she insists; a feminine mystery vouchsafed to all women, a "Lunacy of Light" (J 593/F 627).

Let us examine a famous poem now that puts us back in the emotional atmospherics of her terrorizing pain, a place of *agony* that appears to have sent her into seclusion, to secure her own Balm, the healing ointment of Grace that the Madonna could not heal in her:

> I felt a Funeral in my Brain,
> And Mourners to and fro
> Kept treading—treading—till it seemed
> That Sense was breaking through—   J 280/F 340

The terror she was referring to above was her "sickness-vocation," a shamanic illness that followed the typical shamanic pattern. In Eliade's terms "shamanic vocation is not profane…it does not belong to ordinary symptomatology. *It has an initiatory structure and signification;* in short, it reproduces the traditional mystical pattern."[235]

In another poem, she amplified the meaning of her Brain metaphor further: "Rearrange a 'Wife's' affection! / When they dislocate my Brain! / …Seven years of troth have taught thee / More than Wifehood ever may!" (J 1737/F 267).

Words were her medicine. When her exchange with Bowles heated up and she asserted her power as *"Queen,"* she had been ridiculed and referred to pejoratively as "Queen recluse." The rejection by Bowles stung her to the core, just as the rejection by Susan had felt to her, like "The *Smitten* Rock that gushes!" (J 165/F 181). A further letter to Higginson showed how rebellious she was towards conventional interpretations of Christianity and how searing her criticism was of patriarchal forms of government when she said of her family: "They are religious—except me—and address an Eclipse, every morning—whom they call their 'Father.'"[236]

This statement is filled with wit and paradox, combining Emily Dickinson's greatest literary powers. For here was the most spiritual mind in Amherst, saying to a learned man of letters that she was not only *not* religious in a post-Christian sense but in these Post-Enlightenment times and during the movement afoot for the advancement of women and human rights, that the "Father" had become an "Eclipse!" (It must be kept in mind here, however, as Northrop Frye has aptly remarked: "Emily Dickinson had a great respect for orthodox religion and morality, did not question the sincerity of those who practiced it, and even turned to it for help."[237]) In other words, Emily had an ambivalent relationship to Christianity. She was writing in the Christian myth, but sought to take it further; to help it evolve, to become more inclusive of women's voices and the rights of Mother Nature. In her letters to Higginson, we find no evidence for conventional criteria of clinical psychopathology, moreover, that fits her personality and temperament neatly into a diag-

---

235 Eliade, *Rites and Symbols of Initiation*, pp. 89, 95.
236 *L*, II, pp. 404-405.
237 *Modern American Poetry: Essays in Criticism*, McKay: New York, 26.

nostic category. In fact, when she was in her shamanic character, she actually wrote what she called a "Diagnosis of the Bible!" This shows that her medicine was aimed to administer a good dose of Goddess worship into a Church in which the feminine principle was virtually absent, and when she was present, as in prayers to Mary, could she offer a balm to the Grace that was also missing.

The Funeral she *felt* in her brain was not imagined, then. It was real. She died. Her ego, that is. The theme of the death of the ego is a common feature of the shaman's sickness-vocation. Here is a poem from 1859 that depicts the typical shaman's experience of dismemberment, death, and resurrection during a process of emotional-visioning:

> She died—*this* was the way she died.
> And when her breath was done
> Took up her simple wardrobe
> And started for the sun.
> Her little figure at the gate
> The Angels must have spied,
> Since I could never find her
> Upon the mortal side.   J 150/F 154

What is it that enabled Emily Dickinson to speak with such certainty about her future as an artist whose literary greatness would remain virtually unknown in her lifetime? How is it that she "smiled" when Higginson rejected her most precious poetic gifts? What could she *see* that other poets and critics of her century could not see? The "ever-fixed mark," as Shakespeare said, "That looks on tempests and is never shaken; / ... the star to every wandering bark, / Whose worth's unknown, although his height be taken";[238] this was the magnet to which the needles of her compass were pointing. What did she mean by calling it "north?" As early as 1853, she wrote:

> On this wondrous sea
> Sailing silently,
> Ho! Pilot, ho!
>
> Knowest thou the shore

---

238 William Shakespeare, *The Complete Signet Classic Shakespeare.*

Where no breakers roar—
Where the storm is o'er?

In the peaceful west
Many the sail at rest—
The anchors fast—
Thither I pilot *thee*—
Land Ho! Eternity!
Ashore at last!   J 4/F 3

What Emily Dickinson was referring to here is the experience of shamanic transport to the "Other World"—which, as she said, can be found on the western shore of eternity. Whether we call the "star" to which all needles point, Love, Eternity, Ecstasy, Immortality, or Bliss, she is telling us that she has attained it, as our sailor and pilot, which is a first sign of her acceptance of her designated role as a *Lightning-Shaman of the White Election*.

Emily Dickinson had the capacity to *see* with the eyes of the Serpent what others in her society could not see. In 1865, three years after her struggle with her shamanic illness, Emily traced a childhood recollection of her encounter with "A narrow Fellow in the Grass," whose sudden notice, as we saw, took her breath away when her Sun was at full "Noon."

"Noon" holds a special significance for Emily Dickinson as a symbol for Immortality, poetic trance, Ecstasy, or expanded Consciousness. It is a non-temporal moment when the Self broke through her ego defenses with the *force of Lightning*. In this sense the Serpent is a primary symbol in her poetry as the harbinger of symbolic death, the return to nothingness, and Resurrection. And while Dickinson the so-called "Queen recluse" as she was pejoratively called by Bowles, may not have cared for career and fame in her lifetime, the *Lightning-shaman* within her soul most certainly did: "He fumbles at your Soul / …Deals—One—imperial—Thunderbolt / That scalps your naked Soul—" (J 315/F 477). To be scalped by "Lightning" was the surest sign that a poem rang true for Dickinson. After that awful scalping occurred, she put down her simple wardrobe and started for the Sun, and the Lightning hit her again and again from the transcendent dimension.

Eliade tells us that "the role of lightning in designating the shaman is important; it shows the celestial origin of shamanic powers," and he states, further, that "lightning is sometimes portrayed on the shaman's costume."[239] Lightning and the Sun were Emily's favorite symbols for the *albedo* stage of illumination in alchemy, the whitening—like the whiplash of the Snake that made its appearance and then was gone, leaving her "Zero at the Bone." In a poem written in 1883, she tells us that her head was "scalped" by "Doom's Electric Moccasin," the divine "Bolt" she would not exchange "For all the rest of Life—" (J 1581/F 1665).

The metaphor of scalping indicates that her illumination came from the region of the national unconscious. In a private conversation later recorded by Higginson, Emily stated famously: "If I feel physically as if the top of my head were taken off, I know *that* is poetry."[240] Her decision to dress in white suggests, moreover, that she accepted her role as a poet-shaman, as it was given to her by the supernaturals—or by a process she referred to as the White Election: "Mine—by the Right of the White Election! / Mine—by the Royal Seal!" (J 528/F 411). The assumption of a mythical royal costume or gown was meant to transubstantiate her as a Medicine Woman, transform her, before readers' eyes, into an androgynous Self-aware human being whose aim is to offer healing, like her shamanic predecessors. By assuming her white wedding dress she was essentially assuming the condition of Wife to her "celestial spouse."[241] Here is another poem about lightning that I find breathtaking:

> It struck me—every Day—
> The Lightning was as new
> As if the Cloud that instant slit
> And let the Fire through—
>
> It burned Me—in the Night—
> It Blistered to My Dream—   J 362/F 636

---

239 Eliade, *Shamanism,* p. 19.
240 *S,* p. 566.
241 Eliade, *Shamanism,* p. 168.

American poet-shamans encourage us, as readers, to consciously enter the *symbolic dimension* of the mind, by stimulating feelings, creative imaginations, and emotions simultaneously; thereby demolishing barriers between dreaming and present day reality. A major aim of their work is to lead us to an experience of heightened emotional awareness, which is Ecstatic. This state cannot be taught; it can only be experienced as a destiny inside of one. In short, the experience of Ecstasy comes as an event that upsets the normative functioning of ego consciousness, both in the poet and the reader; "deranging" consciousness potentially, to a point of Illumination.

Emily describes the state of Ecstasy above as Thunderbolt— "That scalps your naked Soul—" (J 315/F 477). This means that it isn't poetry *unless* the top of her head is taken off, and she intends to take the tops of *our* heads off too; for to be "scalped" implies the divine Indian—i.e., the shamanistic state of Consciousness as the "scalper." Like other poet-shamans, her aim is to "scalp" *us* with: "Doom's Electric Moccasin" (J 1593/F 1618) — i.e., the lightning-like, or incantational-like rhythms, images, and blood-quickening metaphors that take our breath away, as we saw in her poem "Snake." Through such quick strikes at the very axis of reality, she awakens the shamanic state of conscious Self-awareness in us as well. This state of divine realization cannot be "taught," it can only be "awakened" by someone in whom it has been *activated*.

The Lightning that precedes illumination by the Self "Struck no one but myself" (J 1581/F 1665). The connection between these ecstatic "instants" and the virginity of her Soul is a favorite theme of the mystics of all cultures; just as the White Buffalo Calf Woman was revered as the most sacred figure to the Plains tribes and as Changing Woman was to the tribes of the South Western United States. This area of Emily's Soul was not to be violated by human touch, but only by the divine hand of God: "He touched me, so I live to know" (J 506/F 349). "Struck, was I, not yet by Lightning—" and "Robbed—was I—intact to Bandit / All my Mansion torn—" (J 925/F 841).

"Surely," writes Holger Kalweit "the most dramatic form of shamanic initiation is initiation by lightning bolt…in tribal cultures throughout the world lightning shamans are often venerated and feared as the mightiest of shamans."[242] So it is with Emily. It is with her Bolts of Melody that she speaks to us most directly today in an effort to wake us up to the realization that the split between the historical human God-image and the inhuman forces of nature must be reckoned with, and Mother earth must be honored if we are not to destroy ourselves and many more living species. What we are doing to the earth and its creatures, in other words, is the real insanity. Now let's take a closer look at the natural wisdom of the "Boy" in her who walked barefoot on Mother Earth and shared in the bounteous beauty of her "Mama's" (J 164/F 130) blessings.

The Boy by the Burying Ground and Transcendence over Fear

Emily Dickinson gave us a number of hints about her poetic quest for Immortality having something to do with a question about an unresolved riddle concerning her early childhood. She said her decision to devote her life to poetry, her commitment to "sing," had something to do with a secret childhood "terror" about which she could tell no one, a "Boy by the Burying Ground," and that someone taught her Immortality when she was a little girl.

In a letter written to Higginson in 1874, moreover, Emily dug deeper into the secret recesses of her childhood memories to a core traumatic memory, from which the inner voice of her poetic vocation appears to have been evoked: "Since my Father's dying," she said after her father Edward's death "everything sacred enlarged so—it was dim to own— When a few years old—I was taken to a Funeral which I now know was of peculiar distress, and the Clergyman asked 'Is the Arm of the Lord shortened that it cannot save?' He italicized the 'cannot.' I mistook the accent for a doubt of Immortality and not daring to ask, it besets me still, though we know that the mind of the Heart must live even if its clerical part do not. Would you explain it to me?"[243] Notice how interested Emily is in theological matters here. Higginson, the reader will remember, was a minister. This interest in questions of theology was alive in her from her very early childhood. By suffering for decades from

---

242 Holger Kalweit, *Shamans, Healers, and Medicine Men*, p. 46.
243 *L*, II, p. 583.

a doubting thought put into her by the Clergyman, she eventually transformed it into a radical truth about the illusions of faith. This doubt was necessary for her experience of Spiritual Democracy.

The notes to "Ode: Intimations of Immortality from Reflections of Early Childhood," William Wordsworth's answer to his colleague Coleridge's "Ode on Dejection," might have offered some solace to Emily. Everyone, Wordsworth believed, could "bear testimony," if "he looked far back enough," to "that dream-like vividness and splendor which invest objects of sight in childhood," to find "presumptive evidence of a prior state of existence."[244] In this passage, Wordsworth captured the experience of Emily in her childhood, when, as a "little girl," her friend taught her Immortality. She mentions elsewhere, in an 1862 poem, in fact, that her vision of Immortality was given to her "by the Gods— / When I was a little Girl—" (J 454/F 455).

For Dickinson, poetry became the means to arrive at this energized world of Immortality—Lightning—Sun—Eternity—Consciousness—Ecstasy—Awe—in preparation for a Life to come. These are all metaphors for the shamanic state of mind. Why she would turn to Higginson to try and solve a problem she had already solved for herself a hundredfold in her art has to do with the vulnerable human problem of the functions of consciousness and the need for their integration in the Self; another reason has to do with the unresolved nature of her childhood trauma, for the words of the Clergyman constellated a painful and perplexing doubt in her. Was it not the clergyman's function to instill hope in the faithful? Her mother's fears of death are certain to have infused her with terror as a little child, moreover, and prayers did not assuage her despair. Even though the Snake and the Lightning Shaman within her *knew* of the reality of Immortality in this lifetime, the vulnerable trembling "Boy by the burying ground" continued to look up to "mentors" for guidance and support, especially for her rational thinking about such things in an age, supposedly of Enlightenment, when there were few reliable guides to instruct her on the problem in question. But what the rational mind could not see distinctly, the Animal Powers

244 Benet & Aiken, *An Anthology of English and American Poetry*, pp. 205-206.

within made up for in the depths of her shamanistic imagination. These were her true poetic ideas, her teachers. It was always the Snake, the Bird, the Spider, the Bee, the Hummingbird, and the Butterfly that led her to create a tapestry of life to transcend Death. Nature herself offered the greatest medicine for what religion could not answer: how to heal herself of the complex of fear from which we all suffer over the reality of death. Out of her fears, came one of her greatest poetic thoughts, an antidote, which is her fearlessness speaking through wellsprings of emotional intelligence in verse:

> Because I could not stop for Death—
> He kindly stopped for me—
> The Carriage held but just Ourselves—
> And Immortality.
>
> We slowly drove—He knew no haste
> And I had put away
> My labor and my leisure too,
> For His Civility—
>
> We passed the School, where children strove
> At Recess—in the Ring—
> We passed the Fields of Gazing Grain—
> We passed the Setting Sun—
>
> Since then—'tis Centuries—and yet
> Feels shorter than a Day
> I first surmised the Horses' Heads
> Were toward Eternity—   J 712/F 479[245]

For Dickinson, as for all of us on this speck of a planet spinning in endless space, death is the great equalizer. As we've seen, the call of the snake in the life of Emily Dickinson was traced to roots in her childhood—to an image of the wounded puer-animus, who led her to sing ("I sing, as the Boy does by the burying ground—because I am afraid.") When the Clergyman italicized the word "cannot"—in reference to a passage about God's power to "save"—Emily "mistook the accent for a

---

245 See Endnote I.

doubt of Immortality," and it was this emotionally charged situation, the presence of a "doubting thought" in her personal unconscious, and in the collective psyche of the whole human race, that led her to follow the shaman's call to ego death, illumination and rebirth.

Emily's childhood illness was eventually healed through her quest for a significant love object, who she referred to as the "Master;" perhaps most significantly, however, through her relationships to mentors, Newton, Susan, and Bowles. Through these friendships, she was enabled to sing her shaman's songs and have them mirrored by people who admired her, to varying degrees, through her poems and letters. All of these relationships provided a place for her transference projections, through which Emily could work out the mystery of her calling as a Lightning-Shaman of the White Election, but it was her less erotically-toned friendship with Higginson that appears to have helped heal her the most.

What ensued (when her love was rejected by Sue and the "Master") was a release of energy, dynamism, and power into the world that expanded her ego to the point of rupture and ultimate transfiguration. When the Snake that took her into the underworld made its first appearance, Emily was sixteen years of age. By the time she reached twenty-eight, she had given her life over almost totally to her art. Somewhere in the late 1850s, she proclaimed to her friends Dr. and Mrs. Holland that her main "business" in life was to "love" and to "sing." It was at this time coincidentally that she met Mr. Bowles. Sewall tells us: "What she seems to have expected from Samuel Bowles, was assistance in the fulfillment of what by now had become a consuming passion: the publication of her poems."[246]

In 1859 she wrote to Bowles: "Success is counted sweetest / By those who ne'er succeed. / To comprehend a nectar / Requires sorest need" (J 67/ F 112), a poem which Helen Hunt Jackson persuaded Emily to publish in 1878, and which had lain in her desk drawer for nineteen years before it ever reached the public's eyes.

The poet-shaman does not wait for some redemption in a future heaven; the time for the Resurrection is at hand, and poetry becomes

---

246 S, p. 475.

the vehicle, the transport to the Kingdom, to which she/he has been "going, all along" (J 324/F 236). In this sense, poetry becomes a means to an experience of death, so that one may begin to live more fully in *this* life. "A *Wounded Deer*" she wrote upon her parting of ways with Susan in 1860 "leaps highest / I've heard the hunter tell— / 'Tis but the ecstasy of *death*— / And then the Brake is still" (J 165/F 181). So too with human life: "'Tis Anguish grander than Delight / 'Tis Resurrection Pain / ....'Tis Transport wild as thrills the Graves..." (J 984/F 192).

It is from the negative or difficult emotions made conscious through reflective awareness that the positive emotions come springing into being. The negative emotions are unified when they are made self-conscious through archetypal imagery. Wading in negative emotions is what led her to the higher emotion of Ecstasy. Ecstasy was the sovereign or supreme emotion that *unified* all the rest. To put it differently, the negative emotions transformed themselves through the aesthetic imagination into One emotion of Ecstasy, or Transport. Ecstasy is made up as much by Woe as by Happiness, as much by Grief as by Joy, yet, she says above that Anguish is more sovereign, and grander than Delight. What does she mean by this?

William James was perhaps the first religious psychologist who properly understood that the goal of the mystical path is the *conjunction* of bitterness and sweetness, Joy and Sorrow. He spoke in *The Varieties of Religious Experience* of a "solemn joy...bitter in is sweetness," or of a "solemn sorrow to which we intimately consent."[247]

With an exquisite feminine sensibility, Dickinson was able to define the shamanic transport—the Lightning Bolt of Ecstasy—as no other poet-shaman before her time. In almost every instance where she describes the experience of mystical rapture, Ecstasy, or Bliss (that most fleeting of spiritual transports) she places its opposite beside it. Peace and violence form a pair of opposites that are experienced by her side by side. In Emily's shamanistic view, the opposites can never be fully separated from one another. Her poems provide empirical justification for Jung's hypothesis that emotion is the chief source of consciousness. Following Heraclitus' law of *enantiodromia* is her similar statement that

247 W. James, *William James: Writings*, p. 64.

sooner or later, everything runs into its opposite: "For each ecstatic instant / We must an anguish pay / In keen and quivering ratio / To the ecstasy" (J 125/F 109).

One learns how to develop the shamanic transport through solitude, pain, and suffering, by remaining "below," upon a "foreign shore— / Haunted by native lands... / And blue—beloved air." "This," she says, "is the Sovereign Anguish! / This—the single woe! / These are the patient 'laureates' / Whose voices—trained—below— / Ascend in ceaseless Carol..." from the "Mysterious Bard!" (J 167/F 178).

What are the "native lands" that haunt Emily? Is this not the national unconscious she is referring to? And who are the "patient 'laureates'" and "Mysterious Bard" Emily is referring to? Surely it is the archetype of the poet-shaman, a creativity of the Self that exists within each of us— accessed in our dreams and creative breakthroughs with their astonishing visionary feelings. In order to learn the shamanic transport, the American poet-shaman, who would consciously identify with this powerhouse of creativity, must enter the "haunted native lands" where identity and forms are no more, and where we return to what we were before our mothers and fathers first conceived us. When Emily has come to the land of the dead, a recurrent theme in the writings of the American poet-shamans, she chants:

> One Blessing had I than the rest
> So large to my Eyes
> That I stopped gouging—satisfied—
> For this enchanted size—
>
> It was the limit of my Dream—
> The focus of my Prayer—
> A perfect—paralyzing Bliss—
> Contented as Despair—   J 756/F 767

The experience of Ecstasy is not something the poet-shaman arrives at all-at-once in a single flash of Illumination, but something that occurs over time, through successive encounters with the *numinosum*; it is an emotional/affective state, which needs to be cultivated in and through the creative imagination, until it begins to catch up with the poet's inner vision. It is at this point in the poet-shaman's psychic development that the technique of shamanic transport becomes a gift of unutterable Bliss: "My Reward for Being, was This. / My Premium—My Bliss" (J 343/F 375). When lived out of the organic seed of wholeness, life itself becomes a *way* to our premium. It is this premium that must be followed, if we are to arrive at a realization of what our true vocation is in its seedbed. The essence of shamanhood is the achievement of a state of expanded consciousness where we are living in the eternal, ecstatic moment of the Self. It involves an extension of the mind, the experience of full stretch, for which poetry becomes the vehicle:

> There is a Zone whose even Years
> No Solstice interrupt—
> Whose Sun constructs perpetual Noon
> Whose perfect Seasons wait—
>
> Whose Summer set in Summer, till
> The Centuries of June
> And Centuries of August cease
> And Consciousness—is Noon.   J 1056/F 1020

"The journey's mythic end," writes Joan Halifax, "is the sun. The shaman flies through the Sun Door to the realm of eternally awakened consciousness. The very act of sacrifice in the domesticated fire of initiation makes it possible for the sacrificed one to enter the realm of the immortal."[248] It is this Noon Consciousness, which is always "aware of Death" that leads one to traverse the "internal / Experience between / And most profound experiment / Appointed to Men—" namely the "adventure" into the secret of our "own identity" (J 822/F 817).

Let us see what happens when the technique of shamanic transport is allowed to mature, and develop over time, when the ego is extended to the rupture point to *become* at-one with the expansive Consciousness of the Cosmic Self:

> I had a daily Bliss
> I half indifferent viewed
> Till sudden I perceived it stir—

---

248 Joan Halifax, *Shaman: The Wounded Healer*, p. 24.

> It grew as I pursued
>
> Till when around a Height
> It wasted from my sight
> Increased beyond my utmost scope
> I learned to estimate.   J 1057/F 1029

Here, Emily's capacity for Ecstasy moves temporarily into a Zone of magnified power, where her *daily* experiences of rapture converge, beyond her "utmost scope" to a sudden "Height." She dares not speak of her "Flood Subject" except in Cosmic terms. "Go Traveling with us!" she says, "Her travels daily be / By routes of ecstasy / To Evening's Sea—" (J 1513/F 1561).

What is clear is that, when a poet of such supreme eloquence learns to cultivate the shamanic transport, it builds to a point that becomes changeless, or eternal. Notice that Emily says: "I had a daily Bliss." Not an occasional Bliss, but a daily habit of thought and mind—a perpetual practice, from which she can no longer retreat with "indifference," once the mystical experience has set in. For Emily, this transport came through her love for the "Amherst girls," Jane and Abiah, and from Newton, Susan, Bowles, and Wadsworth. It is the "mysterious Bard," however, not anyone on the outside, not even the Master, that led her to become the unique person she was meant to be; she discovered Him in the Undiscovered Continent of her Native lands.

In Emily's view, as "Wife," it doesn't matter if fame comes to a person in one's lifetime, for: "Fame is a fickle food / …Men eat of it and die" (J 1659/F 1702) and "Publication—is the Auction / Of the Mind of Man—" (J 709/F 788). What's most important, in Emily's view, is that a person follow one's vocation with a devotion superior to any outward fate; that is, according to the laws of one's innermost Self:

> For love of Her—Sweet—countrymen—
> Judge tenderly—of Me   J 441/F 519

The News she has to share with the world is the news of the Universe which preceded Christ's Birth: "The Bible is an antique Volume— / Written by faded Men" (J 1545/F 1577). Like Whitman and Melville and Jung, she is moving beyond the Judeo-Christian image of God here into the "undiscovered Continent" of the Self: "Soto! Explore thyself! / Therein thyself shalt find / The 'Undiscovered Continent'— / No settler had the Mind" (J 832/F 814).

While everyone experiences the opposites of pleasure and pain, love and hate, rapture and suffering, agony and ecstasy, only rare individuals can experience Joy and Pain, Woe and Bliss, love and violence, Anguish and Ecstasy, as Emily did, "side by side" (J 1168/F 1259). This is precisely what the American poet-shamans bring to bear upon the consciousness of the race: the experience of (creative) freedom from the opposites through the awakening of the Self. Like Walt, Emily realized that America is merely a symbol for the world awakened to a new way of *life*. What is this "new" *way*, in Emily's view? In 1876—the centennial year of America's independence—Emily wrote a poem which sums up her vision for the American future:

> The Heart is the Capital of the Mind—
> The Mind is a single State—
> The Heart and the Mind together make
> A single Continent—
>
> One—is the Population—
> Numerous enough—
> This ecstatic Nation
> Seek—it is Yourself.   J 1354/F 1381

No God-image in history is greater than what resides within one's own "Nation." "Seek—" she says, "it is Yourself." In this poem, Emily says that America is already an "ecstatic nation," and that nation of Ecstasy exists, at least as a possibility in everyone. This is the nation of Spiritual Democracy, which is transnational in scope. However, the meaning of this spiritual boon must be sought in the "Undiscovered Continent," not in an idealized outer world America, which may never come to full fruition as a true Democratic governance; it is to be sought in the Self-realization of the shamanic complex, or symbol, as a democratic spiritual reality in everyone, where each person can become her own shaman, social activist, or feminist, breaking the chains of suffrage. It is an "inner land" of structural representations, living dynamisms that summons one from within to arrive at the sacred marriage. It is not necessarily an external place we inhabit by day; although there are certainly plenty of places in Nature where such experiences may be evoked. We can see such a potential in Emily's progression from the words Continent, Population, to Yourself. She transposes the symbol of the Continent and the land to the race consciousness; then to the Self, locating the Undiscovered Continent in the minds of creative individuals. Rather than following the way of the extraverted hero, Emily chose to walk the path of the holy sage, the Medicine Woman, whose business was to sing and to love and who sought solitude of the Void to gain medicine-powers. There is no general rule as to which path is "right," the way of a successful career, or the way of solitude, for both are potential paths towards the expansion of Consciousness.

While the "splits in Emily's psyche" never completely "swung together in her personal, emotional life," the late Jungian analyst Don Sandner believed: "there was so much vitality and energy" in the "little Force" that exploded within her that her childhood illness was "canceled out" altogether.[249] What did Don mean by this? After Emily's experience with the Electric Moccasin (Lightning) that struck her time and again from the transcendent dimension, her Consciousness, Sandner says, was "changed forever." When her experiences of Illumination broke through her mind in 1862, Emily continued to put on the mask of her naive, vulnerable animus (who she liked to call "the Boy by the burying ground,") yet it was a role she was playing; a mask worn by an actress, as in a Shakespearean drama. Emily transcended the traumatic splits in her personal psyche through the transcendent power of her shamanistic vocation. Shortly before he died, Don Sandner felt that there was enough power in this *vocational* dimension of the American psyche to draw her soul into the Other World; so that the creative "wound" that festered within her "was depleted of its negative charge, and her psyche was healed."[250] "Ecstasy," Don wrote, shortly before his death, "gives us the strength and the will to follow, apart and alone, if need be, our own

---

249 Sandner personal communication, 1995.
250 Sandner personal communication, 1995.

path through life and into death, gratefully and willingly."[251] The sha-man's path is not identical with the way of individuation, yet there are indeed parallels that Jung was well aware of.

As we have seen, Ecstasy was not enough for Emily. She also formed a new symbol for her inner marriage of the soul with the Self that speaks to us today and after her identifications with this archetype ceased, she came back to the ground to find her feet. When Emily said to Higgin-son, "My Barefoot rank is better," she was using her loaded weapon, her "loaded gun," to protect herself from disappointment at having been told by Higginson her poems were *too delicate…*not strong enough to publish"; an experience that must have struck her to the bone. Hearing this must be outraging to most of my women readers and men of a femi-nist persuasion. However, Higginson helped her consciousness evolve, nevertheless, even if he failed to perceive her poetic powers. She appears to have become aware of this when she wrote in her third letter to him, dated June 7, 1862 that "the Verses just relieve" the palsy.[252]

We learn more about her shamanic illness in Emily's second letter to Higginson. She began by saying she is "ill" and she was writing "today" from her "pillow." In this second letter, Emily thanks Higginson for his critical remarks and says ironically: "Thank you for the surgery—it was not so painful as I supposed." Emily appears to have used medical terms here to describe the process by which Higginson helped to "cure" her of her palsy: "Perhaps the Balm, seemed better," she writes, "because you bled me, first."[253] What didn't kill her only made her stronger. As editor and as a "surgeon," Higginson acted paradoxically as a literary healer, a shaman stand in, in the situation of the transference.

Looked at psychologically, her statement about "surgery" reveals a transference situation of patient to an imagined doctor; the difference being that the transference takes place through a literary channel in relationship to her mentor. It is an animus projection with therapeutic roots that goes back to her childhood terror. In her statement, Higgin-

251 D. Sandner & S. Wong, *The Sacred Heritage: The Influence of Shamanism on Analytical Psychology*, p. 10.

252 *L*, II, p. 408.

253 *L*, II, pp. 408-409.

son becomes a literary *shaman,* a medicine man, whose criticism (i.e., surgery) she thinks will make her and her poetry better. Looked at retrospectively, her attempts to heal herself through the practice of her art worked through the refinement of her aesthetic. "Surgeons must be very careful / When they take the knife!" wrote Emily, for "Underneath their fine incisions / Stirs the Culprit—*Life!*" (J 108/F 156). The life force within her knew that Higginson's criticisms about her so-called "too delicate" and "not strong enough" poetry were pure bosh, but in a sexist society where xenophobia and toxic masculinity were oppressing women, speaking out defiantly to him would have only weakened her inner rebellion, if she had lost his friendship.

Through the detachment of her Eros from emotional objects, she eventually arrived at objective cognition through which she could envision for herself a new role as a "Bride" of the nation in which the Divine Masculine would eventually emerge: "Given in Marriage unto Thee / Oh thou Celestial Host— / Bride of the Father and the Son / Bride of the Holy Ghost" (J 817/F 818).

Through her acts of withdrawing projections from Susan and Bowles, she was eventually led to the marriage with the "mysterious Bard," and it was through the quelling of her illusory desires for the outer "Master" in particular that she became who she was and is today:

> There came a day at Summer's full,
> Entirely for me—
> I thought that such were for the Saints,
> Where Resurrections—be—
>
> The time was scarce profaned, by speech—
> The symbol of a word
> Was needless, as at Sacrament,
> The wardrobe—of our Lord—
>
> Each was to each The Sealed Church,
> Permitted to commune this—time—
> Lest we too awkward show
> At Supper of the Lamb.

Sufficient troth, that we shall rise—
Deposed—at length, the Grave—
To that new Marriage,
Justified—through Calvaries of Love—   J 322/F 325

"The future indwelling of the Holy Spirit," wrote Jung in *Answer to Job* "amounts to a continuing incarnation of God. Christ, as the begotten son of God and preexisting mediator, is a firstborn and a divine paradigm which will be followed by further incarnations of the Holy Ghost in the empirical man."[254] In that time of cultural transformation, each will be, as Emily said so eloquently: a "Sealed Church."

---

254 Jung, *CW* 11: ¶ 693.

11

THE CONSCIOUSNESS THAT IS AWARE

Between the years 1850 and 1858, Dickinson was in search of a new technique of visionary consciousness that could revolutionize the world. By 1860, she appears to have arrived at it. Emily suffered greatly because of cultural stereotypes and sexism that chained women to the values of patriarchy. Nevertheless, the Lightning Shaman within her was a powerful force, which was not to be tampered with. When she arrived at the place of ecstatic visioning, her mind was literally on fire:

> Rich! 'Twas Myself—was rich—
> To take the name of Gold—
> And Gold to own—in solid Bars—   J 454/F 455

The years between 1858 and 1862 are generally considered a time of Emily's greatest inner turmoil and we need to consider what was happening to her psychologically. From the appearance of what was taking place in the depths of her imagination and outer friendships, it seems that she experienced a crisis that turned her totally inward.

In this book, I've tended to view the process Emily went through during her "crisis" years (1858 to 1862) as an essential part of her "sickness-vocation," a calling to develop her imaginative capacities out of shamanic structures in the objective psyche.

In a letter to Bowles from about 1860, Emily wrote: "'Faith is a fine invention / When Gentlemen can *see*— / But *Microscopes* are prudent / In an Emergency" (J 185/F 202). The "Emergency" she was referring to had to do with the issue of her career as a supreme poet who was not receiving the recognition from Bowles that she rightly deserved. Her "faith" in Bowles was diminishing and her loss of faith in him coincided with her loss of faith in traditional Christianity. Bowles was interested in changing Emily's poems to suit conventional standards of meter and rhyme of the time; standards being set by such artists as Poe, and Longfellow, who followed standard literary techniques established in Europe, but who were not, like her, masters of freeform. "Written in almost childishly simple patterns—ballad stanzas and rhymed tetrameter quatrains—Emily Dickinson's poems are remarkable for their precision, vivid imagery, and effective use of approximate and slant rhyming," writes Walter Sutton. "Rather than traditional ballads, however, it seems to have been the homely hymns of her Protestant heritage that provided the metrical model for her poems."[255] Of all the poems Emily sent to Bowles, he only selected five for publication. All of these gems were anonymously published, with manufactured titles.

Regardless of her disappointments over publication and career, Emily continued to write prolifically, and her relationship to Bowles only seemed to have made her more creative. Interestingly, in one of her letters, Emily referred to Bowles as "Great Spirit," a term that shows her idealization of him. Yet this reference suggests that she was in touch with shamanic rhythms in Native North America.

Thirty-five letters went to Bowles as "Great Spirit" and nearly fifty poems, one of which involved a reference to a "gentleman" not *seeing* properly. As Andreas Lommel writes: the shaman is "the center, the brain, and the soul" of the community.[256] When the center, the brain and the soul of the shaman-poet is denied, the community that needs her to infuse it with medicine-power is in serious trouble, as we are today.

Regardless of the inadequacy of the fit between Emily and Bowles and regardless of Bowles' inability to *see* properly—he served an important psychological function in his capacity as a mentor, and he was a catalyst for her famous Master Letters. Not anticipating a defeat in her relationship to Bowles, Emily wrote in 1861: "I shall keep singing! /

---

255 Walter Sutton, *American Free Verse: The Modern Revolution in Poetry*, p. 27.
256 Lommel, *The Beginnings of Art*, p. 73.

Birds will pass me / On their way to Yellower Climes— / Each—with a Robin's expectation— / I— with my Redbreast— / And my Rhymes—" (J 250/F 270).

Around this time, something curious happened in her relationship to Bowles. After she ceded her career as a poet in 1862, she wrote six poems across a span of time about Fame, the most volcanic being "Fame is fickle food /…Men eat of it and die" (J 1659/F 1702). Was this angry outburst directed at Bowles? As we have seen, Emily was in an "Emergency" because Bowles could not *see*. He was hesitating with publication and Emily was feeling desperate about her future destiny as a poet. Let us turn now to the symbolism of the Robin as a destiny symbol within her.

The Robin as a Totem Animal

In all of Emily's relationships with mentors—friends, sister-in-law, colleagues, and editors—she was trying to replicate the original "glow" of her early-idealized relationship with Ben Newton; a relationship she was never able to duplicate in her lifetime. In an early attempt to express her idealization of Newton, she used the Robin as an archetypal symbol to represent their friendship. Its first appearance was in an 1853 poem: "I have a Bird in spring," which was written in recognition of Newton's passing sometime after March 24th, 1853. He was thirty-two years old, Emily was twenty-three:

> I have a Bird in spring
> Which for myself doth sing—
> The spring decoys.
> And as the summer nears—
> And as the Rose appears,
> Robin is gone.
>
> Yet I do not repine
> Knowing that Bird of mine
> Though flown—
> Learneth beyond the sea
> Melody new for me
> And will return.

Then will I not repine,
Knowing that Bird of mine
Though flown
Shall in a distant tree
Bright melody for me
Return.   J 5/F 4

It is significant to note that after the loss of Ben, Emily wrote only one poem during a five-year period. The loss of Newton has been greatly underrated by most Dickinson scholars. Most attention has been given to Emily's friendships with Susan, Bowles, Higginson, Helen Hunt Jackson, Wadsworth, and Lord. Yet, in my view this early relationship was pivotal, because Ben was the only man who ever accepted Emily fully and unconditionally. It has been said—after Ben's death—that Emily "seems to have found little to interest her deeply in the other young men of the town, the students, the tutors, the apprentices in her father's office."[257] The "one request" she had in her life, she says, was for the Bird (Robin) she lost.

She said, after Ben's death, that the "Bird in spring" flew "beyond the sea," to learn "melody for me," and after a period of learning, she *knew* he would "return." This is a typical theme of the night sea voyage, where shamanic "learning" takes place in the unconscious, or the Beyond. According to Eliade, the lack of a formal ritual "in no way implies the lack of an initiation; it is perfectly possible for the initiation to be performed in the candidate's dreams or ecstatic experiences."[258] To go beyond the sea implies that this Robin is headed for the Other World; to which the poet-shaman's soul flies away in sorrow, or Ecstasy. In an 1858 poem written to Susan, Emily wrote further:

I had a guinea golden—
I lost it in the sand—

I had a crimson Robin—
Who sang full many a day
But when the woods were painted,
He, too, did fly away—

---

257 *S*, p. 597.
258 Eliade, *Rites and Symbols of Initiation*, p. 87.

> Time brought me other Robins—
> Their ballads were the same—
> Still, for my missing Troubadour
> I kept the "house at hame."   J 23/F 12

In both poems, we see the theme of the "missing friend," who flew away as a central image. Time would bring Emily other Robins (i.e., friends, poems), but none could replace the one "missing Troubadour" for which she kept her "house at hame" (i.e., stayed at home, withdrew into solitude.) In this poem, she was anticipating the Robin's return, however, which cannot possibly mean the return of Ben Newton. What she was referring to I think is the return of the Self (the "guinea golden,") the muse, or creative animus ("crimson Robin") who could free Emily from the creative impasse she was in. It is highly significant, moreover, that she sent this letter to Sue.

The significance of the mentor in the inner evolution of the poet-shaman's art is instrumental in her creative transformation. In fact, without the appearance of mentoring relationships in the life of the poet, the great outpouring of shamanic verses from the fires of her unconscious might never have been tapped from below with such elementary force.

Susan Gilbert became the next significant friend after the death of Newton who encouraged Emily to practice her art. As Sewall tells us, 276 poems are indicated in the *Complete Poems* (1955) as having been written to Sue. This is an astounding number. We can see what role Susan played as a transforming relationship in evoking Emily's life energies towards the road to her inner greatness. In successive correspondences, Sue referred to Emily as "a force of nature ('Gulf Stream,' 'torrid spirit,' 'Avalanche.')"[259] As we have seen, moreover, Emily referred to her inner Susan in 1877 as her "Bliss!"

Paula Bennett explains that Dickinson's poems and letters reveal patterns of erotic imagery that suggests that the poet's "attitude towards female sexual and creative power" was made self-aware in the friendship. Bennett argues that Emily's sexuality and imagination were homoerotic and autoerotic.[260] This is an interesting hypothesis from a psychological

---

259 *S*, p. 209.
260 P. Bennett, *Emily Dickinson: Woman Poet*, p. 21.

standpoint, but I am not convinced that it does justice to her deeper meanings, as I see her affections as bi-erotic. It is not sex that mattered most to Dickinson, moreover, for it is consciousness that "Will be the one aware of Death / And that itself alone" (J 822/F 817) in preparation for her life in the Beyond. For Emily, this meant that her path of evolving consciousness was to be through relationships with friends and through poetry where sex probably played a minimal role in any outward sense. Moreover, it is not clear in my view that the Master was an external person. It is important to advance this hypothesis here because most of the biographies on Dickinson have been preoccupied in solving the puzzle of who the Master was, due to the erotic undertones of love that are effusive in their content. Let us re-visit these Letters, therefore, to see what they actually say about her love problem and how she attempted to resolve it in verse.

The Three Master Letters

In her first Master Letter written perhaps in 1860, she began: "Dear Master, I am ill, but grieving more that you are ill." She says that her beloved "Robin very near, and 'Spring'—they say, Who is she—going by the door— …Indeed it is God's house—and these are gates of Heaven, and to and fro, the angels go, with their sweet postillions—I wish that I were great, like Mr. Michael Angelo, and could paint for you…Listen again, Master. I did not tell you that today had been the Sabbath Day. Each Sabbath on the Sea, makes me count the Sabbaths, till we meet on shore—"[261]

To be sure, this letter has a romantic tone, but it is only mildly sexually charged. It is, as I read it, about Eros in its spiritual accent. She begins by saying that she is ill and that her Master is also ill, and she wants to give him her strength. We also see the symbol of the Robin again, her first male love-object (Ben Newton) and "Spring" is *she* who is going by her door: "This is God's house." She tells her Master, further, that she wishes she could paint for him, like Michael Angelo. Then she asks him to listen again, and that the day she is writing to him is the Sabbath Day. The reader will remember that Emily said that while some religious

---

261 *L*, II, p. 333.

folks go to Church, she keeps the Sabbath staying at Home. She was, therefore, keeping Sabbath in her room. She tells him further that she is in God's House. "Each Sabbath on the Sea" may be the Sabbaths she keeps when she is practicing active visioning through verse, poetry, on the seas of the collective unconscious. She hopes to meet her Master on shore. Shore and Sea may be symbolic of the place of creation, the place of her shamanizing. In other words, the Master may in fact have been an inner figure, a superior teacher and master, like Philemon was for Carl Jung. He may not have been an outer personage at all, therefore, but an interlocutor of her mythopoetic imagination who inspired her greatest poetry.[262] This hypothesis of an inner Master of her soul will be pursued further in what follows. The main thing to keep in mind here is that "Consciousness that is aware" is, from a Jungian standpoint, an objective phenomenon that corresponds to what Jung called individuation, or Self-realization. Dickinson says it is *her Consciousness that is aware of itself, the poet's ability to reflect upon herself objectively through mythopoetic language.* Poetry was the vehicle to this end. Now let us examine some contents from Master Letter two.

In Emily's second Master Letter, written in 1861, we hear a song of a more tragic tune: "Master, If you saw a bullet hit a Bird—and he told you he was'nt shot—you might weep at his courtesy, but you would certainly doubt his word. One drop more from the gash that stains your Daisy's bosom—then would you *believe?* Thomas' faith in Anatomy, was stronger than his faith in faith...I am older—tonight, Master—but the love is the same—so are the moon and the crescent...I wish with a might I cannot repress—that mine were the Queen's place—...Vesuvius dont talk—Etna—dont—...you have felt the horizon hav'nt you... Couldn't Carlo, and you and I walk in the meadows an hour...I used to

---

262 I want to thank Jungian analyst Jean Kirsch for raising this possibility during some personal communications in 2014 and again on August 20, 2015. When Jean told me her insights about the Master-Philemon parallel, it made immediate sense. The Master Letters contain no clear evidence that He was in fact a man in her outside relations. She may have projected the Master onto a few men in her greatest period of creativity. Nonetheless, the three Letters are addressed to an Impersonal figure, perhaps her Muse, mysterious Bard, or God Himself.

think when I died—I could see you—so I died as fast as I could…What would you do with me if I came 'in white?' Have you the little chest to put the Alive—in? …I want to see you more—Sir—than all I wish for in this world—and the wish—altered a little—will be my only one—for the skies…Could you come to New England— [this summer—could] would you come to Amherst—Would you like to come—Master? … Would daisy disappoint you—no—she would'nt—Sir—it were comfort forever—just to look in your face, while you looked in mine—then I could play in the woods till Dark—till you take me where Sundown cannot find us—and the true keep coming—…you did'nt come to me in 'white,' nor ever told me why."[263]

What this letter suggests is that her calling, her destiny factor ("the Queen's place,") was emergent. Her destiny emerged as a way of healing herself through poetry, and here, her soul animal (Bird) had been shot in the breast. This 1861 period, when her psychic trauma emerged in full consciousness, concomitantly with her calling to create shamanic poetry with her greatest intensity and motivation, is the time of her best productivity, when the vocational archetype latent within her (Vesuvius, Etna, Lightning, Thunder) was fully switched on through evocation. Between 1862-1863 she drafted three hundred plus poems in a single year! This is a tremendous output.

In her early relationships to male mentors (Ben, Wadsworth, Bowles, Master) we can see the same images of loss and wounding to a Bird that had originally enabled her to write shamanic poetry, or to sing. Thus, viewed psychologically, the early idealization of her erotic transference onto Newton, symbolized by the Robin, was being shot through her heart (she was heartbroken) by the outward neglect she was now receiving and she was bleeding from a bullet in her ("Daisy's") aching bosom.

In the second Master Letter, moreover, there is a further suggestion of a defeat in the area of her affections by some cruel intervention of fate. Clearly, the Master has disappointed her. Just as she had lost Ben Newton before a love affair could be consummated, now, her erotic desires for a male lover (Master) seems to have been dashed altogether. She appears to be attempting to get the Master to empathize with her

---

263 *L*, II, pp. 373-375.

pain, when she says "If you saw a bullet hit a Bird—and he told you he wasn't shot—you might weep at his courtesy, but you would certainly doubt his word." One more drop from Daisy's bosom—then he, the Master, would *believe.* The next reference to doubting Thomas is also instructive. The "Anatomy" Thomas obviously believed in was the body of Jesus, God made flesh. That incarnation he had faith in. Thomas had faith in the body of the Son that taught the Sermon on the Mount and was crucified on the cross. She mentions faith three times here. Thomas' faith in Anatomy in her letter, however, makes eloquent reference to a science "stronger than his faith in faith." She is brilliant here. As Jesus was crucified and Resurrected, so too was Emily.

She then proceeds to instruct her Master that God made her. She does not know how, but her heart was opened, beyond traditional faith and belief. God built the heart in her and it outgrew her ego, and like a little mother, she got tired holding such an enormous child. This child, as I read her, is winged-Eros ("No Bird—yet rode in Ether.") She then tells her Master further that she asked him for "Redemption" but he gave her something else, the "Scalding One—Sabachthani—" (J 313/F 283). Through the crucifixion of her ego on the cross of her poetic vocation, therefore, He, the Master, altered her—her I—Emily's ego—and she was changed and no longer "tired." She rose, but not as a wounded Bird. She rode the Ether into the air, or sky, as shamans sometimes do. She then says she is older tonight but the love is the same. She is older, but why? Because she has been initiated into Love with a capital L. She then says after longing to breathe where he breathed: "I wish with a might I cannot repress—that mine were the Queen's place—."

The things she writes to her Master are holy things, reverent, sacred things she touches in a hallowed way. She does not want what she writes to be profaned. These words are of the spirit and are from God. Then she returns to a theme we have seen earlier. Let us review it: "persons who pray—dare remark [our] "Father!" This is Awe speaking. Her prayers to God-Goddess cannot be named. Then she proceeds to tell us why: "Vesuvius dont talk—Etna—dont—" Her God was not only a God or Goddess of Love and perfection, like the teachings of Jesus, but also of immense violence, explosiveness, force.[264] This is the Lightning-shaman speaking in her; no mere Daisy! She is not just playing around with words here. She makes every syllable she speaks, have cash value. They pay off.

She is exploding her "little Force" here to open her Master's eyes to the reality of a Divinity so vast it staggers the mind to even try and comprehend it. Only a few syllables are said. She then asks her Master to remember that God is the entire Universe: "you have felt the horizon hav'nt you." I read all of this genius as an inner dialogue with her cre-ative animus, and the Master as a symbol for the Self. She is engaging in what Jung called active imagination, I believe. Thus, it is my hypothesis that Emily was having an inner dialogue with her Master and inviting him to come to Amherst to be with her forever. "Couldn't Carlo, and you and I walk in the meadows an hour," she asks. Carlo, as we have seen, was Emily's trusted companion for sixteen years. He filled her life with excitement and joy. Here, she asks the Master to join them on a walk in the meadows. I do not read the Master to be a man only. He may have been at first. But this letter suggests that He is closer to God. She may have momentarily projected her own inner idea of the Self onto Wadsworth, Bowles, or Lord, but no one could have understood what she was saying, had she mailed this.

Now she proceeds to uncover what her Master gave her instead of redemption: "I used to think when I died—I could see you—so I died as fast as I could." What she may mean is that she actually died to her ego, so that she could be with her Master, the Self. *The Self has a universal vocation; its goal is to be awakened and realized in all human beings.* Emily tells us how: let go of all of your traditional images of God, and be open to the Now of creation in an infinite Cosmos: "Forever—is composed of Nows—" (J 624/F 690). She is speaking with full authority as a Medi-cine Woman here. This is no frail and fragile daisy, but a shaman-poet that has been dismembered and has now transformed the very founda-tion of the Judeo-Christian mythos from the ground up. The Master

---

264 The only other American poet-shaman who takes the violence of the Cos-mos into account, with as much immense force as Emily does is Robinson Jeffers. S. Herrmann, "The Shamanic Archetype in Robinson Jeffers's Po-etry," In *Jeffers Studies*, Vol. 16, Nos. 1 & 2, pp. 1-34.

may indeed have been in part an outer personage. My best hunch would be that the Master was Wadsworth. However, I am hypothesizing that the larger part of what the Master became internally for her transcended anything an outer man could have possibly had to offer in terms of love, friendship, insight, or wisdom. Psychologically, we speak of the process of projection and recollection of the Self as a way that patients in analysis become conscious of themselves. "What would you do with me if I came to you 'in white,'" she asks the Master to consider. "Have you the little chest to put the Alive—in?" She is speaking with the Master as if in a meditation with God, and having it out at the same time with traditional notions of faith. Faith is not for some future Heaven. Faith is for her Now. Faith comes from knowing the Absolute—*feeling* the horizon, boundlessness, infinite, Circumference. She is actually challenging her inner, now introjected animus to see that he needs her feminine wisdom for his very aliveness. Alive is what she is in the moment she wrote it. This Aliveness cannot be repressed. She speaks it, sings it from her heart. Her greatest wish in the world was to see her Master more, and if that were granted, the only desire left for her would be "for the skies." Holding the opposites on the matter of the identity of the Master is without any doubt important. When she asked him if he would come to Amherst, for instance, this appears to be empirical evidence that he was an actual figure. It would seem probable that he was also her own inner animus in a projected and introjected form. Whiteness, as we saw, is a symbol for her betrothal to Divinity. The God of the Bible never told her why He never came to her in white, or why He did not speak up for women's rights. That was her calling: to create a marriage between the Divine Feminine and Masculine long before such concepts were specified for theology in the West.

In the final Master Letter written sometime around 1862, Dickinson refused to accept no for an answer. She spoke forthrightly about the fact that she "never flinched thro' that awful parting, but held her life so tight he should not see the wound…" She then went on to say: "I've got a Tomahawk in my side but that don't hurt me much. [If you] Her Master stabs me more— …Oh how the sailor strains, when his boat is filling—Oh how the dying tug, till the angel comes. Master—open your life wide, and take me in forever, I will never be tired—I will never be noisy when you want to be still. I will be [glad] [as] the best little girl—"[265]

In this third letter to the Master, she tells him that the love she feels for him is so big it frightens her. She asks her Master to open his life wide and take her in forever. These are all the thoughts of a woman who is engaging in a dialogue with an inner figure who she does not name, because he is the mysterious Bard—the poetic genius within her and the theologically-minded woman who has no competitors in the world of male privilege. He is not, as her biographers have speculated, only an outer figure, whether Wadsworth, Bowles, or Lord. As a Jungian, I read these letters as an ongoing conversation with her *medicine-powers*: the medicine of writing, which sustained and redeemed her. In fact, poetry saved her life and her sanity, I believe. Had she not written, she would have no doubt remained neurotic. But the inner voice saved her.

In these three letters that were never sent, one in pencil, and two written in ink, she spoke to her Master, who was ill. But in the second two, her metaphors were intended to be his *medicine*. He remained unnamed because he probably came to her in an impersonal form. In India, such a Master is called a guru, a source of a person's native genius. In all three of them, we can hear Emily speaking to him while he is silent. *Her poetry, I believe, was His Answer.* In the last letter to her Master, we can see a few more facts about Emily as a person, as a pugilist and as a poet.

Firstly, we can see that her feeling was numb— "never flinched... Tomahawk...never hurt me much." Such numbing responses are typical of individuals who suffer from the defensive operations that are secondary to early childhood trauma.[266] In my best estimate as a Jungian child psychotherapist, she suffered from an attachment disorder from early infancy in relationship to her mother. This is perhaps why her emotional relationships with women and with men were so intense: she was seeking a cure of her attachment trauma through love.[267]

---

265 *L*, II, pp. 391-392.

266 Donald Kalsched, *The Inner World of Trauma: Archetypal Defenses of the Personal Spirit.*

267 S. Herrmann, "The Treatment of an Abandonment Trauma," *Journal of Sandplay Therapy*, Vol. 17, No. 2, pp. 51-74.

Secondly, there was an effort to keep her Master from seeing "the wound;" an effort to cover her pain, which may have played a big part in her decision to relinquish her motivation to publish.

Thirdly, there is a clear reference to her never being noisy when he wants her still, so here we see she was attempting to work out her parental complexes through the relationship as his "best little girl."

Fourthly, there is a reference to a possible cultural, or transpersonal *wound* that appears to have been transmitted transgenerationally from her family of origin, her Amherst community and the ground of the Native American earth. We see this in the image of the "Tomahawk" stuck fast in her side.

As we've seen, Emily called Samuel Bowles "Great Spirit" on at least one occasion and the "Tomahawk" may be a further reference to an *injury* she sustained during their parting of ways. Such an injury might best be described as a *shaman's wound*, which comes from the violence of the Self. Such a wound can happen whenever a person is subject to an experience of severe defeat through an intervention of a hostile, or violent fate. The intervention leads the poet-shaman to move beyond the horizontal horizon of her temporal preoccupations with emotional objects, and her temporary love affairs, to a truer, vertical Love of her transpersonal destiny, given to her by Nature and by God.

It is known that three of Emily Dickinson's descendants fought against Native Americans at Deerfield Meadow after the Massacre of 1704,[268] and there are reports from news clippings of retaliatory attacks by Native Americans that she may also have read. Her letters and poems support such a probability. The Native American themes in her poems speak empirically to the possibility that with the withdrawal of her emotional projections and erotic complexes onto women and men in her community, she opened herself up to the deeper shamanistic influences in the American Soul, or what she called the "ecstatic nation." It appears to have been out of this shamanistic domain of the national psyche[269] that the Tomahawk appears to have come to remind her of her destined

---

268 *S*, p. 18.
269 S. Herrmann, "The Cultural Complex in Walt Whitman," *The San Francisco Jung Institute Library Journal*, Vol. 23, No. 4.

tasks. The whole structure of the poet-shaman's personality was altered by the soul-force of her helping spirits and it was through these medicine powers that she would become, once her poems were posthumously published, "poet and artist of [her] group."[270]

The Fourth Figure of Destiny

Earlier in this chapter, I mentioned the correlation between the Master and Jung's inner guru, Philemon. Now I would like to take my hypothesis a bit further. As Jung's autobiography *Memories, Dreams, Reflections* and the *Red Book* reveal, Philemon first appeared in a dream and he then became Jung's interlocutor who taught him "psychic objectivity, the reality of the psyche."[271] What I'd like to advance now is the possibility that an analogous phenomenon may indeed have occurred in the life of Emily Dickinson. The Master may first have appeared in a dream or vision and may then have continued to visit her in her room or garden.

To further illustrate this process, I'd like to refer to Marie-Louise von Franz's book, *Projection and Recollection in Jungian Analysis*. Projections, she says, can lead to disturbances in adaptation. When adaptation is disturbed, an integration of the projected content into the subject then becomes the desirable outcome; introjection then leads to transformation, or the realization of the Self.[272] Projection is a psychological process whereby an inner content of the psyche is transferred onto an external figure that carries the projection for a period of time until it is withdrawn and integrated back into the Self. She also speaks of "the social function of the Self" and "reciprocal individuation," where one gathers around oneself a "soul family"—a group not created by accident and projection, but by something more objective, arranged by the Self.[273]

As Self-figures, therefore, Newton, Wadsworth, and Bowles all became outer transference figures so that the archetypal aptitude of the poet could be switched on through evocation within the relational

---

270 Lommel, *The World of the Early Hunters*, p. 140.
271 Jung, *MDR*, p. 183.
272 Marie-Louise von Franz, *Projection and Re-collection in Jungian Psychology*, p. 7.
273 von Franz, *Projection and Recollection in Jungian Analysis*, p. 177.

matrix between Emily and these three men of letters. Dickinson's psychobiography depicts this process beautifully. The appearance of Wadsworth at Emily's homestead, for instance, on October 1, 1859, shortly after the Philadelphia pastor's mother had died, shows how pivotal this time of destiny was for Dickinson. As Jay Leyda suggested, Dickinson had begun writing to Wadsworth to inquire about his mother's illness as early as 1858.[274] At the age of thirty-two, four years later, Dickinson learned, in 1862, that Wadsworth was called to a new Church in San Francisco, California. Just as she experienced the loss of Newton through death, and the loss of Bowles to his marriage, so too, did she suffer a defeat over this loss of Wadsworth. These three successive blows of fate ultimately led her though her agony and pain to the very source of her destiny pattern as the poet and Medicine Woman, and the Master served as the channel for her transport to Spirit. In other words, the Master was evoked relationally through the projection and recollection of the Self onto these three destiny figures.

What ultimately crystallized out of the three relationships and their frustrations was an inner, fourth figure, the inner, great teacher of insight and Wisdom, who named himself Master. Along with the objective knowledge that emerged from her active visioning with Him we can also observe the regressive and infantile complexes that were part and parcel of her unanalyzed developmental stages that remained partially unintegrated and immature.

It is my hypothesis, therefore, that the *higher destiny of the transpersonal Self in Dickinson's life is what was projected onto the Master. He, finally, is the fourth figure who led her to become superior to fate.* We do not see this kind of spiritual idealization in any of her outer relationships except perhaps Wadsworth. The archetype of the Poet that had been constellated in Dickinson's youth had been seeking to latch itself onto literary and religious types, men of letters who could direct her towards a *higher destiny.* Newton, Wadsworth, and Bowles all played pivotal parts in helping to evoke the Self as a figure of great inner Light in Dickinson.

---

274 *S*, pp. 452-453.

As I've hypothesized, this process of Self-awakening occurred in a relation-al matrix, in four consecutive stages: 1) Emily and Newton, 2) Emily and Wadsworth, 3) Emily and Bowles, and 4) Emily and the Master. Wadsworth's departure for California led Emily beyond the narrow horizons of her youthful idealizations. By the time she met Bowles, the archetype of the Self was fully activated. By withdrawing her projections, she was led by the Master to a realization of her *higher transpersonal destiny*. She eventually encountered the figure of the Master as an objective reality within and without, and had conversations with him. It was the Master who taught her to follow the Self-path. Dickinson's discovery of a soul society to support her individuation led her to an experience of liberation, illumination, and democracy, as a poetess of Liberty.

I Know that He Exists

I believe she was cured of her creative illness[275] through the writing of shamanic poetry itself. Poetry and letter writing became her *cure*. As Emily wrote to Higginson: "I felt a palsy, here—the Verses just relieve—"[276] By this time in her development, she no longer looked to Jane, Abiah, Kate Scott Anthon, Wadsworth, Bowles, or Susan, to fulfill her erotic desires, dreams, or longings for union, or publication; for she had found her deeper *solace*—comfort from an agency within herself: "Destiny," "Balm" or "Dew," through which her *healing* powers came.

Once her childhood wound surfaced interpersonally in her second Master Letter, Emily was able to withdraw the projections of her soul-image onto women and men and come to the full realization of the shamanistic "Inheritance" that was inborn in her:

> Inheritance, it is, to us—
> Beyond the Art to Earn—
> Beyond the trait to take away
> By Robber, since the Gain
> Is gotten not of fingers—
> And inner than the Bone—   J 321/F 334

---

275 See Endnote J.
276 *L*, II, pp. 408-409.

"A real and great shaman," writes Lommel "will generally possess this measure of power from birth."[277] So, it wasn't so much Higginson or Susan or Wadsworth or whoever who *healed* her from her "palsy," as much as it was the "verses," her "Destiny" and the "Dew." As Sewall says: "Her growing sense of the healing power her verses had for others now joined with her awareness of how necessary they were to her own health of mind and spirit; how (as she wrote Higginson in her third letter, June 7, 1862) the Verses just relieve" the illness, how their "jingling cooled my Tramp—"[278] Higginson acted as a master shaman of initiation in the situation of the transference by "bleeding" her first.

Thus, Higginson's critical "advice" helped, in a metaphorical way to drain (bleed) the infection (i.e., the shaman's wound) that was festering within Emily Dickinson's heart. He came along as a "surgeon" precisely at the time when she needed him most, at a point after the imagined loss of the Master; and at the same time, not incidentally, of increasing tensions with Susan Gilbert. In fact, Emily's relationship to Higginson may have been the one relationship in her life that "saved" her from her neurosis most because it helped her arrive at the deepest activation of her capacity for creative birth-giving: "The Robin for the Crumb / Returns no syllable / But long records the Lady's name / In Silver Chronicle" (J 864/F 810).

In another letter, this one written to Bowles in 1862, we can see how her newly found friendship with Higginson may have led her to get over her dependence on Bowles. Emily wrote: "Victory comes late, / And is held to freezing lips / Too rapt with frost / To mind it! / How sweet it would have tasted! / Just a drop! / Was God so economical? / His table spread too high / Except we dine on tiptoe! / *Crumbs* fit such little mouths—/ *Cherries*—suit *Robins*— / The Eagle's golden basket—*dazzles them*! / God keep his vow to '*Sparrows*,' / Who of little love—know how to starve!" (J 690/F 195).

It is hard not to read the anger in these poems. This letter shows that this poet-shaman from Amherst was not just playing around with language in an effort to please: she meant business. She was ready and

---

277 Lommel, *The World of the Early Hunters*, p. 75.
278 *L*, II, p. 408.

willing to forgo publication if need be. Here, Emily makes use of a theme that is common to shamans across all cultures of the Far North, the Ecstasy too "rapt with frost." We see it again in another poem she sent to Bowles: "The Needle—to the North Degree— / Wades—so— thro' polar Air!" (J 792/F 187). Amongst Siberian shamans, the experience of initiation sometimes takes place in a little snow hut, where, for months at a time, the neophyte remains with little food and sometimes only a little blanket to keep himself or herself warm. Here, however, the drought of victory is not drunk, or at least so it appears; the marriage wine cannot be drunk, because her lips are frozen. Victory comes, but it comes late in a "solitude of space," which she refers to in a relatively late poem as "That polar privacy / A Soul admitted to itself— / Finite infinity" (J 1695/F 1696).

Victory is possible, but only in the future. "A Wife—at Daybreak I shall be— / …How short it takes to make a Bride— / …Unto the East, and Victory—" (J 461/F 185). Triumph can still come from within by way of the Self and its calling to vocation and this experience is arrived at through ego-death, acceptance of her fate, and defeat in the field of her career and love relationships: "As he defeated—dying— / On whose forbidden ear / The distant strains of triumph / Burst agonized and clear!" (J 67/F 112). In so many of these poems, she is clearly in anguish, suffering greatly, and outraged. This is what today we call poetry therapy.[279]

Emily's life and work was devoted to relieve others from the pain of unrequited love, and from the anguish of one who is not properly mirrored by the conventional masculine standards in which a woman is living: "Why make it doubt—it hurts it so. / So sick—to guess— / … That Something—it did do—or dare— / Offend the Vision—and it flee / And they no more remember me— / Nor ever turn to tell me why— / Oh Master, This is Misery—" (J 462/F 697). Such a defeat for her ego was nevertheless a victory for the Self in the transpersonal domain of her art, as she kept right on writing, up until her triumphant end:

---

279 Herrmann, "Whitman, Dickinson and Melville—American Poet-Shamans: Forerunners of Poetry Therapy," *Journal of Poetry Therapy*, Vol. 16, No. 1.

If I can stop one Heart from breaking
I shall not live in vain
If I can ease one Life the Aching
Or cool one Pain

Or help one fainting Robin
Unto his Nest again
I shall not live in Vain.   J 919/F 982

Here we hear a different tune: intending to stop a single bleeding heart from breaking and help the fainting Robin that needs to get back into her nest again, so she can sing the songs of her truest Nature. This, again, is shamanism, only her aim is to cure the heart of a single person. On the other hand, through her healing work on the souls of individuals, one reader at a time, she is also ministering a therapeutic transpersonal medicine to theology. Her aim is to offer readers, woman and men and children alike, her own personal theology, her own myth:

The Bible is an antique Volume—
Written by faded Men
At the suggestion of Holy Specters—
Subjects—Bethlehem—
Eden—the ancestral Homestead—
Satan—the Brigadier—
Judas—the Great Defaulter—
David—the Troubadour—
Sin—a distinguished Precipice
Others must resist—
Boys that "believe" are very lonesome—
Other Boys are "lost"—
Had but the Tale a warbling Teller—
All the Boys would come—
Orpheus' Sermon captivated—
It did not condemn—   J 1545/F 1577

She does not need to "believe," she knows. "*I know that He exists.*" (J 338/F 365)[280] she says, because of her lyrical resonance with a "warbling" Teller. She becomes, after Higginson's surgery, a Snake-doctor. She titled this remarkable poem "Diagnosis of the Bible, by a Boy!"

---

280 Italics mine.

Thus, she doctors what she sees to be the disease in the Bible with her doctor-animals. The Bible's *disease* is that it expurgated the dispensation of the Goddess. She has left the Judeo-Christian tradition behind here, following her fierce grapple with the Hebrew "God," the God of Jacob, and has by this time become an Orpheus, a Nature poet, whose ecstatic tunes captivate. They do not condemn; they electrify us. She has, by this time (1882) become an American Orpheus. "Ties more Eleusinian I must leave you—" she wrote to her nephew, Ned, "Deity will guide you—I do not mean Jehovah—The little God with the Epaulettes I spell it in French to conceal it's temerity."[281] The poet-shaman, like the modern analyst, remains what she is: a wounded-healer. She does not heal from all of the wounds of her development, from infancy onwards. Her wounds remain open. But from her receptivity to them, from her vulnerability and pain, she gains the inner strength to offer healing to the world. One of her greatest gifts is her example of how to mourn, as we can see in the following poem from 1862:

> I measure every Grief I meet
> With narrow, probing, Eyes—
> I wonder if it weighs like Mine—
> Or has an Easier size.   J 561/F 550

Lots of pain here, pools of it as she once said. We hear of it again in the following lines, written in the same year: "After great pain, a formal feeling comes— /...A Quartz contentment, like a stone—" (J 341/F 372). Here, she expresses a pain that is most ancient and constant in human suffering: the pain of unrequited love. Was it the love she never felt from her mother or father? Perhaps. But I think it goes much deeper. This is her shaman's wound, the cross she carried. What she is measuring through the eyes of the Goddess is the *measure* of grief in the eyes of everyone she meets. We all share in the human condition and are grieving over the damage that is being done to our environment. Her pain and her grief are not merely personal: "I could not tell the Date of Mine—/ It feels so old a pain—" (J 561/F 550). It is an ancient pain. She cannot tell the date because it is prenatal and precedes her birth. It is an ageless wound of the shamans who suffer the fate of the tribes. It is

---

281 *L*, III, p. 880.

the grief of all women and men, whose connection to the Self has been lost in the turbulent seas of unconscious projections onto futile and illusory loves. She grieves for the fate of girls and mothers. She looks with open eyes into our souls. She remembers the wound and reminds us of its antiquity. How old it is she does not know, but she feels with empathy into its source of pain.

It is the *grief of all nature.* The grief that "feels so old" is the grieving of the human species over our loss of a guiding myth that places Nature at its center. This is the dowry our American poet-shaman, the Medicine Woman, bequeaths to us. It was through her capacity to grieve and to grieve deeply that she was led to the "Consciousness that is aware" (J 822/F 817). For these gifts of love that she has to offer us, we must be grateful.

12

DEATH TO THE EGO

The precise dates of the Master Letters are not known, yet, as we've seen, it has been generally assumed that they were written between the years 1858 to 1862. We've taken a quick look at some sections from these three Master Letters in the last chapter. Now, let's consider some themes of loss and death to her ego that are contained in letters two and three. We examined losses of significant love-objects—whether a Bird, such as in the case of her Robin; or to some imaginary death within herself (i.e., to a Death *in* her "Brain,") which suggests the temporary loss of her *logos* function. In the following poem, written in 1859, we can hear that she had an experience of a death to her ego: "She died—*this* was the way she died" (J 150/F 154). We have to take her at her word here.

The "simple wardrobe" she took up when she headed for the sun was undoubtedly a reference to the statement in her second Master Letter: "What would you do with me if I came to you in 'white'?" It points to the fact that she was in the process of transit from one mode of existence to another. The precise experience that changed her life is not certain; yet, we've seen an anticipation of something building, a "little Force," as she named it, Vesuvius, or Etna, that could explode into full Consciousness to nullify the former oppositions in her God-concept that were too small.

"In his techniques of ecstasy," wrote the California poet William Everson, "the shaman returns to the primordial wound and revives his vocation by recourse to interior pain. He seeks isolation because the relativity of life becomes excruciatingly distractive, and the 'great solitude,' the uncrossable ice floe of his interior landscape, enables him to concentrate on the essentiality of his pain, which is his obsession…the shaman maintains interior stability in the face of his obsession only by shamanizing…The calmness of the shaman in the tribal midst is the witness of cosmic unity."[282]

In such a process of interior pain, which came with the withdrawal of her emotional projections onto women and men, she was able to arrive at the place that her destiny had in store for her. In 1861 Emily wrote: "I can wade Grief— / Whole Pools of it— / I'm used to that— / But the least push of Joy / Breaks up my feet—" (J 252/F 312). Another poem, during the same year, takes this theme a little further. The mood is "solemn": "A solemn thing—it was—I said— / A woman—white—to be—" (J 271/F 307). Here we can see the image of the white wedding gown again. White, as we've seen, is a symbol of death.

Grief is the sister of Joy. Clearly the cavalier was not to be mistaken for the Master. This Cavalier was the Holy Ghost that she wed—the Comforter. She was speaking of her *coniunctio* with the "mysterious Bard": the bard of her poetic imagination. We now come to an even more solemn image, also from the same year, which is one of her most famous poems, the Funeral she *feels* in her Brain. The death to her ego led her to assume a new immortal body: "I felt a Funeral, in my Brain / …And when they [the Mourners] all were seated / A Service, like a Drum— / Kept beating—beating—till I thought / My Mind was going numb—" (J 280/F 340).

This four-line stanza suggests that she was hearing a shaman's drum, beating, beating with its steady rhythms. The drums make her think her mind is going numb. The Drum is also a reference to the Drums of Civil War that she was hearing in 1861 when the poem was written. The "Plank" of "Reason" breaks and she drops "down, and down" until she hits "a World, at every plunge, / And Finished knowing—then—" (J 280/F 340).

The "Sense" was now "breaking through" with loss of her normative way of "knowing":

---

282 William Everson, *The Excesses of God: Robinson Jeffers as a Religious Figure*, pp. 111-114.

One Crucifixion is recorded—only—
How many be
Is not affirmed of Mathematics—
Or History—

Our Lord—indeed—made Compound Witness—
And yet—
There's newer—nearer Crucifixion
Than That—   J 553/ F 670

Jung has shown that when the libido formerly invested in love objects is withdrawn into the unconscious, the surplus energy streams back into the psyche to activate the "primordial images;" amongst them is the God-image: "the symbolic expression of a particular psychic state, or function, which is characterized by its absolute ascendancy over the will of the subject" and can "bring about or enforce actions and achievements that could never be done by conscious effort."[283] Dickinson had by this time tapped into a new feminist God-image that would not surface in the culture completely for another hundred years, with the rise of the second wave of feminism. This is how far ahead of her times I believe she was.

Beneath the symbol of the Robin's broken heart was an archetypal God-image of the *coniunctio* that was in the process of transformation. As a visionary artist, Dickinson strove to conjoin the dust behind to the disc before: "The Dust behind I strove to join / Unto the Disc before—" (J 992/F 867 a). She was clearly seeking a new God-image when she wrote this. What did she mean by Disc? I think she meant the Cosmos as an expansion of the traditional image of the Deity. The soul's "Society" she selected for herself, furthermore, was an archetype of wholeness, an image of the supraordinate personality, the Feminine Self in all women and men, a source of her awesome Wildness. Listen:

Wild Nights—Wild Nights!
Were I with thee
Wild Nights should be
Our luxury!

---

283 Jung, *CW* 6: ¶ 412.

Futile—the Winds—
To a Heart in port—
Done with the Compass—
Done with the Chart!

Rowing in Eden—
Ah, the Sea!
Might I but moor—Tonight—
In Thee!   J 249/F 269

"Ah, the Sea!" She is swimming in the collective psyche here. Her words are bathed in Ecstasy. After Samuel Bowles died in January of 1878, Emily wrote to his wife Mary Bowles: "As he was himself Eden, he is with Eden."[284] She was rowing in the calm depths of her soul that she had shared with many women and men, the waters of Eternity. "From Homer and Milton to Whitman," writes Paula Bennett, "the concepts of creative power have been intertwined in the masculinist literary tradition,"[285] and yet Dickinson's calling was directed at a future wave of feminism that is just on the horizon now. I have called it a fourth wave to distinguish it from the "third," which feminists identified with a movement that emerged from the early 1990s in our nation to the 150th anniversary of the Seneca Falls Convention in 1998. The "fourth" wave will be a wave of the Feminine that will not only insist on equal rights, but on equal *power* for women in economics, politics, and religion. "Cherish Power—dear" the poet wrote to Susan Gilbert in 1878, after the death of Bowles. "Remember that stands in the Bible between the Kingdom and the Glory, because it is wilder than either of them."[286]

In my view, Emily was a solitary one, a snake-visionary, with tremendous medicine-power for women in her day and today. These are the words of a woman who knows she is empowered by both King and Queen in her psyche. She tells us that she is a giver of a new wine, a new Liquor that was never brewed before. She takes the Goddess religions and the Bible at full stretch, and creates out them her own meanings,

---

284 Mabel Loomis Todd, *Letters of Emily Dickinson*, p. 189.
285 P. Bennett, *Emily Dickinson: Woman Poet*, p. 153.
286 *L*, III, p. 631.

her own new myths. By reaching down into the Native American earth, her soul burns pure in a *white heat*.

Of course, her ego never fully dies. It is only sacrificed in its heroic stage of development for a fuller maturity of midlife transitions. When she said "She died," she meant the early identification with her childhood fears and complexes that kept her quiet and still. Following her ego death, the Self emerged and reached the goal of her deepest yearnings, which was to give birth to her mature Voice.

Sickness-Vocation

On April 25, 1862, as we have seen, Emily Dickinson made reference to publication as being foreign to her thought "as Firmament to Fin," and of "fame" not belonging to her, etc. All of these statements are without precedent in the known history of letters. What is it that made this letter so *extra-ordinary*? When we generally think of shamans, we think of persons with *archaic*, or marginal mentalities, who engage in trance, dissociation, or possession states at will, who isolate themselves from their communities, who are "technicians of the sacred," masters of the "technique of ecstasy."[287] She had no choice. She had to follow her call to ecstasy and Bliss. As Eliade points out, "shamanic vocation" is "obligatory; one cannot refuse it."[288] To infer that a poet-shaman can serve the same function as a medicine person in a complex pluralistic society implies that they serve a function of *healing* in their communities.

Poet-shamans emerged in nineteenth and 20th century art as leaders and guides to the secret mysteries of the divine and as revealers of things yet to come. What distinguishes poet-shamans from other members of the community is the acquisition of a method of Ecstasy and visioning that is sacred, and used to transport *us* to the Other World. The experiences of Ecstasy sweep over the poet and leave her soul stunned and rapt in Awe. Yet part of Dickinson's greatness is that, from the inception of her vocation, she was empowering women as well in whatever limited way she could. Abiah Root was advised, for instance, at fourteen: "Don't

---

287 Eliade, *Shamanism*, p. 4.
288 Eliade, *Shamanism*, p. 18.

let your free spirit be chained."[289] Thus, from the start she was an artist par excellence and a powerful Medicine Woman who was fighting for women's liberation.

This portrait that I've been painting of her may understandably be questioned by some Dickinson scholars who have speculated that she was not interested in the American Democratic process, and concerned herself primarily with her own psyche's individuation, and what happens after death, as well as with the souls of people in her own immediate environment; in this view the assumption has been that she was not interested in the politics of the nation, or the larger world. I do not share this view because as a Jungian psychotherapist, it is my sense that the political concerns that she was preoccupied with run parallel with the aims of modern democracy. *As a poet-shaman, I believe she was attempting, in her individual way, to provide a therapy for the modern world.* One of the passages from her letters that has led to such a basic assumption that she was apolitical was written to Mrs. Holland, during the Presidential campaign of 1884. After hearing that the campaign was being spoken about through a cliché phrase as an "open secret," she wrote forcefully: "What a curious Lie that phrase is! I see it of Politicians—Before I write to you again, we shall have a new Czar—Is the Sister a Patriot? …'George Washington was the Father of his Country'—'George Who?' That sums all Politics to me—but then I love the Drums, and they are busy now—"[290] To Joseph Lyman, she wrote further: "My Country is Truth…it is a free Democracy."[291]

As I have been attempting to make clear in this book and am hopefully succeeding in my efforts, Dickinson's political poetry was an embodied therapy for a divided nation. Not long after Lincoln signed the Emancipation Proclamation, for instance, Dickinson penned one of her most political poems about race, creed, color, and class, which were all stripped away, she says, by "Death's large—Democratic fingers":

> Color—Caste—Denomination—
> These—are Time's Affair—

---

289 *L*, I, p. 104.
290 *L*, III, p. 849.
291 *S*, p. 654.

Death's diviner Classifying
Does not know they are—

As in sleep—All Hue forgotten—
Tenets—put behind—
Death's large—Democratic fingers
Rub away the Brand—   J 970/F 836

As early as the age of fourteen, she saw clearly enough that her calling was not to become involved in the conventional preoccupations of
women, or men, but to stay true to her main business, which was to
sing. As a rebellious teen, she wrote to Abiah Root that she could be a
housekeeper "very comfortably" if she knew how to cook, but then she
added with her characteristic wit and irony that her situation was sort
of like "faith without works, which you know we are told is dead." She
then ended: "Excuse my quoting from the Scripture, dear Abiah, for it
was so handy in this case I couldn't get along very well without it."[292]
The reference to faith without works comes from James 2:17, "faith, if it
hath not works, is dead being alone." As we've seen, she saw herself as a
"Bride of the Holy Ghost" (J 817/F 818). By this she meant her poetic
vocation to transform religion from the ground up by shamanizing.

To *shamanize*, according to Lommel, means to subordinate the spirits or render them subservient to one's vocation.[293] The aim of the poet-
shaman's art is to "capture" an animal's "soul-force," its medicine-power,
and to use it not for personal aggrandizement, but strictly in the service
to the community, and for the sole purpose of *healing*. The soul-force of
the helping spirits is what give shamans his or her medicine-power and
the spirits can be animate or inanimate. As Sewall writes, poets "like
Emily Dickinson may 'lie' in their hyperbole and exaggerated rhetoric.
They may strike poses and don masks and speak through personae. But
in their basic structures, where they begin, where they end, and how
they got there, they do not lie."[294]

---

292 *L*, I, p. 31.
293 Lommel, *The World of the Early Hunters*, p. 10.
294 *S*, p. 24.

Her calling was to enlighten us with a new revelation of the spirit: "Light—enabling Light / The Finite—furnished / With the Infinite—" (J 906/F 830). Dickinson had caught the wave of science and rode it into ceaseless Circumference. Like modern psychotherapists, she was an empiricist, for whom death was not something to be feared and seen as final, for she paid close attention to dreams, statements of the dying, and near-death experiences. Death to her is the greatest equalizer of humans and of all living creatures. Death is what makes us all equal. *Death was to her democracy's Voice, as it had inaugurated a Revolution.* "Science will not trust us with another World," she wrote in a letter in 1873; and then she added: "Guess I and the Bible will move to some old fashioned spot where we'll feel at Home."[295]

Always, her political poems are directed at freedom and Liberty. Her higher Biblical criticism was made possible by the social forces of Darwinian science and yet she felt that she had proof in her own experience of her soul's immortality. Not through faith in God was redemption made possible to her when she entered Death's chariot, but through actual resurrection of her spirit in this life. Speaking of those who have faith but not equivalence in works, she wrote tellingly: "Those—dying then, / Knew where they went— / They went to God's Right Hand— / That Hand is amputated now / And God cannot be found—" (J 1551/F 1581). The men in her Amherst community and all across her nation had a political interest in keeping the old-time religion of her forefathers alive. Yet to her, in Vinnie's Garden, as Paula Bennett says, there had never even been a fall. "In the semi-final draft of 'The Bible is an antique Volume'" Dickinson had titled it "Diagnosis of the Bible, by a Boy."[296] The Boy was the Boy by the Burying Ground.

I am not the first to have named the current movement of feminism, which I think Dickinson was the first American woman poet to envision for us as Liberty as "fourth wave." The American Journalist, Diana Diamond, for instance defined "fourth-wave" feminism as a movement that "combines politics, psychology, and spirituality in an overarching

---

295 *S*, p. 620.
296 Bennett, *Emily Dickinson: Woman Poet*, p. 87.

vision of change."[297] This kind of change is what Spiritual Democracy is all about. However, while the political is usually named the spiritual component, the transpersonal dimension is usually not present in most definitions of the term according to *Wikipedia*. For this reason, we need to go a little bit further in our attempts to explain what we mean in using it now.

The new movement that has been conceived by a number of women authors focuses primarily on technology, such as on-line feminism through Facebook, Twitter, YouTube, and other forms of social media. What is missing in many of these blogging efforts is a language that is equivalent to the message of change it hopes to impart as regards to women's empowerment and advocacy for equal rights on a transpersonal level of experience, which includes reflections of our modest place in the Cosmos on this green-blue planet spinning in infinite space.[298] It is here that Dickinson soars as a visionary poet to meet the current requirements with an overwhelming excellence for spiritual precision, impeccable mastery of American English, and concise word choice with regards to feminist politics. The reader will remember Adrienne Rich having said that her calling was to "retranslate her own unorthodox, subversive, sometimes volcanic propensities into a dialect called metaphor: her native language." Metaphor was an invincible weapon in women's empowerment. Here is another exquisite example: "When Thrones accost my Hands— / With 'Me, Miss, Me' / I'll unroll Thee / Dominions dowerless—beside his Grace— / Election—Vote— / The Ballots of Eternity, will show just that" (J 343/ F 375).

Women did not have the right to vote until 1920, yet as we've seen, Election has a double meaning in Dickinson's poetry. I would argue as a Jungian, therefore, that there can be no organized leadership in this "fourth" direction that attains to the level of achievement the movement rightfully deserves without a *visionary* who excels in the spiritual domain through language and my ballot, in literature, is cast for Emily

---

297 Diana Diamond, *Fourth Wave Feminism: Psychoanalytic Perspectives*, pp. 213-223.

298 Herrmann, "William James & C.G. Jung: The Emergence of the Field of Transpersonal Psychology." In *Integral Transpersonal Journal of Arts, Sciences and Technologies*, No. 8, June 2016, pp. 22-57.

at a transpersonal level of achievement. She outsoars any other poet writing in American English. Jungian analyst, Andrew Samuels, wrote in his marvelous book *The Political Psyche*, "Politics is also a transpersonal activity and, like most transpersonal activities, politics points in what can only be described as a spiritual direction."[299] In the realm of spiritual thought, Dickinson simply outstrips her field. She has no competitors as an American poet. *Poets like Emily are needed, therefore, to help empower the movement that is currently afoot, but most importantly, I feel, to heal it.* "Depth psychology wants there to be a therapy for the world," says Samuels.[300]

That Dickinson wrote poetry for the nation is a testament to her political stance as a patriot for Liberty, but that she also hoped to reach the world is a testimony to her embrace with an audience of global citizens in the present and future, who could truly understand her and accept her, just as she was, in a new day. Liberty was for her the best symbol for Spiritual Democracy, because it is portrayed as feminine. Liberty appears far more frequently than does the word Democracy in her poetry and letters. As we've seen, Emily was a poet for Liberty. She fought her fiercest battles for Liberty, in the hearts and callings of every person's souls. Her aim was to infuse Liberty, as an archetype of Freedom and Peace, into the World Soul. Liberty was a medicine for the Soul's "Bandaged moments" (J 512/F 360) that we all suffer from in space and time.

> No Rack can torture me—
> My Soul—at Liberty—
> Behind this mortal Bone
> There knits a bolder One—   J 384/F 649

Consciousness is captive in our mortal frame, but the Soul (Self), the One is always at Liberty behind this mortal Bone. Looking back at her moments of Ecstasy, in the peace of her room or garden in Amherst, she wrote, during the agonies of the Civil War: "It feels a shame to be Alive— / When Men so brave—are dead— / …In Pawn for Liberty—"

---

299 A. Samuels, *The Political Psyche*, p. 337.
300 Samuels, *The Political Psyche*, p. 339.

(J 444/F 524). Here, Liberty is cruel as Fate is: Liberty's Pawn. With democratic fingers, Death touches us all to the Bone. Yet in this very life, she asserts authoritatively because she has experienced ego death and returned from the land of the Dead:

> The soul has moments of Escape—
> When bursting all the doors—
> She dances like a Bomb, abroad,
> And swings upon the Hours,
>
> As do the Bee—delirious borne—
> Long Dungeoned from his Rose—
> Touch Liberty—then know no more,
> But Noon, and Paradise—   J 512/F 360

Imbibing Emily's medicine might help to give women and men (who are also part of the fourth wave of feminine movement in the world), a head start; a transport into democracy's *true* future in a time of tyranny in the United States. This is the time, therefore, for all of us to speak up as members of a participatory democracy, whose ultimate aim is liberation, Liberty, Freedom, and Equality for all, including wildlife and salmon in our California Rivers, and bees, and butterflies, and the ruby-throated hummingbirds that Emily loved so much.

13

A SOUL AT THE WHITE HEAT

What poet-shamans do, at least since Melville's, Whitman's and Dickinson's days, is to teach us to attune ourselves to the psychological and aesthetic *processes* of visioning. By stimulating the creative powers of the imagination and deep emotional structures of the shamanic personality; in which the poet-shaman's ego swims, often ecstatically, like a great fish in the sea; they seek to lead us on a visionary journey to transcendent experiences of the Self, a union of paradoxical opposites. One metaphor for the experience of soul purification that recurs throughout Emily's *oeuvre* is the symbol of *whiteness*. Listen again:

> Dare you see a Soul *at the White Heat?*
> Then crouch within the door—
> Red—is the Fire's common tint—
> But when the vivid Ore
> Has vanquished Flame's conditions,
> It quivers from the Forge
> Without a color, but the light
> Of unanointed Blaze.
> Least Village has its Blacksmith
> Whose Anvil's even ring
> Stands symbol for the finer Forge
> That soundless tugs—within—
> Refining the impatient Ores
> With Hammer, and with Blaze
> Until the Designated Light
> Repudiate the Forge—   J 365/F 401

In this poem, Dickinson makes her purpose clear from the start. What she is speaking about here is her own Soul's blazing *whiteness* and the potential whiteness—which is to say the illuminative *capacity*—that exists within each of us. The central idea of this poem is that, through the Forge of the poet-shamans refining Art, we too may begin to partake of the imaginal and emotional realities of the Soul. We too may be filled with a white heat of Ecstasy as a *living experience*. It is "probable," writes Eliade, that the state of

> pre-ecstatic euphoria constituted one of the universal sources of lyric poetry. In preparing his trance, the shaman drums, summons his spirit helpers, speaks a "secret language," or the "animal language," imitating the cries of beasts and especially the songs of birds. He ends by obtaining a "second state" that provides the impetus for linguistic creation and lyric poetry. Poetic creation still remains an act of perfect spiritual freedom. Poetry remakes and prolongs language; every poetic language begins by being a secret language, that is the creation of a personal universe, of a completely closed world. The purest poetic act seems to re-create language from an inner experience that, like the ecstasy or religious inspiration of "primitives," reveals the essence of things. It is from such linguistic creations, made possible by pre-ecstatic "inspiration," that the "secret languages" of the mystics and the traditional allegorical languages later crystallize.[301]

Through her shamanizing, Emily attempts to guide us to the *emotional-symbolic dimension* of the "Soul," or what is known analytically as the shamanic psyche. There is no disguise about what she is attempting to do in this poem; no literalism, no concretization, no hidden agendas. She bids us "crouch" at the "door" "within—" and *see* what quickens there, from the inner Forge of her Soul—the Center—of the shamanistic imagination.

We enter this door by way of the "Anvil's even ring." It is not the outward image of the Blacksmith, but the "even ring" of his anvil that draws us inward and onward, which is to say to the Blacksmith's rhythm, tune

---

301 Eliade, *Shamanism*, pp. 510-511.

or steady beat. By entering the state of "pre-ecstatic euphoria," which Eliade says is the impetus for linguistic creation and all lyric poetry, Emily obtains a "second state," by which she is able to articulate a vision of the Self that applies to each of us, through an alchemical metaphor that is both imaginal and *rhythmic*. The "symbol for the finer Forge / That soundless tugs—within." As well as serving a refining purpose for Emily's own individuation, it calls to us as an archetypal image, as a musical Forge of vocation: the state of *imaginatio* and *song* through which we may be re-born from blackness and darkness of our ordinary minds into the blazing "Light" of Creation.

Literalism might lead us to conjecture that she is talking about the process of metallurgy here, as opposed to something symbolic, emotional, affective, and rhythmic, but she is careful to choose her metaphors here with precision. As Eliade points out further, the craft of the Blacksmith ranks immediately after "the shaman's vocation in importance" and "the 'secrets of metallurgy' are reminiscent of the professional secrets transmitted amongst the shamans by initiation."[302] Thus, she is speaking metaphorically of the refining Light of the shamanistic personality and of her songs to act as a Forge of inner transformation *both* on herself and the consciousness of the world as well. The alchemical metaphor of turning base metals into gold was present in American poetry at least as far back as Emerson's time and undoubtedly played a part in informing Dickinson about the basic operations of alchemy. Thus, the idea of the Blacksmith of the Soul, who is—like the shaman—preoccupied with soul-purification, was probably known to her.[303] Yet the idea of the Blacksmith's anvil and its "even ring," as "symbol" for something finer, tugging at us from the inside of the Soul is something born entirely out of her own creative imagination. Poetry as song, as sung by the poet-shaman during states of trance and visionary consciousness, becomes a means for a purification of the Soul that is not only imaginal, however. It is emotional as well. It is the "Anvil's even ring" that stands symbol for the "finer Forge," not the image itself. As such, it serves as a Zen gong to awaken us to Enlightenment. It is this Light of a purified Soul that Emily wishes us to *see* within ourselves ("Dare you see," she says). What

---

302 Eliade, *Shamanism*, pp. 470, 474.
303 I would like to thank John Beebe for pointing this out to me in 1995.

she is describing when translated through the lens of analytical psychology, is the experience of the *albedo,* following the intense heating up of
calcinatio. About this state of the soul's operations, Edward Edinger says:

> the end product of *calcinatio* is a white ash. This corresponds
> to the so-called "white foliated earth" of many alchemical
> texts. It signifies the *albedo* or whitening phase and has para-
> doxical associations. On the one hand ashes signify despair,
> mourning, or repentance. On the other hand they contain
> the supreme value, the goal of the work.[304]

Emily refers to this "whitening phase," or "fire bath of immortality,"
as the place where the "impatient Ores" are refined, and where the Forge
of the Soul is repudiated. The word "repudiate" comes from the Latin
root *repudiare,* which means to cast off, reject, or divorce. This could
mean psychologically that to *see* a "Soul *at the White Heat*" requires a
rejection of a former value, which the Forge represents. In this view,
the Blacksmith's Forge is *symbolic* of an inner place in the Soul through
which each may be purified during an individuation process. It is a collective archetypal image inside each of us that needs to be repudiated.

Shamanism can influence the post-modern West in imagination, yet,
in the poet-shaman's view, it is not enough. If shamanism is to become
a movement in the West, it must also return through rhythm, poetry,
and song that is lyrical and *emotionally attuned.* The expansion of consciousness through the cultivation of shamanic states of awareness, in
other words, cannot be complete without the integration of archetypal
affects, rhythmic attunements, and emotional visioning that is centered
in the shamanic psyche, and hence, in melody. Thus, Emily enables us
to revision Ecstasy as an ambivalent principle, which is as much concerned with the downward journey of individuation (i.e., *calcinatio*),
as with the upward ascent to Illumination (i.e., *albedo*). On this point,
Emily is even more explicit than Whitman: *there can be no ascent without descent, no Joy, without Anguish and Pain, no Illumination without
suffering, despair and darkness.* "To learn the Transport by the Pain—"
(J 167/F 178) she says is one way to describe the *calcinatio* experience;

---

304 Edinger, *Anatomy of the Psyche,* p. 40.

another way is depicted in the following lines: "'Tis so much joy! 'Tis so much joy! / If I should fail, what poverty! / And yet, as poor as I, / Have ventured upon a throw! / Have gained! Yes! Hesitated so— / This side the Victory!" (J 172/F 170).

These two poems, written in 1860, are descriptive of the stage of individuation in which the ego must endure the "descent of consciousness into the animal realm," through identification with the "fiery energies of instinct."[305] "Whether one gets through such a *calcination*" experience, says Edinger, "depends on whether one is acting on ego motives or Self motives."[306] In Edinger's view, experiences of pain or joy can be *coagulated* in either a positive or a negative way, based on one's early relation to the parental images of childhood. Emily Dickinson can be described as having experienced an *ambivalent yet transcendent* relationship to the Self, where Joy and Pain, Grief and Woe, suffering and Rapture (she likes her capitals!), were often experienced side by side. In the early *calcinatio* stage of her poetic journey, her ego had difficulty containing these paradoxical emotions. She wrote in 1860: "A Transport one cannot contain / May yet a transport be— / Though God forbid it lift the lid— / Unto its Ecstasy!" (J 184/F 212).

At least for a period of time, while she was still engaged in her projections of Eros onto Sue, Bowles, and the Master, Emily's ego could not *contain* the opposites of calcinatio and albedo because: "the opportunity to experience the archetypes mediated and personalized through human relationships"[307] had not yet been vouchsafed to her. "The transference," writes Jung, "is far from being a simple phenomenon with only one meaning, and we can never make out beforehand what it is all about."[308] Her childhood relational patterns had "to be broken up," as Edinger says and "recoagulated under more favorable circumstances."[309] Dickinson describes this state of affairs wonderfully:

---

305 Edinger, *Anatomy of the Psyche*, p. 19.
306 Edinger, *Anatomy of the Psyche*, p. 24.
307 Edinger, *Anatomy of the Psyche*, p. 99.
308 Jung, *CW* 16: p. 175.
309 Edinger, *Anatomy of the Psyche*, p. 99.

I can wade Grief—
Whole Pools of it—
I'm used to that—
But the least push of Joy
Breaks up my feet—
And I tip—drunken—
Let no Pebble—smile—
'Twas the New Liquor—
That was all!   J 252/F 312

Taken out of context, this poem might appear to point to an exclusively negative relation to the parental imago, but when looked at in the context of her entire *opus,* this 1861 poem can be seen as a transitional one. "This whitening (*albedo* or *dealbatio*)," says Jung, "is likened to the *ortus solis,* the sunrise; it is the light, the illumination, that follows the darkness…The spirit Mercurius descends in his heavenly form as *sapientia* and as the fire of the Holy Ghost, to purify the blackness."[310]

As an intuitive introvert, Emily's poetic initiation was experienced internally at the ecstatic dimension: by the Self. As a woman of great passion and aliveness, her inner greatness was never to be confirmed by a man on the outside. Only from Newton and Susan did she receive some unconditional support and mirroring that her early art deserved, but the truly magnificent poems were never fully appreciated. The road she had blazed for future poets of America, without anger, bitterness, or hate for having been almost completely overlooked, was the simple path that Nature told of her tender majesty. All of the bitter hardships and shocks of fate at the career level were burned pure, finally, by the blazoning whiteness of the inner Forge that had purified her.

The Stars are old, that stood for me—
The West a little worn—
Yet newer glows the only Gold
I ever cared to earn—
Presuming on that lone result

---

310 Jung, *CW* 16: ¶ 484.

> Her infinite disdain
> But vanquished with her my defeat
> 'Twas Victory was slain.   J 1249/F 1242

The only success Emily ever really cared to earn was the alchemical "Gold" of the West, which she called "Immortality." Through the refinement of her poems, she was not seeking Ecstasy for ecstasy's sake; she was in it for a *telos,* a purpose, and that purpose was her *integrity*.[311] She wrote, in 1859:

> Flowers—Well—if anybody
> Can the ecstasy define—
> Half a transport—half a trouble—
> With which flowers humble men:
> Anybody find the fountain
> From which floods so contra flow—
> I will give him all the Daisies
> Which upon the hillside blow.
>
> Too much pathos in their faces
> For a simple breast like mine—
> Butterflies from St. Domingo
> Cruising round the purple line—
> Have a system of aesthetics—
> Far superior to mine.   J 137/F 95

And again, in the same year:

> The Lark is not ashamed
> To build upon the ground
> Her modest house—
>
> Yet who of all the throng
> Dancing around the sun
> Does so rejoice?   J 143/F 86

---

311 Personal communication from John Beebe in 1995.

So many animals, birds, flowers, and insects were alive to Emily Dickinson that it is difficult to say whether she had a favorite totem animal. The Animal Powers were a living part of her Soul. These natural powers of her psyche were given voice late in her life in an image of *integrity*:

> After all birds have been investigated and laid aside—
> Nature imparts the little Blue-Bird—assured
> Her conscientious Voice will soar unmoved
> Above ostensible Vicissitude.
>
> First at the March—competing with the Wind—
> Her panting note exalts us—like a friend—
> Last to adhere when Summer cleaves away—
> Elegy of Integrity.   J 1395/F 1383

Emily Dickinson lived a life of *integrity*, which came from giving voice to the animals—which included amphibians, reptiles, and birds—of her Soul. In her early 1859 poems, her "system of aesthetics," she says, was *not* co-equal with that of either the Butterfly, or the Flower. Only later, when her ego-investment and ego's-thirst for publication had been banished by the "distain" of the Self did she feel that she was performing an important role in the transformation of Nature through art.

Such reflections raise an important question about the process of individuation, which is latent in the Christian-Protestant tension surrounding the idea of *integrity* and "works" (i.e., *vocation*), and their relation to the journey toward the soul's Immortality. The central question seems to be whether the *opus* has a refining purpose.[312] While Jung said that the artist's individuation is in his work, John Beebe has remarked that: "the artist's individuation is in his or her *style*. This is the link between Jungian psychology and literary criticism."[313]

In Beebe's view, the individuation of integrity can be seen as the central aim in Emily's work. In this sense, we can see that it is the refining nature of Emily's *style* upon the moral development of humankind which doesn't change over time and which the elegy of Emily's integrity

---

312 Personal communication from John Beebe in 1995.
313 Personal communication from John Beebe in 1995.

ultimately holds.[314] As we saw in "Dare you see a Soul *at the White Heat?*" Emily noted that there *might* be a refining purpose in her art, a *telos.*

Despite the sometimes-negative reactions Higginson may evoke in us, it is important to keep in mind that as an extrovert, he opened the way into the larger community for a more complete understanding of the meaning of her soul's opus by evoking what was at the foundation of Emily's quest for Immortality and Selfhood, namely the incarnation of a new God-image through the phenomenon of the transference.

"The transference phenomenon," writes Jung,

> is without doubt one of the most important syndromes in the process of individuation; its wealth of meanings goes far beyond mere personal likes and dislikes. By virtue of its collective contents and symbols it transcends the individual personality and extends into the social sphere, reminding us of those higher human relationships which are so painfully absent in our present social order, or rather disorder.[315]

In my view, it was through the refinement of her style and character that Emily achieved her defining purpose, the individuation of *integrity*; for through her poems, she was working not only for the immortality of *her* soul; but also for the Immortality of the collective Soul of humankind.

> The Poets light but Lamps—
> Themselves—go out—
> The Wicks they stimulate—
> If vital Light
>
> Inhere as do the Suns—
> Each Age a Lens
> Disseminating their
> Circumference—   J 883/F 930

---

314 Personal communication from John Beebe in 1995.
315 Jung, *CW* 16: ¶ 539.

When the Lady Lies in Ceaseless Rosemary

The disorders of childhood that are present in every creative artist may actually be burned away and consumed—even if only temporarily—in the fires of *albedo*, by the One who makes it to the "further shore" of Immortality, Transport, Vision or Bliss. This is not to say that every artist is capable of such transformations as we witness in the life, works, and art of Emily Dickinson, but the *potential* for it, at least, exists in everyone. The question now is how to achieve it optimally on an individual basis, perhaps less optimistically, on a collective basis. Emily Dickinson had the capacity to *see* with the eyes of the Serpent what others in her society could not see: "My barefoot rank is better."

Rather than running frantically after success, Emily preferred her "barefoot rank," which she claimed to be "better" than "fame." By studying under Higginson, by becoming his friend, the surest way to stay true to her vocation was vouchsafed. Only when the conscious sacrifice of ego became a reality could her symbolic death, nothingness ("Zero at the Bone—") lead her to Resurrection.

Like Whitman, Dickinson was unique. She was herself—an individual with her own unique vision to offer the world. That Emily wrote for publication (i.e., that she wrote for the sake of a *career*) is a certainty, yet it is also an afterthought. Emily knew, beyond a shadow of a doubt, that her works would be immortalized. She knew also, as Albert Gelpi has rightly stated, that "her immortality depended upon it."[316] And yet, in 1863, one year after her decision to forego publication, she said: "The General Rose—decay— / But this—in Lady's Drawer / Make Summer—When the Lady lie / In Ceaseless Rosemary—" (J 675/F 772).

Here again, we see the metaphor of noon in the full zenith of "Summer," when the rosemary is in fullest scent. The "Lady's Drawer" is a reference to her finely sewn packets of poems that she left for posthumous publication. Why else would she have written over 1775 poems—360 of which were written in a single year! —if she did not feel secure about their eventual publication? And while Emily Dickinson, the so-called recluse may have forsaken a career in her lifetime, the Lightning-shaman within her most certainly did not forsake her: "He fumbles at your Soul

---

316 Albert Gelpi, *Emily Dickinson: The Mind of the Poet*, p. 150.

/...Deals—One—imperial—Thunderbolt / That scalps your naked Soul—" (J 315/F 477).

As we know from observing Nature, moreover, Lightning is always accompanied by water, clouds, moistness, or "dew;" which as Jung tells us, is synonymous with the "*aqua permanens* or the *aqua sapientiae*":

> After the ascent of the soul, with the body left behind in the darkness of death, there now comes an enantiodromia: the *nigredo* gives way to the *albedo*. The black or unconscious state that resulted from the union of opposites reaches the nadir and a change sets in. The falling dew signals resuscitation and a new light: the ever deeper descent into the unconscious suddenly becomes illumination from above. For, when the soul vanished at death, it was not lost; in that other world it formed the living counterpole to the state of death in this world. Its reappearance from above is already indicated by the dewy moisture. This dewiness partakes of the nature of the psyche.... dew is synonymous with the *aqua permanens,* the *aqua sapientiae,* which in turn signifies illumination through the realization of meaning.[317]

In an 1872 poem, Emily describes this dewy state as a process occurring also in Nature: when "A Dew sufficed itself—/...And felt 'how vast a destiny'—" and was "Abducted" by "Day," or "emptied by the Sun;" or when it passes "Into the Sea / Eternally unknown / Attested to this Day / That awful Tragedy / By Transport's instability / And Doom's celerity" (J 1437/F 1372). (Celerity means to come suddenly, with speed, or rapidity.)

As Jung said about the switch from *nigredo* into *albedo,* when the dew comes, illumination follows from above. Emily experienced this swift coming of the state of Transport by the vastness of her destiny in 1862. Following her creative breakthrough, she made frequent associations to the coming of "Doom." In another 1862 poem, she writes:

> Doom is the House without the Door—
> 'Tis entered from the Sun—

---

317 Jung, *CW* 16: ¶ 493.

And then the Ladder's thrown away,
Because Escape—is done—   J 475/F 710

One cannot escape. "What would the Dower be," she asked, "Had I the Art to stun myself / With Bolts of Melody!" (J 505/F 348). The Dowry is the Lightning Bolt of Melody from the center of her shamanic psyche. Holger Kalweit tells us that "among the peoples of the Andes, the appearance of *chukiilla*—lightning or 'spear light'—is an initiation experience for the shaman and the *curandero*."[318]

In all of these poems, her Bolts of Melody are bursting forth page after page with pure electricity; her mind is on fire and she is literally being struck day after day by strikes, ravishments that scalp her. This is Ecstasy—liquid Quartz. She is distilling the Dew and her Dower is the "Rainbow's Way" —Delight— "Flung colored, after Rain," and for her "glee," she takes "Rainbows as the common way" (J 257/F 317). She is writing like Rilke, a modern Orpheus. Both poets were born to anxious and depressed mothers. Like Rilke's *Sonnets to Orpheus*, Dickinson's poems act for readers today as a beacon of creative transformation and hope from which we may draw deep feeling, meaning, and inspiration. She asks us first to see a soul at the white Heat. By seeing her soul on fire, she may light our minds on fire too. She is our teacher in this respect and our guide.

---

318 Holger Kalweit, *Shamans, Healers, and Medicine Men*, p. 47.

14

RESURRECTION, IMMORTALITY, AND THE MEANING OF SPIRITUAL MARRIAGE

As Emily Dickinson says in her description of the shamanic state of consciousness, Ecstasy is an admixture of rapture and pain, joy and suffering, bliss and woe—emotional states that cannot be separated from one another, and, just as life and death appear from our limited plane of normative consciousness as a pair of irreconcilable opposites, so too are they unified at a higher field of order through Rapture, Illumination, Eternity, and Bliss.

In Emily's view, poetry became the means to overcome death, and the poet-shaman's task was to convey such an experience to the listening public through art; the idea being that she serves as a bridge over which her soul may pass into a domain where the opposites are resolved. "The nearest Dream recedes—unrealized— / The Heaven we chase, / Like the June bee—before the School Boy, / Invites the Race— / Stoops to an easy Clover—" (J 319/F 304). The goal of life, as she says so eloquently, is to realize for the world the *reality* of the nearest Dream as it recedes unrealized, yet by following the path of Mother Nature, as does the "School Boy" (her childlike animus) everything becomes easy.

From such a perspective, pleasure and pain, illness and health, rapture and woe, life and death, good and evil, peace and violence, are seen—not as principles to be feared, or shied away from, but to be *experienced*—with the humblest reverence in one's very life. Only when we have arrived at this "sea in the West," termed "Immortality," can we overcome the terror of death, and even then, the fear of death is always with us in the background of our awareness throughout the advancing years of our mortal frailty.

The experience of Ecstasy and eternity Emily is referring to in so many of her poems is not something that happens to a person simply at the end of life, but something that can take place in the *here* and *now* of existence, in the eternal moment of creation. Emily says that America is essentially an "ecstatic nation." However, the undiscovered continent, as we've seen, is not an idealized outer world America. It is an "inner land," that summons us from within, not necessarily an external place we inhabit by day during our occupational rounds. The aim of life, our destiny as individuals and a world, is the expansion of consciousness:

> A Spider sewed at Night
> Without a Light
> Upon an Arc of White.
>
> If Ruff it was of Dame
> Or Shroud of Gnome
> Himself himself inform.
>
> Of Immortality
> His Strategy
> Was Physiognomy.   J 1138/F 1163

"The spider," writes Gelpi, "is Emily Dickinson's emblem for the craftsman spinning from within himself his sharply defined world... He is 'an Artist,' whose 'unperceived Hands' mysteriously and skillfully weave tapestries from the private resource of his hidden 'Yarn of Pearl'— tapestries whose beauty and design originated in himself."[319]

Transcendence over Fear

Despite all of the raptures achieved during her lifetime, Emily was plagued by a doubt about life after death because there was no one in Amherst who could mirror for her a reflection of who she was as an Individual. Only the Animal Powers within her, such as the Spider ("Himself

---

319 Emily Dickinson, p. 151.

himself inform") and the Bird (Robin) could reflect for her an image of what her true individuality was, a reflection of the Self: "And then he lifted up his Throat / And squandered such a Note / A Universe that overheard / Is stricken by it yet—" (J 1600/F 1663). This poem represents the influence of a woman's suffering upon the Creator. She wrote the following poem to Helen Hunt Jackson after Helen had asked Emily if she could be her literary executor in 1884. "Take all away from me," Emily wrote to her, "but leave me Ecstasy, / And I am richer than all my fellow Men—" (J 1640/F 1671).

As Emily herself said in her first letter to Higginson: "The Mind is so near itself—it cannot see distinctly—" and unlike Whitman, who had the blessing of Emerson to transmit to him the mantle of his own spiritual greatness, Emily had only Newton, Susan, Bowles, Higginson, and Helen Hunt Jackson, and a few others to mirror her art. The fact that Higginson was a former clergyman must certainly have complicated the matter. (Higginson was a minister of a Free Church in Worcester, Massachusetts, in 1852). From another point of view, however, Higginson carried precisely the image Emily needed in the situation of the transference to evoke a lifeway of mythmaking in a post-Christian age. By representing the collective problem of the Church, as an extroverted thinking type, Higginson acted as a transference object onto which Emily could project an infantile emotional conflict that would only have led to neurotic dissociation if her psychological functions had achieved only an "incomplete realization." About this partial realization of the archetype of the Self, Jung writes: "it is very easy for the modern mind to get stuck in one or other of the functions and to achieve only an incomplete realization...Nor is the realization through feeling the final stage."[320]

As in alchemy, the resolution of the problem of Immortality, which had been constellated in Emily's childhood in relationship to the parental imagos could only be resolved by the "imaginative activity of the fourth function—intuition, without which no realization is complete."[321]

In a letter written to Higginson in 1874, Emily wrote: "I am glad there is Immortality—but would have tested it myself—before entrust-

---

320 Jung, *CW* 16: ¶¶ 490, 492.
321 Jung, *CW* 16: ¶ 492.

ing him" [i.e., her father, who had recently died].[322] Intuitively, she *knew* the answer to her childhood question about Immortality. However, she turned to Higginson, both hopefully and teasingly, in an attempt to develop her thoughts into a personal theology of her own. This was the burning question she set out to answer for herself, and which she had already answered many times over, in her poems. The wounded child in her did not know what the Lightning Shaman knew—about the *reality* of life after death—namely that there is a *symbol* latent in the repressed rememberings of our childhood that typically seeks consciousness through an imaginal *reality* outside the field of ordinary awareness. This symbol, which I have called the *nuclear symbol*, is often associated with positive or negative alignments with the parental images of childhood. If it is properly integrated into consciousness, however, as it was in Emily's case, it has the potential to lead a person to an experience of Ecstasy and vision through what Jung called the "transcendent function."

In order for Emily to move through her primary ambivalence towards her parental images, to a more positive orientation towards the Self, she needed to correct her emotional relationship to her imaginative fourth function, intuition, which had been wounded in childhood. James Hillman said in this regard: "the main trauma of early abuse is the damage it does to imagination…The way out of the box which has trapped imagination is by means of imagination…I'm suggesting that the restoration of the imagination is the correct response to disordered emotions."[323]

How true in Emily's case! "The self," writes Jung, "wants to be made manifest in the work, and for this reason the *opus* is a process of individuation, a becoming of the self."[324] Self-realization through the *opus* of individuation was known in alchemy as the quintessence. In order for Emily to achieve this state, her childhood relation to the parental images had "to be broken up" through a transference of the nuclear symbol (embodied in the *image and emotional "distress"* of the "Boy by

---

322 *L*, II, p. 528.

323 J. Hillman, cited in D. Noel, *The Soul of Shamanism: Western Fantasies, Imaginal Realities*, p. 191.

324 Jung, *CW* 16: ¶ 531.

the burying ground," and her "doubt of Immortality") onto self-objects in her environment.

In providing a projection screen for Emily's projections, Higginson was working not only for his own *integrity*—by immortalizing Emily's poetry through posthumous publication—but for the moral and spiritual progress of humanity as well. He was indeed working "for the moral and spiritual progress of mankind…and in so doing," he was perhaps "laying an infinitesimal grain in the scales of humanities soul."[325]

In "Introduction to 'The Beyond,'" Jungian analyst Barbara Hannah speaks of the ancient Chinese conception of life after death, reported by Richard Wilhelm. She says:

> Wilhelm points out that the physical body itself is quite willing to die when its time comes but that there is an inner aspect of the body that possesses consciousness and it is this aspect which is constantly imagining how death will be before it comes. It is this aspect that gives rise in many, if not most individuals to a profound desire for immortality, and which is constantly imagining how death will be…this subtle body is made up of 'thoughts and works' and above all of energy, which we must detach from earthly things.[326]

For Dickinson, poetry became the means to arrive at this energized world of Eternity—Consciousness—in preparation for the Life to come. The Snake-Goddess, or the Spider-Woman within her *knew*—through "thoughts," "works," and energy—of the reality of Immortality in this life, even though the trembling "Boy by the burying ground" looked to Higginson to enlighten her on the problem in question; this is the paradox of human existence, when realized to the full.

Through dying to her ego and experiencing Ecstasy, the feeling of Immortality was crystallized in Emily's mind and this became her central most theme. "There came a day at Summer's full," she wrote, "Entirely for me— / I thought that such were for the Saints, / Where Resurrections—be—" (J 322/F 325). Was she looking into the far-off future

---

325 Jung, *CW* 16: ¶ 449.
326 B. Hannah, "Introduction to 'The Beyond,'" pp. 42, 44, 47.

when she said, "Each was to each The Sealed Church?" She seems to be saying that the time when we arrive at "that new Marriage" we all will be "Justified—through Calvaries of Love—" (J 322/F 325). Let us hope so.

Does the Opus have a Refining Purpose?

In conclusion to this chapter, let us return to "Dare you see a Soul *at the White Heat?*" and ask whether the *opus* has a refining purpose. Through the refinement of her art, did Emily achieve her defining purpose, the individuation of *integrity?* I believe Emily's life reflects this purpose in two ways:

1) From an introvert's point of view, it would seem that by fulfilling the pattern of individuation in her lifetime that was enough in the fulfillment of Emily's responsibility towards the Self. But from another point of view, Emily's preoccupation with her own individuation was not enough. There was also a collective need, a *telos* in society that needed to be fulfilled, and I think Emily knew this. I believe there was a part of her (the Lightning Shaman) that *knew* her works would be immortalized and that her individuation indeed depended upon this. While Mable Loomis Todd and Higginson helped to preserve the work through posthumous publication, literary critics have preserved her character and style by returning her *Complete Poems* to their original unaltered condition. This points to the necessity of preserving the style and character of a consummate artist as the signature of his/her *identity*, without alteration; the style and character comes from an eternal pattern in the collective Soul of humanity; a pattern that does not change over time, because it is eternal. Despite Higginson's well-intended efforts to "smooth rhythms, regularize the meter, delete provincialisms, and substitute 'sensible' metaphors,"[327] Emily refused to compromise her integrity, and thereby preserved her moral character for all times. Through her conscious sacrifice of her drive for publication, she was then led to a deeper and more satisfying commitment to her *vocation to the Self.* By the emphasis she placed upon the transformation of humanities Soul in her poems ("This ecstatic Nation / Seek—it is Yourself") she was, there-

---

327 From Thomas H. Johnson's Introduction.

fore, in her role as poet-shaman, concerned "with the fate of the singular human being—that infinitesimal unit on whom the world depends, and in whom, if we read the meaning of the Christian message aright," says Jung, "even God seeks his Goal."[328] This is to say that the part of her that wrote for the collective knew also that the transformation of humanities Soul depended upon her achievement of public renown in order to advance the style and character of American poetry. In this sense, she was concerned with individuation in a broader collective sense, the individuation of American speech.

Emily's life and work has helped us see that it is *vocation*—the calling—that matters most in the process of individuation to an introvert. While career may have been viewed as a secondary phenomenon, Emily's suffering had a refining purpose on the consciousness of the collective. For the ultimate goal of the poet-shaman is the transformation of the Self within Humanity's Soul.

2) Even if her works had remained unpublished in her lifetime, it is still possible that her poetry would have had a refining purpose on the Self. As Erich Neumann writes: "The inexplicable fact that man's very center is an unknown creative force which lies within him and molds him in ever new forms and transformations, this mystery which accompanies him throughout his life, follows him even into death and beyond."[329]

The Meaning of Spiritual Marriage

"The Stars about my head I felt / About my feet the sea /…This gave me that precious Gait / Some call Experience" (J 875/F 926). This poem captures the meaning of what I've called Spiritual Democracy in her "Experience" of the real-world through art. The stars about the poet's head are symbols for religious Freedom and Liberty. How to achieve universal religious equality for all people in a way that is open to all faiths is the central question of my book *Spiritual Democracy*. Whether the Global Village will become democratized spiritually in the near future is unclear.

---

328 Jung, *CW* 10: ¶ 588.
329 E. Neumann, "Mystical Man," p. 48.

The idea that there are people—they're rare—on this planet of seven billion humans, people who can drop down into the field of Spiritual Democracy and have perceptions of it, really began to fascinate me about twenty years ago, when I wrote my first essay on Emily Dickinson in 1995. There's a vision in her perceptions I feel, that world-culture needs right now. Dickinson's time, I feel, has come. Dickinson provides answers to the question of what equal rights really means. She cuts to the chase.

Seven poems were published out of 1775! This is staggering. Such a supreme gift for elocution, for language-creation, for metaphorical thinking. To have silenced such a natural gift for poetry in her lifetime is tragic. Her rebellion was American to the bone; her revolution through language *against* the forces of sexist oppression in a patriarchal-dominated society goes back to the American revolution of 1776. She was, like Whitman and Melville, a rebel for Spiritual Democracy. She would not submit to external standards of authority. Dickinson's penetrations to cosmic awareness in her breakthrough moments are stunning.

Her main business, as she famously told Higginson, was *Circumference*. "Perhaps you smile at me. I could not stop for that—My Business is Circumference."[330] To another friend she wrote: "Pardon my sanity, Mrs. Holland, in a world *in*sane, and love me if you will, for I had rather *be* loved than to be called a king in earth, or a lord in Heaven."[331] Again: "Seven years of troth have taught thee / More than Wifehood ever may!" (J 1737/F 267).

What I find fascinating, moreover, is the recurrence of the number seven. For the forty booklets containing her pentalogy were assembled across the span of a period of her greatest productivity, which lasted seven years (1858-1865).[332] Let us examine one more specimen of a love letter written to Susan Gilbert in 1852: "Only think of it, Susie; I hadn't any appetite, nor any Lover, either; so I made the best of fate, and gathered antique stones, and your little flowers of moss opened their lips and spoke to me, so I was not alone."[333]

---

330 *L*, II, p. 412.
331 *L*, II, p. 329.
332 *S*, p. 537.
333 *L*, I, p. 202.

One more love that filled her in her later life and that we have only briefly considered was with Otis Phillips Lord. Lord was appointed to the Supreme Court in 1859, and it may have been in that year that a warm relationship began with Emily. "My Sweet One" she wrote to Lord later in a letter, "for your great sake—not mine—I will let you cross—but it is all yours, and when it is right I will lift the Bars, and lay you in the Moss—You showed me the Word."[334]

Clearly, Emily was in love with life. From her first letters to Jane and Abiah, we have seen that her affection was transgressive and filled her, by 1860, with feelings of a blissful marriage. She seems to have kept her "Secret" to the end of her lifetime and several months before her death, during her final grappling with Grave's Disease, she reveals her audacity in asserting her usurpation of the title of "Wife" from the Biblical Jacob: "Audacity of Bliss, said Jacob to the Angel 'I will not let thee go except I bless thee'—Pugilist and Poet, Jacob was correct."[335] Again, about two weeks before her death, she wrote to Mrs. Tuckerman, who was in profound bereavement over the loss of her husband: "How ecstatic! How infinite! Says the blissful voice, but a vision, 'I will not let thee go, except I bless thee.'"[336] Emily was, like Whitman and Melville, an early visionary of Spiritual Democracy. She gives us her medicine of Liberty.

In "I taste a liquor never brewed—" (J 214/F 207) she enters the imaginal body of a Bee, or a Butterfly, sipping from flowers. To her cousin, Eudocia Flynt, she wrote further: "Depths of Ruby, undrained—/ Hid, Lip, for Thee, / Play it were a Hummingbird / And sipped just me—" (J 334/F 380).

The Medicine Woman of supreme power did not respect doctrines, as we've seen, mostly the doctrine of original sin: "'Heavenly Father'— /…We apologize to thee / For thine own Duplicity— (J 1461/F 185).

---

334 *L*, II, p. 617.
335 *L* III, p. 903.
336 *L* III, p. 898.

15

AFTERWORD AND CONCLUSION
EMILY DICKINSON'S ANTI-TOXIN
FOR OUR TIMES

C.G. Jung's greatest work on spiritual marriage is found in his master-piece on Western alchemy, *Mysterium Coniunctionis.* In his "Foreword," Jung stated clearly that alchemy is a "spagyric art" represented by the oft-repeated saying "solve et coagula" (dissolve and coagulate), or, in psy-chological terms to bring hostile, warlike enmity, or intense interpersonal conflict, back into a state of harmony; to create, in other words, a world of inner and outer order out of chaos.[337] The master-notion Jung chose for completing this process of organization in psyche and the globe was borrowed from Gerhard Dorn's term, the *unus mundus,* or "one world."

In Emily Dickinson's poetry, we have examined in the foregoing chapters her metaphorical dissolution of our previous notions of mar-riage and a rebirth of something surprisingly new. The dissolution of traditional stereotypes of marriage in any of the world's religions may be accompanied by a confrontation with incompatible affects, or clashes in religious values, due to the persistence of the toxic values of patri-archy. At first, confronting turbulent emotions around marriage in a patriarchal culture may meet with enmity in any individual, group, or creed that is resistant to change and clings to the outworn values of men in economic or religious or political power. There may be a feeling of death in the atmosphere being created by the world's millennials. Toxic emotions may surface that can at first poison the psychic atmosphere of

337 Jung, *CW* 14: p. xiv.

any group that is in the process of transformation out of sexist biases. Eventually, over time, however, healing emotions may spark a deeper and more satisfying acceptance of changes that are afoot.

Dickinson was part of a sacred lineage of carriers of a healing medicine that extends far back to shamanism. As we've seen, the great transformations of her consciousness were preceded by a *nigredo* experience, likened in alchemy to a "wounding of the heart."[338] The remedy for such a heart-wound was found in *alexipharmic agents* in her psychic blood stream; anti-toxins were produced primarily through her poetry. Jung's writings make it clear that acknowledging heart-wounds is a way we can begin the process of healing through psychotherapy. Oftentimes our hearts have been broken not only by a partner in love, but also by "God" in a conventional religious sense. Dickinson was wounded in the breast by her Master, who was probably not a man, but an inner interlocutor. Her vocation, as we've seen, was to save as many broken hearts as she possibly could, and to ultimately heal them through love.

> Crowned—Crowing—on my Father's breast—
> A half unconscious Queen—
> But this time—Adequate—Erect,
> With Will to choose, or to reject,
> And I choose, just a Crown—   J 508/F 353

We have considered this poem before, but let us postulate a further hypothesis: *Wounding by women and by men was necessary for her individuation.* Dickinson had not only to leave her Mother behind, to transcend her mother complex, she had also to leave her Father behind, and the transcendence of her father complex only took place through what Jungian analyst James Hollis has called "necessary wounding."[339] In all psychotherapeutic processes the excruciating agonies of broken hearts have their analogy with violent clashing together of human emotions that results in an alchemical reddening (*rubedo*), where, through an intense heating up of primary affects, new insights, images, or ideas may

---

338 Jung, *CW* 14: ¶ 24.
339 James Hollis, *Under Saturn's Shadow: The Wounding and Healing of Men*, p. 65.

suddenly burst forth and set in motion healing antibodies to fight toxic infections in one's culture. The new integrated wisdom-medicine may be used to help change the world. The medicine Dickinson produced is a balm of bi-erotic marriage possibilities to help us solve the sickness of homophobia and the toxic atmosphere of sexism and xenophobia worldwide. But it also goes further than where we are today. She is still I think ahead of our times. Writing against the tide of discrimination in her culture, she dispensed a medicament for healing heart's hurts, where no other remedy could be found in her day. "But this—in Lady's Drawer / Make Summer—When the Lady lie / In Ceaseless Rosemary—" (J 675/F 772).

The concept of marriage has been expanded in a non-discriminatory way today to include most people. A recent Supreme Court ruling legalizing same-sex marriage in all fifty States has led to a radical change in modern psychology and public policy. The changes that are currently afoot are being instanced, moreover, by a miraculous occurrence of what Jung called *synchronicity*. The archetype of bi-erotic marriage that Whitman and Melville and Dickinson all incarnated and foresaw for us is becoming an integrated spirit-soul substance in the body politic of many nations. The Self is converging—to use Dickinson's metaphor again— upon a center. "Each Life Converges to some Centre— / Expressed—or still— / Exists in every Human Nature / A Goal—" (J 680/F 724). We see a miraculous thing happening that is radically altering the way we think. It is not only a fourth wave of feminism that we are witnessing in our culture, but a fourth wave of male liberation from patriarchy and sexism, made possible by women. Not only the Divine Feminine, but the Divine Masculine too is emerging in our culture, side by side. A fourth wave of the men's movement may also be arising as an antidote to heal the toxic masculine that pervades our culture.

As Dickinson said in a poem enclosed in a letter to Samuel Bowles, she felt that she was in an "emergency" in getting her poems published and hoped men could *see*. I, too, feel an urgency in getting this book out now, when the toxic masculine is again poisoning our nation. Dickinson needed the Self to wake up during the Civil War, so that men could see her antidote to sexism. She created a revolution in Liberty that needs to become part of a global movement in the march towards spiritual democracy. "Faith," she said is "a Revolution / In Locality" (J 972/F 839). Her doubts about democracy helped ignite a revolution of Liberty in an imagined future that could help radicalize feminists in America and the world, who might take instruction from her about the validity of despair, grief, and angst regarding our lack of civil liberties even during a psychological age. In my view, her momentary depressions were a direct result of the suppression of her little life-Force by a bigoted society of men who could not see her worth properly. Liberty was not vouchsafed to women in an equalizing way with men and her intellectual property was not protected through publication. This made her vulnerable to periods of psychic instability. Her grief helped her stay true to herself. This is sometimes overlooked: the necessity of accepting the bitterness of suffering, when one's truths are not believed, is a common human experience. Accepting her despair and hopelessness about her works ever being properly seen by men in her lifetime led her to embrace her fate and its inevitable tragedies and agonies, and to arrive late at a victory through defeat. Her outrage was a legitimate response to her soul's woundings. Such a one as this was able to fearlessly assert to herself in her own solitude: "I am not my fate and its inevitable pains and sufferings. *I am my own destiny*. I have freedom of choice." She had the courage to choose her destiny rather than auctioning her mind and succeeding at the cost of her integrity. She was not what we would consider to be a social activist. She was a leader in the domain of religious and scientific ideas and a defender of Liberty. She spoke up for the Divine Feminine, for women and men worldwide. The fourth wave of the men's movement that I am postulating alongside woman feminists seems to presage the sacred marriage of men and women at a new level of psychological and spiritual experience that is unprecedented. What it means is that we are each responsible for the fulfillment of our destiny and have to stop blaming our mothers and women for our moral shortcomings. When Samuel Bowles called her "Queen recluse" I believe this was a form of unconscious sexism, therefore, because it was attempting to oppress what he feared most: his own feminine side, discovered in solitude. Men and women usually fear solitude that is so necessary for personal individuation. As James Hollis has written: "This is what Nietzsche meant by crossing the abyss on the tightrope of ourselves. The energy is there, the task is to risk walking further into space. In that space is more freedom. A greater amplitude of soul; it is where we are meant to be."[340] One unified world can only be created through individuals who are brave enough to go out alone with Dickinson: "A Speck upon a Ball— / …upon Circumference— / Beyond the Dip of Bell—" (J 378/F 633).

Jung makes it clear that the *unus mundus* is a metaphysical concept, which is to say that it transcends consciousness. Its empirical equivalent may be found in the central point of mandala symbolism as the ultimate unity of all archetypes in the phenomenal world. Such mandalas are represented by a unity of the Microcosm with the Macrocosm.[341] Jung went on to say, moreover, that, "if mandala symbolism is the psychological equivalent of the unus mundus, then synchronicity is the parapsychological equivalent."[342] We have seen a number of Dickinson's mandalas at play in this book. Her most recurrent image is represented by flowers as emblems of her Resurrection. As she wrote in a letter: "When Flowers annually died and I was a child, I used to read Dr. Hitchcock's Book on the Flowers of North America. This comforted their Absence—assuring me they lived."[343]

> The Lilac is an ancient shrub
> But ancienter than that
> The Firmamental Lilac
> Upon the Hill tonight—
> The Sun subsiding on his Course
> Bequeaths this final Plant
> To Contemplation—not to Touch—
> The Flower of Occident.
> Of one Corolla is the West—
> The Calyx is the Earth—
> The Capsules burnished Seeds the Stars
> The Scientist of Faith

---

340 James Hollis, *Swamplands of the Soul: New Life in Dismal Places*, p. 139.
341 Jung, *CW* 14: ¶ 661.
342 Jung, *CW* 14: ¶ 662.
343 *S*, p. 348.

His research has just begun—
Above his synthesis
The Flora unimpeachable
To Time's Analysis—   J 1241/F 1261

How Dickinson can be said to have foreseen current developments in world culture might best be explained by Jung's theory of synchronicity.[344] In his postulate of a "foreknowledge of some kind" Jung preferred to call it "absolute knowledge."[345] Meaningful equivalences, such as I have attempted to bring forth in this book on Dickinson, can be amplified by calling strong attention to the current changes that are taking place in our understandings of the marriage archetype; the changes point to the existence a transcendental background that is the domain of virtually every religion of the world. Yet while all three of the American poets—Whitman, Melville, and Dickinson— tapped into the archetype of marriage, only Dickinson took it to a transcendent theological level in her theorizing. As she wrote about her poetry in general: "let not Revelation / By theses be detained—" (J 1241/F 1261).

In Western alchemy, the medicament was believed to be a unity of spirit and soul contained in the body, where the body was said to be made one with the *unus mundus*.[346] To my knowledge, there was no alexipharmic (antidote) provided for the toxins of homophobia in comparative religions worldwide before Whitman and Melville and Dickinson emerged on the scene. The most "powerful medicine for uniting the unus mundus with the body"[347] can be found in *antitoxins* that

---

344 For instance, at the precise moment in time that I received my permissions to quote from Emily Dickinson's poetry from Harvard University Press, which led to my being able to move forward with the signing of my contract with Fisher King Press, via Mel Mathews, *A Quiet Passion* was released in the movie theatres nationwide. Emily was clearly depicted as a feminist who was far ahead of her times. I saw the movie with my wife Lori and we loved it. The release of this move at this pivotal moment in time was extremely improbable, as so few films on Dickinson have been made. This is one of those acausal coincidences that Jung called *synchronicity*.

345 Jung, *CW* 8: ¶ 931.

346 Jung, *CW* 14: ¶ 664.

347 Jung, *CW* 14: ¶ 690.

correct for what is lacking in the world. Interestingly, Jung mentions the antitoxin of "rosemary flowers" or *Rosmarinus* (sea-dew), which, for the alchemists was an analogy for the *aqua permanens*.[348] The Self, he wrote, as the *total personality* was considered to be a healing and "whole-making" medicine that is "recognized even by modern psychotherapy" and it "was combined with spiritual and conjugal love, symbolized by rosemary."[349] Rosemary, as we've seen, is the herb she said she would lie in ceaselessly in her immortal nature. It is, therefore, a symbol for the medicine she bequeaths to us for our collective healing.

We might conjecture, furthermore, that the marriage archetype was conjoined through a more complete spiritual marriage in Dickinson's poetry than in any other American bard because *her marriage was with the whole Cosmos.* "Enchantment's Perihelion / Mistaken oft has been / For the authentic orbit / Of its Anterior Sun" (J 1299/F 1375). The word perihelion comes from the ancient Greek words *peri*, meaning "near," and *helios*, meaning "sun." In astronomy, the "perihelion" is the point in the orbit of a celestial body where it is nearest to its orbital focus, generally a star. Jung asserted that "everything divided and different belongs to one and the same world," by which he meant that even "the psychic world," which has "its roots outside the one cosmos is evident from the undeniable fact that causal connections exist between the psyche and the body that point to their underlying unitary nature."[350]

This notion of the inseparable unity of psyche and Cosmos can alter our ideas about marriage worldwide. Jung's reflections on the *unus mundus* can help us see, furthermore, that the Self is always in a state of continuing incarnation no matter how evolved religions may appear to be at any given time in human history. The absolute knowledge of the Self cannot, in other words, ever be fully conveyed to the human ego and like the Cosmos, from which we all evolved, its infinite extent will always remain a mystery. There is, therefore, no Absolute to which humanity can cling in any of the world's revealed religions as regards to marriage: all are merely attempts to give form to what is forever formless.

---

348 Jung, *CW* 14: ¶ 701.
349 Jung, *CW* 14: ¶ 706.
350 Jung, *CW* 14: ¶ 767.

Dorn had a name for an antitoxin in the body that I am suggesting Dickinson carried in her medicine bundle, as a sort of absolute fore-knowledge of what our patriarchal religions desperately need today, namely a *caelum*: the prefiguration of the Self, or desired realization of a whole woman, or man, which Dorn described as a "universal medicine."[351]

In alchemical terms this universal medicine might best be described as a strengthening *elixir*, an archetype of union that is being integrat-ed politically and spiritually in a bi-erotic union of the Sacred Mascu-line with the Divine Feminine, after the long legal battles for marriage equality.[352]

From a psychological view, the external changes in society have been motivated not only by Civil Rights, Women's Liberation, and Gay Rights, but also by internal shifts that have occurred in the soul-con-cepts of individuals. This is precisely where Whitman and Melville and Dickinson come in. As bi-erotic people in a homophobic society, Whit-man, Melville and Dickinson foresaw the current developments. Not only did they anticipate the transformations we are seeing in our culture today, but, by awakening the archetype of Sacred Same-Sex Marriage[353] within their readers, many, if not most of whom have been and continue to be heterosexuals, they evoked changes in our soul-concepts and Self-concepts: gay, bisexual, and straight.

Not only do these great American shaman-poets encourage men and women to bring their sexuality and spirituality out in courageous ways through poetry, they also encourage heterosexual men and women to let their bi-erotic selves come into full consciousness to dissolve the illness of homophobia that has been dividing the World Soul and plaguing us since time immemorial because of a fundamental misunderstand-ing about the nature and structure of the soul as contrasexual. Whit-man, Melville and Dickinson were amongst the first American poets to embody, materialize, and incarnate the archetype of Same-Sex Marriage

---

351 Jung, *CW* 14: ¶ 770.
352 Matthew Fox, *The Hidden Spirituality of Men: Ten Metaphors to Awaken the Sacred Masculine*, pp. xxi, xxiv.
353 Herrmann, "Melville's Portrait of Same-Sex Marriage in *Moby-Dick*." In *Jung Journal: Culture & Psyche*. Vol. 4, No. 3, pp. 65-89.

as a syzygy and they created a completely new myth out of their inner unions by 1860. They inaugurated a cultural revolution in the idea of the World Soul that has to do with the emergence of emotional dynamisms that are not mere Platonic ideals, but long-standing archetypal fields that are active in the American psyche and the World. These electrical sexual-spiritual fields (as evidenced in Whitman's "I Sing the Body Electric" and Dickinson's "Depths of Ruby, undrained— / Hid, Lip, for Thee, / Play it were a Hummingbird / And sipped just me—" (J 334/F 380) were active in our myth of the bi-erotic Self one hundred years prior to the emergence of gay liberation. It is highly probable that the changes in the concept of the soul in world culture today are being patterned in part, therefore, on numinous nodal points of human thought, fantasy, and emotion that are emergent ideational powers (Animal Powers) in the World Soul. What we are seeing surrounding the fiery debates on same-sex marriage is a paradigm shift so fundamental that it may rock the cradle of the world's civilizations and enlarge our conceptions of the soul and Self to include the Cosmos.

While we have seen the archetype of same-sex marriage emerge in nations of the world in isolated ways before, we have never seen such grand changes taking place in the soul-concept, with such wide sweeping potential for impacting our world religions, world politics, and world's social and legal institutions. The changes foreseen by Whitman, Melville and Dickinson in the soul-concept predicted a collective movement with tremendous potential to inaugurate a paradigm shift that may reverse the axis of the world, hopefully, turning the institution of marriage upside down. This does not mean that Dickinson's poetry should be read as free of violence. When she was told by Higginson her poems were "*too delicate*…not strong enough to publish" her soul erupted into violence because her integrity had been violated. When she wrote that her life had stood a loaded gun, what she was saying, therefore, is that her life could be potentially violent, because her soul had been desecrated. If any of us looks deeply into the source of our own rage, it is not hard to see that she has much to teach us with her medicine-powers. "Dig deeply into any man" writes Hollis, "and one will quickly find not only that lake of tears but a mountain of rage, layers of anger accumulated since childhood, slowly pushing its magma toward the surface, there to erupt."[354] "Violate a man's soul and some part of him becomes violent," he continues.[355] I have found the same to be true of women patients expressed in similar and different ways. When Dickinson says, "I'm Czar—I'm 'Woman' now— / It's safer so—" (J 199/F 225), what I think she means psychologically is that her ego has put traditional marriage, wifehood, and domesticity aside and has consciously *chosen* political empowerment through an integration of the collective shadow. Choice is crucial here as a vehicle of her destiny. "Destiny" writes Hollis, "repents one's potential, inherent possibilities which may or may not come to fruition. Destiny invites choice."[356]

Bringing forth the Self from within regardless of outer circumstances requires a strong and resilient ego that can say yes to fate and destiny through freedom of choice. To fail to do so will only lead to self-destruction. The inner voice can never be heard in the noise of society and the answer to neurosis, therefore, can only be found in solitude. Dickinson teaches us to say yes to solitude as a conscious choice to heal our sense of loneliness. Being alone is a precondition for poetry. Political power rested with the Czar in Russian history and Dickinson the poet knew this. Her vocation was to transform the Czar, as an archetype of political upheaval and revolt in the World Soul into a transnational revolution of Liberty that could free women and men worldwide from the chains of serfdom. She transformed the shadow of patriarchy (that such a Czar as Peter the Great may have represented to her, for instance) into spiritual empowerment as a "Wife" of women and men who could usher in new waves of women's liberation in the future: "What Liberty / A loosened spirit brings—" (J 1587/F 1593)!

Dickinson's spirit is still with us today. I think that the quest for the Sacred Marriage is very alive and well in my book on Dickinson. The marriage of the Divine Masculine and Divine Feminine is what we need, especially now that the Goddess has returned and that the women's movement has brought forth the power of the role of the Divine Feminine in a fourth wave of feminism that has just begun to rise; now

---

354 Hollis, *Under Saturn's Shadow*, p. 79.
355 Hollis, *Under Saturn's Shadow*, p. 106.
356 James Hollis, *The Middle Passage: From Misery to Meaning in Midlife*, p. 92.

we have to detoxify and clean up the role of the toxic masculine by taking in Dickinson's sacred medicine.

Spiritual Democracy, therefore, is an attempt to get outside all creeds to the "one Cosmos" that Dickinson and Jung had in mind. Creeds were, in fact, a frequent target of Jung's pen; as was the Bible, for Dickinson: "The Bible is an antique Volume— / Written by faded Men" (J 1545/F 1577). Wrote Jung: "Every theologian speaks simply of 'God,' by which he intends it to be understood that his 'god' is the God."[357] This was an incisive criticism of all faiths being finally forever limited.

Since individuation is being driven by the Self, in an attempt to become ever more aware of Itself in individuals, nations, and groups in all cultures, anyone who comes into contact with Its numinous energies is vulnerable to psychic infections. Jung refers to such contagions as psychic *toxins*. The safeguard Jung offered for such infections are not to get identified, or swept up with any archetype and become, rather, vehicles for their transformation in the evolution of the World Soul. The numinosity of the Self, Jung wrote, might appear to be viewed by "naïve" people as "God."[358] For Dickinson, such numinous energies are an ecstatic nation that must be sought inside by everyone, while God or the Goddess is always cosmically Infinite.

Spiritual Democracy complements our images of a united Self in contemporary society by offering a solution, a medicine for the problem posed by the limitations of religions. Marriage as a collective organization in our globalized world needs a medicine to cure the illness of homophobia and sexism and bigotry in all nations. The time for new religions may be over in an age of modern psychology and contemporary spirituality. Yet, as religions have always been inspired by poets, perhaps the poetry of 19th century, America might offer insights from the foundation of the World Soul about the way ahead? A more complete representation of the Divine is currently needed.

The relativity of the marriage archetype, in a changing climate of legal, civil, and religious unions that are in the process of integration in the Anima Mundi, towards a more complete incarnation of the *unus*

---

357 Jung, *CW* 14: ¶ 781.
358 Jung, *CW* 14: ¶ 781.

mundus, is something that was foreseen a century and a half ago by Emily Dickinson.

Conclusion

Twenty-one years ago, I began this book by writing a seventy-page essay about Dickinson. Only recently, in 2012, 2015, and 2016, did I return to the text, after an accident arranged by Fate, and expanded it for post-modern times. I have not attempted a full exegesis of all of Dickinson's poems in this book, but provided an interpretation of some of her most basic metaphors in light of the current needs of readers in the 21st century. I have done my best to paint her as an intellectual genius, a woman poet who was far ahead of her times, and who may even be more relevant to the climate of our current world affairs than when she was alive.

My book has been about Spiritual Democracy, women's rights, and equal rights. I spoke up for Dickinson as an advocate for what she taught in a down-to-earth psychobiography that put her in cultural context as a Medicine Woman for our times. I attempted to do this from a *psychological* and a *spiritual angle.* I demonstrated how her aims as a Medicine Woman were to disseminate a shamanic cure to a creedal culture that could not agree on doctrinaire matters and that desperately needed her comfort and wisdom, as I think we also do today. What I attempted to make clear in my psychobiography on Dickinson is the fact that as a poet-shaman, she was in dialogue with her soul and that an archetype of wisdom spoke directly out of her from the ground of the Native American psyche. It is to the archetype of the shaman that I turned in my psychobiographical sketch to illustrate how she can function as a visionary artist for a fourth wave of feminism and men's liberation that began to emerge at the precise moment in time when I was writing my book *Spiritual Democracy* between 2011-2013. I showed how Emily gave birth to *the explosive power of her vocation* vouchsafed to her through a union with God and the Goddess, as complementary archetypes symbolizing her marriage with the Cosmos. I trust my readers will agree that her poetry is simply breathtaking and that jewels, such as this one, about a ruby-throated hummingbird are works of art that can be celebrated for all times.

A Route of Evanescence
With a revolving Wheel—
A Resonance of Emerald—
A Rush of Cochineal—
And every Blossom on the Bush
Adjusts its tumbled Head—
The mail from Tunis, probably,
An easy morning's Ride—   J 1463/F 1489

From my writing desk in Montclair, Oakland, I have often pondered the beauty of "A Route of Evanescence" and her poems about birds, bees, butterflies, and flowers. I have planted many rosemary plants in our garden, and I love watching swarms of honey bees come to drink their sweet nectar when the white-blue flowers are in full blossom. I have also learned to cultivate flowers that hummingbirds love and find nourishment in all across our property. I owe my love for plants, flowers, and bees to Emily. Snakes and Butterflies, I have loved since I was a boy.

She has been a great teacher of mine, and hopefully yours. But mostly, she has given me an appreciation for poetry in ways I never quite expected. When she wrote to her cousin, Eudocia Flynt "Depths of Ruby, undrained— / Hid, Lip, for Thee, / Play it were a Hummingbird / And sipped just me—" (J 334/F 380), what she was saying, I think, is that she saw herself as a healing flower that others could drink from. To sip her ruby or purple flower, the "Purple Democrat" (J 380/F 642), is to drink deep droughts of her medicine-powers from Mother Nature. It is this power to heal that she bestows upon us: the medicine of Spiritual Democracy. The plant Dickinson was writing about is the common American clover, a "sturdy little" blossom bursting with sweet nectar and that bees, butterflies, and hummingbirds love, and were scattered all around her garden in Amherst.

The story surrounding her writing of "A Route of Evanescence" is a good note to end this book on. In this book, I have been speaking about a vision of what I'm calling Spiritual Democracy. The term Whitman had used for this notion was "Religious Democracy." This is a concept that coincides beautifully with C.G. Jung's attitude toward religion and also with Melville's and Emily Dickinson's. I have used this term, therefore, because I recognize the need for a contemporary language that can be applied cross-culturally to everyone, regardless of whether a person identifies with a religion or not. For post-modern individuals, Spiritual Democracy seems to me to be the right term. As we've seen, Dickinson's use of the word Liberty was also essentially a religious idea, one I would place at the core of what I am calling Spiritual Democracy. Liberty was certainly *numinous* for her—a product of what Jung called the "religious function of the psyche." In talking about Spiritual Democracy today, I want to link Dickinson's and Jung's visions of a spiritually democratized world grounded in a sense of the common reality of the psyche with the great 19th century explorer Alexander von Humboldt's feeling for the immense unity-in-diversity that he perceived when contemplating the entire Cosmos. Humboldt called this the "feeling of the infinite" and Jung called it the "feeling for the infinite." I draw this connection between Humboldt and Jung, great figures on either side of Whitman, Melville, and Dickinson, in an effort to give the reader a synoptic view of how the notion of Spiritual Democracy incubated itself throughout the 19th and 20th centuries. From a strictly scientific standpoint, it is an empirical view that emerged for Humboldt through his pragmatic development of such natural sciences as geology, for Dickinson through poetry and for Jung through the practice of medical psychology. For Whitman, it was a cornerstone of his poetry.

As a Jungian, I would argue therefore that Spiritual Democracy is the logical outcome of an important line of the later Jung's thought, since behind it lies the idea Jung selected to focus upon in his culminating explorations of the mystery of the alchemical *coniunctio*. As we've seen, this was the idea which he took from the Paracelsian Dorn of the *unus mundus*, Latin for "one world," the result of bringing spirit, soul, and body together in a transformative, alchemical synthesis. This was natural philosophy's master notion for what Jung, and Whitman before him, and Humboldt before both, saw as the basis for a rare convergence of science, poetry, and religion that could unite the world. A question arose for me as I was writing this book on Emily Dickinson. It is this: "Do we need to consider as Jungians today whether Jung's empirical studies on the phenomenology of the Self entitles us to draw a broader circumference for the possible meanings of individuation to include the cosmological domain of religious phenomena?"

It was the American psychologist, William James, who stated in his 1902 book *The Varieties of Religious Experience,* that the "real backbone of the world's religious life" is not creeds, schools, or theories, but *experience* first and foremost. James in his youth had travelled with Humboldt's student Louis Agassiz to South America. Agassiz had produced the first scientific evidence of an ice age and he knew firsthand that experience means, experience of the world and engagement in both its present reality and its inevitable geological transformations. James had followed Agassiz's call to establish in America a better natural science, and he had chosen to look upon psychology as such a science. In 1902, James asserted as a matter of empirical psychological observation that it is the religious life of humanity as a whole, that is our "most important function,"[359] meaning the function of psychological life. Jung was well aware of William James. He had read *Varieties* and specifically sought James out for a personal meeting on his first trip to the United States in 1909. For anyone else who has read James' *Varieties*, it will be clear that the religious function—the *life* granted by our psyches to the world's religions as a whole—is also coincident with a *cosmic function*, part of the natural history of the universe to be observed by an empathically participating psychological consciousness.

The cosmic function of the universe in its individuation (e. g. in geology) is also expressed in the cosmic intuition that so frequently accompanies altered states of consciousness, and it's a concept that was certainly "in the air" by 1900, when the Canadian born psychiatrist, Richard Maurice Bucke, M.D. published his sensational book *Cosmic Consciousness.* Bucke, moreover, was one of the chief disciples of Walt Whitman and he placed Whitman's work among the supreme examples of "cosmic consciousness." William James quotes both Bucke and Whitman liberally in *Varieties.* James quotes Bucke as saying, for instance: "The prime characteristic of cosmic consciousness, is a consciousness of the cosmos, that is, of the life and order of the universe."[360] What he

---

359 William James, *The Varieties of Religious Experience*, p. 17.
360 James, *The Varieties of Religious Experience*, p. 388.

doesn't quite say is that such consciousness is generated by the Cosmos and belongs as much to It as the egos of the people privileged to participate in It.

As I have mentioned, William James was a member of an expedition up the Amazon in Brazil with the great naturalist, Louis Agassiz. On this expedition, James traveled and slept in a hammock next to Agassiz, who was perhaps the most invigorating and influential scientist during the heyday of the American lecture circuit fancifully called (after Aristotle's peripatetic school) the lyceum. Agassiz had been an early and ardent admirer of Humboldt. While in Europe, he held a professorship, which Humboldt helped him secure at Neuchâtel, Switzerland. Agassiz was known for his breathtaking vision of geological formations of high mountain Alpine glaciers, which led to his seminal postulation of an ancient ice age, now an established scientific tenet. This theory influenced Emily's teacher, Hitchcock.

Long before Agassiz's entrance into the mainstream of American academic life at Harvard, where he held a prestigious professorship in zoology, he had undertaken a study of Brazilian fish fossils, which he published in his vastly illustrated *Recherches sur les Poissons Fossiles*. Agassiz finally came full circle to describe at Harvard the whole of creation as an exalted expression of "divine thought," a vision of the individuation of the Cosmos of which those geological and biological instances of developmental change were only instances.[361]

Thus, a trip to Brazil with Agassiz was important for James' own feeling for the cosmic range of human individuation. As one of the fathers of American pragmatism, he found it sensible to unite empirical science and the transcendent intuitions that are grounded in religious experiences because, for him, they belonged to the same universe of thought. But Agassiz's vision, as we've seen, was directly influenced by the works of Alexander von Humboldt, whose book *Cosmos* had sold eighty thousand copies by the year 1851, when Whitman's contemporary Herman Melville published *Moby-Dick,* a masterpiece of truly cosmic range, and when Dickinson had only just begun to compose poetry.

---

361 David McCullough, *Brave Companions: Portraits in History*, pp. 20-36.

Cosmos, as I have indicated, popularized the natural sciences and stirred the imaginations of mid-19th century people to such an extent that it actually made Humboldt the most famous man in the world by the time of his death in 1859. Humboldt's lectures giving evidence for his Cosmos hypothesis had their inception on the high slopes of the Andes, between 1799 and 1804, where the only bird in sight was the condor.

Cosmos itself first began to take shape in 1805, in Humboldt's *Essay on the Geography of Plants*, a work of Romantic science dedicated to Goethe. Goethe's visionary imagination had introduced into his poetry a picture of the immeasurable Universe and its interconnectedness, and this was picked up by Humboldt, whose *Cosmos* was one of the key inspirations for Emerson's essay "Nature." Goethe himself hailed Humboldt's cosmos lectures at the University of Berlin between November 1827-April 1828 (sixty-one of them in total) by declaring without any doubt that "the immeasurable abyss has been fathomed" and "that the great work, beyond all belief, has truly been done."[362] Nearly three decades would pass, however, before *Cosmos* was made available to the general public.

Emerson was among the first Americans to read the first German edition of 1844, and he commented on it that same year in his essay "The Poet." Whitman was later to read that essay and fulfill its promise as the American bard Emerson had called for, while Dickinson was completely overlooked by her contemporaries. Nevertheless, one of the most heated debates while Emily was in her mature years, centered on the geological and astronomical question concerning the "igneous" or "aqueous" origins of our planet earth. In a late poem, dated about 1884, she seems to have sided with her teacher Hitchcock in favor of fire, when she wrote:

> Though the Great Waters sleep
> That they are still the Deep,
> We cannot doubt—

---

362 Laura Dassow Walls, *The Passage to Cosmos: Alexander von Humboldt and the Shaping of America*, p. 217.

No vacillating God
Ignited this Abode
To put it out—   J 1599/F 1641

In this poem, we can see how scientific she in point of fact was. She had an acute appreciation for the igneous sublime. In Volume 1 of *Cosmos*, Humboldt had declared: "The feeling of the sublime, so far as it arises from a contemplation of the distance of the stars, of their greatness and physical extent, reflects itself in the feeling of the infinite, which belongs to another sphere of ideas included in the domain of mind."[363] By "mind" Humboldt meant the human mind, yet for Emerson, the domain of the mental took on an entirely different meaning since (anticipating Jung) he speaks of what he calls the "Universal Mind." This same idea was expressed in such lectures of Emerson's as "The Philosophy of History," "Nature," and his famous "Divinity School Address." In another essay "The Individual," he went so far as to say that "*Religion* is the emotion of reverence which the conscious presence and activity of the Universal Mind inspires."[364] The "emotion of reverence" is what Jung, following Rudolph Otto, would call the *numinous*. For Emerson, backed by Romantic science, it seemed possible for the individual mind to *become* at-one with the Cosmos, at which point it becomes a Universal Mind. The psychological step was for the individual mind, as Chai says, "to perceive the Universal Mind within itself." Then the individual can feel himself become a "representative" of the Universal Mind, a form of "translucence" in thought made possible through the symbol.[365] This was Emerson's view, and it strongly influenced Whitman and Dickinson. Let's look briefly at Jung's vision of Spiritual Democracy to see where Humboldt, Agassiz, Emerson, Whitman, Melville, Dickinson, James, and Jung all converge on a cosmological vision of an interconnected unity between psyche and matter, the *unus mundus* that is also the Ground of the collective unconscious and its frequently announced presence through synchronicity.

---

363 A. von Humboldt, *Cosmos*, 1: 40.
364 Leon Chai, *The Romantic Foundations of the American Renaissance*, p. 251
365 Chai, *Romantic Foundations*, pp. 253-254.

I have surveyed Jung's comments on psyche, matter, and Cosmos throughout his collected writings and it is evident that he believed that collective consciousness could evolve once this universal ground was in place and speaking to it. Jung's notion of the Self as a Cosmic Consciousness extends from the furthest galaxies of the stars to the innermost depths of the *psychoid* background of the psyche itself. The *psychoid* (for instance, personality's ultimately astrological nature) offers a way of seeing the mind that transcends the split between the universe and how it is perceived. From this perspective, even the split between scientific and religious worldviews can be resolved. Jung says this, for instance: "The decisive question for man is: Is he related to something infinite or not? That is the telling question of his life…The feeling for the infinite, however, can be attained only if we are bounded to the utmost."[366]

Such a *feeling for the infinite* as something we are inextricably bound to is an essentially Humboldtian view. What enables us to be "bounded to the utmost" is our embodied experience, which we share with the world. Embodiment is another term for what Whitman means by the experience of Religious Democracy, and Dickinson means by Liberty. As we've seen, no one captures Jung's meanings better than Emily does: "A Soul admitted to itself— / Finite infinity" (J 1695/F 1696); "The Finite—furnished / With the Infinite—" (J 906/F 830); "How ecstatic! How infinite! Says the blissful voice, but a vision, 'I will not let thee go, except I bless thee.'"[367]

In addition to the figures in her life that we have considered, who kept Emily bounded to the finite, it is important to mention Carlo in this context, for the big Newfoundland dog had been her companion for sixteen years. Her dog was, therefore, a medicine for her. He helped relieve her of her loneliness, her moments of despair, doubt, and anxiety. Carlo also kept her grounded in reality. When he died, in the winter of 1865-1866, shortly after the end of the Civil War, she wrote sadly to Higginson: "Carlo died— E. Dickinson Would you instruct me now?" In the summer of 1866, she wrote further: "I explore but little since

---

366 Jung, *MDR*, p. 325.
367 *L*, III, p. 898.

my mute Confederate [died]."[368] By Confederate, she means her Ally. For Dickinson, Carlo was one of Nature's democratic citizens and the noblest work of Her Art. "The Dog is the noblest work of Art, sir. I may safely say the noblest—his mistress's rights he doth defend." If by "his mistress's rights" she meant her own rights, then Carlo had protected one of the greatest poetic and literary integrities ever. He was her associate, assistant, ally. Carlo was in this sense a soul-guide in life and into the afterlife, a bridge between the finite and the Infinite, her small body and the Cosmos.

The inseparable unity between psyche and physics was expressed further by Jung in *Memories, Dreams, Reflections*, where he said specifically: "Our psyche is set up in accord with the structure of the universe, and what happens in the macrocosm likewise happens in the infinitesimal and most subjective recesses of the psyche."[369] Thus, for Jung, Spiritual Democracy is not just one of the deepest goals of the psyche, it already exists at least in potential everywhere around us.

"True democracy," Jung says "is a highly psychological institution;"[370] thus, we need a psychology of the depths in order to define what democracy is at a spiritual level and where order and totality may be experienced in conjunction with the natural harmony of things. One way to further define Spiritual Democracy, therefore, is through Jung's psychological reflections on the *psychoid*: the psychophysical dimension of reality that reaches from the instinctive ground of human nature to the farthest depths of the Cosmos. Jung says for instance: "And just as the cosmos is not a dissolving mass of particles, but rests in the unity of God's embrace, so man must not dissolve into a world of warring possibilities and tendencies imposed on him by the unconscious, but must become the unity that embraces them all."[371] Whatever this unity is that embraces everything, it is, at bottom, what Jung and the physicist Wolfgang Pauli called a *psychophysical* reality, neither wholly physical nor psychic, but a third thing transcendent of the opposites.

---

368 *L*, II, pp. 450-451.
369 Jung, *MDR*, p. 335.
370 Jung, *CW* 18: ¶ 456.
371 Jung, *CW* 16: ¶ 397.

A pair of synchronicities that crossed my path in a meaningful way helped me see what such a union of opposites might look like in a natural context as it applies to my work on Emily Dickinson. Both coincidences appeared in a way that for me lends weight to Jung's theory that it is "probable that psyche and matter are two different aspects of one and the same thing."[372] The coincidences through which we explore the correspondence between archetypes with the environmental Cosmos in which archetypal forms naturally emerge, is a link that would not have surprised Humboldt, Whitman, Melville and Dickinson, and that Jung rediscovered in the 20th century. Significance, or what Jung called meaning, may thus of course be found both inside and "outside the psyche."[373] It exists in a "self-subsistent,"[374] "transcendental"[375] domain Jung called the psychoid. By "psychoid" Jung meant to imply a foundation for emergence that was both psychic and cosmic. This was what Bucke called "Cosmic Consciousness," though for most of us it is a consciousness that operates unconsciously.

The two coincidences—one on each side of the Unites States—made me finally see what Jung was talking about. It's the enormous capacity nature accords any living being to bring the two sides of its existence together. These sides, rather artificially called by us inner and outer reality, come together as we move forward in accord with our instinctive prerogative to individuate, which is to realize the union of psyche and environment in a Spiritual Democracy of consciousness that gives equal weight to both.

Synchronistic occurrences may be more regular in fact than they are rare. This may be true particularly when we are engaged in meaningful work, which leads us to touch taproot in a vocational archetype of great significance to our life and destiny. Coincidences may happen, in other words, more often than we tend to think.

On December 9, 2012, my wife Lori and I were painting our bathroom together and it was also the first day of Hanukkah, so we were

---

372 Jung, *CW* 8: ¶ 418.
373 Jung, *CW* 8: ¶ 915.
374 Jung, *CW* 8: ¶ 944.
375 Jung, *CW* 8: ¶ 915.

mindful of the holiday. Lori lit the first candle that evening. After we finished painting, she took out a little purse that she had kept from Israel and there were some coins in it, mostly foreign currency, and she showed this money to me. As I looked in her hand, I said, "What's that?" As I looked at a coin, I saw it was a Liberty silver dollar minted in the USA! I saw immediately, moreover, that it was minted in 1885! It's probably only worth about $35 to $40, as there were about seven million minted, so it's not a rare coin. But let me report what was going on for me when she handed it to me.

First, I noticed it says *e pluribus unum*—"one from many"—from the Great Seal of the United States. Well, this sacred inscription is at the core of Spiritual Democracy: the oneness of all religions. That's very American. And it's in the First Amendment, too: the freedom of religion, religious Liberty. What's most interesting to me is the symbolic dimension I found myself in during the moment I first examined the coin. A lot of the imagery of the Seal comes from Rosicrucian and Masonry symbolism. Ben Franklin played a pivotal part in shaping the ideas that went into the creation of the Great Seal. I'd always been impressed with silver dollars as a boy and I didn't have one. And at the time that this event happened, I was returning to my manuscript on Emily Dickinson to expand it into a book form. I was working on some letters she had written to Helen Hunt Jackson. Jackson was an American poet who was a contemporary of Dickinson. She's remembered mainly through her letters to Emily today, not because of her extra-ordinary stature as a poet and novelist; her works are not of supreme stature. Anyway, as Jackson was nearing death, she came to Santa Monica, California. She was on the Pacific Coast, in other words, and she and Dickinson had been corresponding. Dickinson had written about the great sea in the West that she called "Immortality," a great mythological motif. The Western sea is symbolic of immortality. Moreover, we see it in a lot of myths and poems. So, Jackson was looking out (as Dickinson said in a letter) to Japan from the West Coast. Then, Emily penned this marvelous poem in the letter she wrote to Jackson in 1885!

Dickinson was approaching her own death, which was a year later. She wrote: "Take all away from me—but leave me Ecstasy, / And I am richer—than all my Fellow Men." Here she was proclaiming her wealth, her infinite riches, in the simple Ecstasy she *felt*, near the end of her life, as she was now 54 years old and suffering from kidney disease. She died as I've said at 55. I received the coin on Sunday, which was the 9th of December, on the eve of her birthday: December 10th! I was flabbergasted. I don't have any coins with that date on them, or that old. In fact, that is my only US coin from the 19th century. I thought: "What an interesting coincidence!" As a poet-shaman, she really spoke for Ecstasy. Nobody illustrates this technique in verse better than Emily does. She has taken the top of my head off on many occasions.

To return to my story, Jackson had encouraged Emily to publish her poems so that they wouldn't be published merely posthumously, but in her own lifetime. Dickinson then wrote back: "Take all away from me— but leave me Ecstasy." She was thinking, I've published several poems in my lifetime, but that doesn't matter much; I'm so rich in gold, in Ecstasy, in the ecstatic dimension of art, that I am infinitely richer than all my fellow men. That's enough, she thought, that's sufficient.

The only people who tried to recognize her greatness were her sister-in-law, Susan; Bowles; and her mentor, Higginson. Also, a few of her trusted friends, whom she wrote letters to and who she blessed with poems. But Jackson clearly recognized Emily's magnificence and felt that her poetry should in fact be in print.

I think such coincidences as my receiving the Liberty dollar from Lori are based on destiny factors that are relatively opaque during such exquisite moments, and the actual occurrences lead one to formulate ideas about human fate and destiny that otherwise could not have been possible. It bespeaks the fact that there are figures in world, and vocations people have—specific callings, such as marriage, and the unions Emily and Susan and her brother Austin and Helen and the poetess all shared—people that are in the field of our ecstasy, our greatest Happiness. Helen, who was so well-known at the time Emily was alive was in the field of her Ecstasy, the literary field.

The intersection of various vocational fields converges on a center. That center is, I think, what Jung called the Self. For Dickinson, her favorite subject was what she called her "flood subject," the great water of the West, Immortality. From Santa Monica, on the West Coast, waves of feminism washed all the way across the USA, from California to Amherst; the feeling of a mutual connection between the two writers, Helen and Emily, connected them in spirit.

The interesting thing about Dickinson is that she seemed to be very curious about people who are approaching death, near-death experiences. She wanted to gain as much information as she could about what it was like, either from a person who was ill or who had been on the verge of dying and came back; or from family members, who were close to a person who had just passed. What we've seen is a reaching out in her letters and her giving confidence to family members or to a person who was on the verge of passing over—to convince them that the soul does in fact have a life that continues after death. So, she's a real shaman-poet of near-death experiences.

The poet-shaman often has a connection with death. Her poem about Ecstasy is about this sense of completion, of fulfillment in life, a sense of satisfaction in a work well-accomplished and well-done. Dickinson exudes this confidence and fearlessness and strength to her friend Helen. She conveyed this power of *knowing* to the recipients of some of her best letters in a way that is very convincing; that she had indeed touched an infinite domain of absolute knowledge and knew what she was talking about in a bounded way. She wasn't just talking about a faith in the coming Rapture that we hear some fundamentalists ruminating about.

Yes, she had read the Old and New Testaments up and down. She came from the Protestant and Puritan biblical traditions, but it was not the kind of faith she wanted. She had to have experiential knowledge of the Infinite while being fully embodied. This is very psychological and transcendent.

To comprehend her, someone needs to know about the nectar in her flowers of speech. I think she had a sense that she was exuding a kind of essence. She had it. She had her fingers on it, because it was a destiny factor within her, given to her by the gods when she was a little girl, as she said. There's this sense in her poetry that she's teaching something that is beyond belief, beyond faith. That's what I love most about her.

Let me return now to the 1885 coin I found in Lori's purse to take final note of the second synchronicity. Dickinson wrote in the same year

"A Route of Evanescence." This is also a poem she sent to Helen. Jackson had asked for a bird poem, about a bluebird. Dickinson sent her a poem describing the actions of this bluebird to a T. Then she wrote a poem about an Oriole and added, "I add a Hummingbird and hope they are not untrue—"[376]

So, here's my connection: Sunday evening, after finding the coin, I was watching a Nature show with Lori, and there was this special on hummingbirds. Now, one of the things I learned from the show about hummingbirds is, the ruby-throated hummingbirds of the East Coast migrate up from Central America. What I also learned about many of the hummingbirds that we have here in our gardens in California is that, in the spring and summer, they fly up from South America on their way to Alaska, and these hummingbirds return to our precise gardens!

I bought some hummingbird plants for them to drink from. They have returned to our garden for the last four years. What I have learned from writing this book is that if one stays true to one's destiny then things work out in the end. Fate and destiny then work together. I think that in rare moments, we can see that the fate that we've been given is precisely the fate that we needed to have. To split fate and destiny as opposites, to think that fate is bad and destiny is good, is a terrible mistake. Superiority to fate means one has accepted one's destiny and can love one's fate. Love of one's fate is the capacity to accept life just the way it is. Helen's envy and hate[377] of Emily's amazing abilities to portray a precise picture of a bluebird, to the exact proportions of Nature, shows how much the voice of the Self had spoken through her Amherst friend with feminine eloquence.

As Susan Dickinson wrote in her obituary of the poet in the *Springfield Republican*: "To her life was rich, and all aglow with God and immortality. With no creed, no formulated faith, hardly knowing the names of dogmas, she walked this life with the gentleness and reverence of old saints, with a firm step of martyrs who sing while they suffer."[378]

---

376 *L*, II, p. 639.
377 Wolff, *Emily Dickinson*, p. 528.
378 Wolff, *Emily Dickinson*, p. 535.

The poet was buried on Wednesday, May 19, 1886. Higginson came to Amherst for the funeral, to pay her body, soul, and spirit a final tribute. Emily's body was dressed in white and laid to rest in a white casket with violets draped all over it. The casket was carried out of the back door of Emily's house through the yard, where the still and cold body passed her beloved buttercups and wild geraniums, and across the meadow she went, to the graveyard, where she was carefully lowered into the sod, beside her mother and father.[379] Dressed in white the body lay—metaphorically and spiritually—in the anti-toxin of "ceaseless Rosemary"—just as she had wanted.

---

379 Wolff, *Emily Dickinson*, p. 535.

SEVEN WAYS TO TAKE IN DICKINSON'S MEDICINE AND HELP TRANSMIT IT TO OTHERS

Taking in Dickinson's medicine and transmitting it to others begins at *home*! Seven ways to learn from her style and stay true to your vision in life are listed below.

1. *Read as many Verses as you can from Emily's Complete Poetry.* We owe it to ourselves to read Dickinson deeply in order to gain a greater capacity for language and to become more attentive to inner voices and callings as poets, environmentalists, spiritual activists, psychotherapists, and scientists. It may require one to contemplate one poem at a time, as in a meditation. Emily is one of our greatest international teachers of the value of listening to the small still voice of conscience within, and her verses are an anti-toxin against psychic infections, such as sexism, homophobia, xenophobia, and bigotry. Reading her can heal us from the contagions of our time.

2. *Immerse Yourself in Nature's Gardens.* Being in nature's gardens with Emily can facilitate your connection to the earth, the environment, and the Cosmos. Take trips into the wilderness, look up at the stars, plant some flowering shrubs bees and butterflies and hummingbirds can enjoy. Keep your eyes out for snakes! Be not afraid. Enjoy some essential oils or rosemary tea with white-blue flowers. Recite her prayer:

> In the name of the Bee—
> And of the Butterfly—
> And of the Breeze—Amen!

3. *Practice poetry.* Buy a journal and an attractive pen and evoke the muse in Nature or in the solitude of your own room. Experiment with poetry. Suspend your critical judgement, shut the door, and stay

254 EMILY DICKINSON: A MEDICINE WOMAN FOR OUR TIMES

true to your natural rhythms and style! Make sure to consult your companion lexicon!

4. *Learn the Art of Metaphor and Melody.* Memorize a few of your favorite Dickinson poems and recite them as lyrical meditations before bed, share them with family, children, or friends. Let a couple of her poems scalp a colleague or two at a cocktail party with her powerful Bolts of Melody! Feel the Lightning.

5. *Reflect Creatively on Your Own.* Come up with your own hypotheses about her life and its meaning for our times, and think about how her art can best be applied to the illnesses of our world, such as the rape of Mother Nature, the spraying of toxic chemicals on our almond orchards, where bees love to dance and play and gather their sacred pollen before returning to their colonies to make the honey we enjoy.

6. *Speak up for Women's Rights and Men's Liberation from the Toxic Masculine.* Taking Dickinson into the public and political and spiritual domains means staying in dialogue with people who love her or have been prejudiced to see her as a mad woman who stayed only in her room, someone who was weird, or weak, or too "delicate" and "not strong enough" to publish. Show others how she advocated for women's empowerment and prepared the forty packets of 800 poems for posthumous publication to become our national bard and a visionary for our times.

7. *Introduce Others to Dickinson.* Find ways to raise awareness about Dickinson's medicine-powers in conversations with others. For example, talk to people about her as a shaman-poet. Show family, children, mentors, therapists, religious teachers, and others in your social network how she can assist us in becoming more conscious and fully related to Nature and the Cosmos. Bring her playfulness, creativity, and wisdom into your experience of reading her verses. Allow yourself to take in her Ecstasy, her fearlessness as a woman writer, and her superiority to Fate, and how she offers an antidote to the malaise of our times by offering us her sacred medicine.

DEFINITION OF SPIRITUAL DEMOCRACY

35 Elements of Spiritual Democracy

1. Spiritual Democracy is the big idea of worldwide religious equality.

2. Spiritual Democracy is an American notion; it is related to the Iroquois myth of the Peacemaker and can also be found in early American poetry.

3. Spiritual Democracy is based on the principles of religious Liberty, equality, and individual freedom.

4. Spiritual Democracy exists in three stages: political, economic, and religious.

5. Spiritual Democracy is a dispensation of the Divine Feminine, or "Nature's God;" it is transcendent of gender, bierotic, and free of the chains of patriarchy.

6. Spiritual Democracy is linked to the cosmic science of 19th century naturalist Alexander von Humboldt, whose work Whitman, Melville, and Dickinson were aware of.

7. Although it is archaic and found in the rites and symbols of initiation in all shamanistic cultures across the globe, Spiritual Democracy exists in the Now.

8. Spiritual Democracy is supported by a *Deus Quadriune*, a four-sided, or quaternary God-image, a symbol for wholeness.

9. Spiritual Democracy is informed by the writings of America's poet-shamans and by the pragmatism of William James and C.G. Jung's psychology of the Self.

10. Spiritual Democracy is founded on an equality of being in Nature; an experience of being human in relationship to the Self, or the Divine, to which every person has access.

11. Spiritual Democracy is neither patriarchal, nor matriarchal; it places the Cosmic Self in the center of its worldview and asserts that the Divine Feminine, Nature, is present in everyone.

12. Spiritual Democracy is the realization that we are all centers for the transformation of global consciousness.

13. Spiritual Democracy is the realization that we are each a microcosm of meaning in a macro cosmic power that absorbs everything, where meaning is born from a search each person undertakes; whether in the city, at home, or in the solitude of Nature.

14. Spiritual Democracy is a change in attitude that can facilitate solutions to problems of war, genocide, bigotry, and prejudice.

15. In the Near East and the West the origins of the concept of Spiritual Democracy lies in the writings of the Old Testament prophet Isaiah, who was a beacon of world Peace.

16. Spiritual Democracy is universal, transnational, and transpersonal. It places no God- or Goddess-image above what waits to be Self-realized within you.

17. Spiritual Democracy is a way to personal and cultural liberation.

18. Spiritual Democracy is born from a mystical marriage between the body, soul, and spirit with the Cosmos.

19. Spiritual Democracy is a way to sacred action, whether through political activism, through advocacy for the environment, or through the writing of poetry or prose in the solitude of one's own home.

20. Spiritual Democracy is a way to become aware of the Self's ultimate meaning, which is the aim of evolution.

21. Spiritual Democracy is a vocation from the Self, a calling, or destiny to live by, that puts a person in accord with Nature's God.

22. Spiritual Democracy is born through techniques of vocalism and other expressions of contemplation and art, such as meditation, yoga, the writing of poetry, or active visioning.

23. Spiritual Democracy is a path of nonviolence through the integration of the shadow and human evil.

24. Spiritual Democracy is the calling to advocate for equal rights for all people; women's rights, civil rights, LGBT rights, and it does not discriminate on the basis of ethnicity, gender, or sexual orientation.

25. Spiritual Democracy is an advocate for many paths to marriage.

26. Spiritual Democracy is a way to speak up for what one knows from the inner most depths of the psyche and the earth.

27. Spiritual Democracy is a path with a heart, a way of love, compassion, and human affection.

28. Spiritual Democracy is a vocation to preserve the psychic integrity of the community in connection with the earth and its native species.

29. Spiritual Democracy is a way to develop our divine nature.

30. Spiritual Democracy is a global phenomenon that takes place in one individual at a time, or in groups that place a premium on the transformation of human consciousness.

31. Spiritual Democracy is patterned upon an instinct of activity in the human psyche, the instinct of vocation, or impulse for Holy or Sacred Work.

32. Spiritual Democracy aims at world peace through non-violent means; revolution, war, and political uprising through peaceful means of protest.

33. Spiritual Democracy is a psychology of vocation, a personal theology that places its greatest emphasis on attending to the call from within.

34. Spiritual Democracy is a personal and global consciousness that sees, feels, and experiences the unity of the Cosmos in all forms of life.

35. Spiritual Democracy is not antagonistic towards any person's religion. It respects the dignity of all human paths and practices tolerance; it advocates responsibly living out one's vocation as a path of sacred action.

BIBLIOGRAPHY

Beebe, J. *Integrity in Depth.* New York: Fromm International, 1995.

Benét, W.R. & Aiken, C. *An Anthology of English and American Poetry.* New York: The Modern Library, 1944.

Bennett, P. *Emily Dickinson: Woman Poet.* Iowa City: University of Iowa Press, 1990.

Bogan, L. "A Mystical Poet." In *Emily Dickinson: A Collection of Critical Essays*, (Richard Sewall, ed.). Englewood Cliffs: Prentice-Hall, 1963.

Campbell, J. *Historical Atlas of World Mythology Vol. 1: The Way of the Animal Powers.* New York: Harper & Row, 1988.

———. *The Hero with a Thousand Faces.* Princeton: Bollingen, 1972.

Chai, L. *The Romantic Foundations of the American Renaissance.* Ithaca: Cornell University Press, 1987.

Dassow Walls, L. *The Passage to Cosmos: Alexander von Humboldt and the Shaping of America.* Chicago: University of Chicago Press, 2009.

Davis, D. *Religion and the Continental Congress 1774-1776.* New York: Oxford University Press, 2000.

de Chardin, T. *Hymn of the Universe.* New York: Harper & Row, 1965.

Diamond, D. *Fourth Wave Feminism: Psychoanalytic Perspectives*, 2009.

Dickinson, E. *The Complete Poems of Emily Dickinson,* (Thomas Johnson, Ed.). New York: Little, Brown and Company, 1951.

Dickinson, D. *The Letters of Emily Dickinson*, 3 Volumes, (Thomas H. Johnson and Theodora Ward, Eds.). Cambridge Mass.: Harvard University Press, 1958.

Edinger, E. *Anatomy of the Psyche.* La Salle: Open Court, 1985.

Eliade, M. *Rites and Symbols of Initiation.* New York: Harper, 1958.

————. *Shamanism: Archaic Techniques of Ecstasy.* Princeton, NJ: Bollingen, 1964.

Ellenberger, H. *The Discovery of the Unconscious: The History and Evolution of Dynamic Psychiatry.* New York: Basic Books, 1970.

Everson, W. *The Excesses of God: Robinson Jeffers as a Religious Figure.* Stanford: Stanford University Press, 1988.

Fox, M. *The Hidden Spirituality of Men: Ten Metaphors to Awaken the Sacred Masculine.* Novato: New World, 2008.

————. *The Coming of the Cosmic Christ.* San Francisco: Harper & Row, 1988.

Franklin, R.W. *The Poems of Emily Dickinson: Variorum Edition.* Cambridge Massachusetts: The Belknap Press of Harvard University Press, 1998.

Gelpi, A. *Emily Dickinson: The Mind of the Poet.* New York: Norton, 1965.

Habegger, A. *My Wars Are Laid Away in Books: The Life of Emily Dickinson.* New York: Modern Library, 2001.

Halifax, J. *Shaman: The Wounded Healer.* Singapore: Thames and Hudson, 1982.

Hannah, B. "Introduction to 'The Beyond.'" Chicago: Chiron Publications, 1992.

Henderson, J. *The Wisdom of the Serpent: The Myths of Death, Rebirth, and Resurrection.* New Jersey: Princeton University Press, 1963.

Herrmann, S. "William James & C.G. Jung: The Emergence of the Field of Transpersonal Psychology." In *Integral Transpersonal Journal of Arts, Sciences and Technologies.* No. 8, pp. 22-57, June 2016.

————. *William Everson: The Shaman's Call, Expanded Edition.* New York: Eloquent Books, 2016b.

————. "C.G. Jung and Teilhard de Chardin: Peacemakers in an Age of Spiritual Democracy," In *Pierre Teilhard de Chardin and Carl Gustav Jung Side by Side,* (Fred Gustafson, Ed.). Cheyenne: Fisher King Press, 2015a.

———. *Spiritual Democracy: The Wisdom of Early American Visionaries for the Journey Forward*, Foreword by John Beebe. Berkeley: North Atlantic Books (Sacred Activism Series), 2015b.

———. "Teilhard de Chardin: Cosmic Christ." In *Encyclopedia of Psychology and Religion*, (David A. Leeming & Stanton Marlan, Eds.). Springer Publications, Article ID: 306726, Chapter ID: 9128, 2014e.

———. "The Shamanic Archetype in Robinson Jeffers's Poetry." In *Jeffers Studies*, Vol. 16, Numbers 1 & 2, 1-34, Spring and Fall, 2012.

———. *Walt Whitman: Shamanism, Spiritual Democracy, and the World Soul*. Durham: Eloquent Books, 2010a.

———. "Melville's Portrait of Same-Sex Marriage in *Moby-Dick*." In *Jung Journal: Culture & Psyche*. Vol. 4, No. 3, 65-89, 2010b.

———. *William Everson The Shaman's Call*. New York: Eloquent Books, 2009a.

———. "The Case of Clare: The Emergence of the Self in a Six-Year-Old Girl." *Journal of Sandplay Therapy*. Vol. 18, No. 2, 111-132, 2009b.

———. "Colloquy with the Inner Friend: Jung's Religious Feeling for Islam." *Jung Journal: Culture and Psyche*. Vol. 3, No. 4, 123-132, 2009c.

———. "The Treatment of an Abandonment Trauma." *Journal of Sandplay Therapy*. Vol. 17, No. 2, 51-74, 2008.

———. "The Transformation of Terror into Joy." *Journal of Sandplay Therapy*. Vol. XVI, No. 2, 101-113, 2007a.

———. "Emergence of the Bipolar Cultural Complex in Walt Whitman," *The Journal of Analytical Psychology*. Vol. 52, No. 4, 463-478, 2007b.

———. "Walt Whitman and the Homoerotic Imagination." *Jung Journal: Culture and Psyche*. Vol. 1, No. 2, 16-47, 2007c.

———. "A Conversation with William Everson: Shamanism, American Poetry, And the Vision Quest." *The San Francisco Jung Institute Library Journal*. Vol. 24, No. 4, 2005.

———. "The Cultural Complex in Walt Whitman," *The San Francisco Jung Institute Library Journal*. Vol. 23, No. 4, 2004.

————. "Melville's Vision of Evil." *The San Francisco Jung Institute Library Journal.* Vol. 22, No. 3, 2003a.

————. "Whitman, Dickinson and Melville—American Poet-Shamans: Forerunners of Poetry Therapy." *Journal of Poetry Therapy.* Vol. 16, No. 1, 2003b.

————. "Donald Sandner: The Shamanic Archetype." In *The San Francisco Jung Institute Library Journal.* Vol. 21, No. 2, 2002.

————. "Donald Kalsched: The Inner World of Trauma." *The San Francisco Jung Institute Library Journal.* Vol. 19, No. 2, 2000.

————. "Murray Stein: The Transformative Image." *The San Francisco Jung Institute Library Journal.* Vol. 17, No. 1, 1998.

————. "The Visionary Artist: A Problem for Jungian Literary Criticism." In *The San Francisco Jung Institute Library Journal,* Vol.16, No. 1, 1997.

Hollis, J. *Swamplands of the Soul: New Life in Dismal Places.* Toronto: Inner City Books, 1996.

————. *Under Saturn's Shadow: The Wounding and Healing of Men.* Toronto: Inner City Books, 1994.

————. *The Middle Passage: From Misery to Meaning in Midlife.* Toronto: Inner City Books, 1993.

James, W. *William James: Writings 1902-1910.* New York: The Library of America, 1987.

————. *The Varieties of Religious Experience.* New York: Image Books, 1978.

Jung, C.G. *Collected Works of C.G. Jung,* 20 Volumes, (William McGuire, Ed.). Princeton: Bollingen.

————. *The Red Book,* (Sonu Shamdasani, Ed.). New York: Norton, 2009.

————. *Children's Dreams: Notes from the Seminar Given in 1936-1940.* Princeton: Princeton University Press. Philemon Series, 2008.

————. *Psychology of the Unconscious: A Study of the Transformations and Symbolisms of the Libido,* (Beatrice M. Hinkle, Trans. in 1916). Princeton, NJ: Bollingen Series XX, 1991.

————. *Nietzsche's Zarathustra: Notes of the Seminars Given in 1934-1939*, 2 Volumes, (James Garrett, Ed.). Princeton: Bollingen, 1988.

————. *Dream Analysis: Notes of the Seminar Given in 1928-1930.* Princeton: Bollingen, 1984.

————. *The Visions Seminars*, 2 Volumes. Zurich: Spring Publications, 1976.

————. *Memories, Dreams, Reflections*, (A. Jaffe & R. and C. Winston, Eds. and Trans.). New York: Vintage, 1961.

————. *C.G. Jung Letters*, 2 Volumes, (Gerhard Adler, Ed.). Princeton: Bollingen, 1953.

Kalsched, Donald. *The Inner World of Trauma: Archetypal Defenses of the Personal Spirit.* New York: Routledge, 1996.

Kalweit, H. *Shamans, Healers, and Medicine Men.* Boston: Shambhala, 1992.

Loomis Todd, Mabel. *Letters of Emily Dickinson.* New York: Dover, 2003.

Lommel, A. *The World of the Early Hunters.* London: Evelyn, Adams & Mackay, 1967.

McCullough, D. *Brave Companions: Portraits in History.* New York: Simon & Schuster, 1992.

Neumann, E. *The Place of Creation.* Princeton: Bollingen, 1989.

————. *The Great Mother.* Princeton: Bollingen, 1963.

————. "Mystical Man." New York: Spring Publications, 1961.

Noel, D. *The Soul of Shamanism: Western Fantasies, Imaginal Realities.* New York: Continuum, 1997.

Otto, R. *The Idea of the Holy.* New York: Oxford, 1950.

Oberhaus, D. *Emily Dickinson's Fascicles: Method & Meaning.* University Park: Pennsylvania University State University Press, 1995.

Rich, A. "Vesuvius at Home: The Power of Emily Dickinson." *Parnassus: Poetry in Review.* V, No. 1, Fall-Winter 1976.

Samuels, A. *The Political Psyche.* London: Routledge, 1993.

Sandner, D. & Wong, S. *The Sacred Heritage: The Influence of Shamanism on Analytical Psychology.* New York: Routledge, 1997.

Sewall, R. *The Life of Emily Dickinson.* Cambridge, Mass.: Harvard University Press, 1980.

———. *The Life of Emily Dickinson*, 2 Volumes. New York: Farrar, Strauss and Giroux, 1974.

———. *The Lyman Letters: New Light on Emily Dickinson and Her Family.* Amherst: The University of Massachusetts Press, 1965.

Shakespeare, W. *The Complete Signet Classic Shakespeare.* New York: Harcourt Brace Jovanovich, 1972.

Stein, M. *Transformation: Emergence of the Self.* Texas A & M: College Station, 1998.

———. "'Divinity Expresses the self'…An Investigation." *Journal of Analytical Psychology.* Vol. 53, 2008.

Stonum, G. *The Dickinson Sublime.* Madison: The University of Wisconsin Press, 1990.

Sutton, W. *American Free Verse: The Modern Revolution in Poetry.* New York: New Directions, 1973.

Von Franz, M. *Projection and Re-collection in Jungian Psychology.* La Salle: Open Court, 1980.

Von Humboldt, A. *Cosmos: A Sketch of the Physical Description of the Universe*, Vol. 1. Baltimore: John Hopkins, 1997.

Wilhelm, R. *The I Ching or Book of Changes.* The Richard Wilhelm Translation rendered into English by Cary F. Baynes. Princeton: Princeton University Press. Bollingen Series XIX, 1950.

Whitman, W. *Leaves of Grass.* New York: Library of America/Vintage, 1992.

Winhusen, S. "Emily Dickinson and Schizotypy," In *The Emily Dickinson Journal*, Vol. 13, No. 1, 2004.

Winters, Y. "Emily Dickinson and the Limits of Judgment." In *Emily Dickinson: A Collection of Critical Essays.* Englewood Cliffs: Prentice-Hall, 1963.

Wolff, C. *Emily Dickinson.* New York: Alfred A. Knopf, 1987.

ENDNOTES

A   In a final meeting with Donald Sandner, on March 24, 1997, a week before he died, he said to me: "The idea of shamanism in American poetry has been around for a long time, but people haven't really understood it. This one concept is beautiful. It takes your breath away. It's been around for a while, but to my knowledge, it has never been brought together in a single work. To suddenly see this new shamanic viewpoint in your paper is really electrifying. It is new and thrilling enough to carry the whole book. No one has developed the idea, as you have done in your chapter on Emily Dickinson! Bring the complete quote of Emily's poem 'Take all away from me, but leave me Ecstasy' (J 1640/F 1671) up front and let it stand out on its own." These were the last words Don spoke to me, before a massive heart attack on Easter morning. Months after his funeral, his wife Mary Sandner told me that the Ecstasy poem was on his lips the night before he took his last breath. There is a hidden synchronicity behind these meaningful coincidences that I will elaborate upon in notes ahead.

B   In the summer of 2015, I presented my paper "C.G. Jung's Vision of Spiritual Democracy" at the IAAP/IAJS Conference at Yale University, where Jung spoke to a crowd of twenty-five hundred people in 1937 on the subject of psychology and religion.

C   "Essential Oils—are wrung—/ The Attar from the Rose / Be not expressed by Suns—alone—/ It is the gift of screws—The General Rose—decay—/ But this—in Lady's Drawer / Make Summer—When the Lady lie / In Ceaseless Rosemary—" (J 675/F 772). The name Rosemary comes from the Latin words "dew" (*ros*) and "sea" (*marinus*), or "dew of the sea." It is a native plant from areas in the Mediterranean and Asia. It may be in constant bloom in warm climates. Its flowers may be white, purple, or deep blue. According to Greek mythology, it was draped around the goddess Aphrodite when she arose from the sea, after being born from the semen of Uranus. In Christian mythology, the Virgin Mary is said to spread her blue cloak over the white blossoms of a rosemary bush while she was in repose and its flowers then turned blue. The herb then became known as the "Rose of Mary." Since ancient times Rosemary has been a symbol for friendship, love, and remembrance. Brides were said to have worn Rosemary wreathes as a symbol of their affection, believing that this beautiful herb was a gift from the goddess of love and beauty, Aphrodite. Rosemary is considered to be an herb of remembrance because of its stimulating effects on the brain. It has been shown medically to increase the flow of oxygen-rich blood to one's head, which is why it is considered to be a memory booster. The medicinal uses of its essential oils are widespread; from anti-bacterial uses, to boosting the immune system, to fighting deadly skin cancer or melanomas. I think that it's highly probable that Emily Dickinson had an instinctual wisdom about the curative property of Rosemary and other herbs, flowers, and plants. When she wrote that the "Lady lie / In Ceaseless Rosemary—" I think she was well aware of the healing properties of this plant. The things that we now know about Rosemary today were also ancient intuitive wisdom. The shamans of old, the *medicine women*, who gathered the herbs *knew* of the plant's curative powers: the power of flowers to bring optimal health, hair and skin beauty, and general well-being. For Dickinson, it was also a symbol for her Immortality as an American poet.

D On the 19th of February, 1954, Jung wrote a reply to a question asked by some members of a seminar that was held in Los Angeles on Jung's book *Aion*, led by Dr. James Kirsch. Several of the group members stated that they had not found any commentary in Jung's writings on the idea of Resurrection, the ultimate event in the Christ story. Kirsch wrote Jung a letter to this regard and Jung answered with a piece "On Resurrection." What Jung says in this brief is that although the fact of the Resurrection is historically doubtful, those who were said to have witnessed Christ's transfiguration were probably participating in a parapsychological phenomenon. Whether Jung fully grasped the significance of the phenomena for theology is questionable. Nevertheless, he did say that "The better we understand the archetype, the more we participate in its life and the more we realize its eternity or timelessness…The realization of the self also means a re-establishment of Man as the microcosm, i.e., man's cosmic relatedness. Such realizations are frequently accompanied by synchronistic events. (The prophetic experience of vocation belongs to this category.)…Resurrection as a psychic event is certainly not concrete, it is just a psychic experience." (*CW* 18: ¶¶ 1572-1574).

In the Spring of 1991, when I was beginning to answer my calling to write about the phenomenon of shamanism in American poetry under the tutelage of William Everson and Don Sandner, I did some journaling. Out of my journaling efforts, I put together a poem, which I edited later on, after reading Dickinson in 1995. Little did I know at this time how much my efforts to meditate on the meaning of the Resurrection archetype through journaling would play itself out in my fate and destiny patterns over the next two decades. No poet I have read focuses so intensely on the *experiences* of Crucifixion, Death, and Resurrection as significantly as Emily does. My attempts to amplify the meaning of the archetype in my journal were fully illuminated when I read her. Everything I had written four years prior was confirmed and extended—a hundredfold—by her! For here was a poetess who truly understood the meaning of the archetype! When she says, for instance: "Twas just this time, last year, I died" (J 445/F 344), I had to ask myself whether this death she sensed and felt inside of her was really "just psychic." No, "It was not Death, for I stood up, / And all the Dead, lie down—" (J 510/F 355) she said. Clearly, she was talking about something *real*, more than just psychic. I believe she may have been perceiving the fact of her own immortality as a poet post mortem, through a *trans-psychic experience.*

Now, I will present my poem, then, I will attempt to take Jung's ideas on Resurrection a little bit further.

Meaning of the Resurrection
What is the meaning of the Resurrection of Christ?
What does the Resurrection mean to me?
The Resurrection of Christ,
That He arose from the dead—
Rose to life—and bestowed upon us—
A vocation to live by.
He is revealed to the world
Through the creative Act.
This means He must become creative in us—
Christ—who was hidden in all things.

By losing his career on the Cross,
Christ attained the Light of his Vocation—
His final Resurrection—for all Eternity.
To suffer with Christ
Means that we too are in pursuit of the Light.

The Cross is the Destroyer of all created forms—
The destroyer of everything the empirical ego clings to—
In the career-world of multiplicity.
The wise person knows:
"Greater works than these" are being done daily
As we approach the New Age.
But we keep our vigil
And daily watch for the Redeemer nevertheless,

Because we cannot see the meaning
Of the Resurrection in ourselves.

Were we to see the unformed image of the Resurrection
There would be no need to go any further in our quest.
For we would have found the Light that is no light,
The Sound that is no sound,
The very flood and source of the Godhead that underlies Reality.
There, we would see Christ on the Cross, suffering the anguish
Of his Crucifixion and Joy of his Resurrection
For all Eternity—the non-dual-Symbol of the life-energies of the Cosmos
Destroying and renewing themselves
Throughout all Creation.

"What does it matter" wrote Meister Eckhart,
"That the Birth of God took place in Christ, Jesus,
 If that Birth does not also take place in Me?"
Christ must be reborn in the Soul—
Must endure the torment of his Crucifixion in our careers
If we are to realize the meaning of the Resurrection ourselves.
It is our callings that make this Transfiguration possible in us;
It is also our vocations
That lead Christ to be Crucified and Resurrected again
Within us.

What does it matter
That we have "faith" in Christ Jesus—
That we believe in His Crucifixion—
If He is not also Crucified
And Resurrected
In our innermost hearts?
O, take the journey into oblivion
My friends;
There is no other way
To the Resurrection of the World!

I wrote this poem in my thirty-fifth year. In his book, *The Wisdom of the Serpent*, Jungian analyst Joseph L. Henderson wrote beautifully: "*Finally, we have the mysterious power of the feminine in connection with resurrection,*" p. 203. He later adds, before quoting two Dickinson poems: *"Poets more than prose writers express clearly and poignantly the mythological theme of death and its archetypal corollary, rebirth, or of the quest for the certainty of an after-life, namely, resurrection,"* p. 235.

Of all of the American poets who wrote about Resurrection (Whitman and Melville included), no one surpasses Dickinson in her comprehension of the archetype. She knew the passion of the Self in its cosmic dimensions and lived out its mystery in the field of her calling and career like no one else. She confirmed, beyond any shadow of a doubt—at least in me—that there is a cosmic dimension to the meaning of the archetype, an experience of Universal Oneness, beyond the archetypal symbol. When she says, therefore, she died and arose from the dead, I do in fact believe her. This is the basic experience of shamanistic dismemberment. Writes Mircea Eliade: "almost everywhere in North America, initiation rites into secret societies (shamanic or other) involve the ritual of the candidate's death and resurrection," *Shamanism*, p. 55. Somehow, I knew, before reading Dickinson, that I would have to wrestle with her central metaphor of standing up in white after her fierce grapple with Death, before I was called to engage with her. *Medicine Women can summon us this way—I believe—through a timeless premonition, recorded in writing before a temporal event is "perceived."*

E As I was in the process of beginning to edit this chapter for my book's eventual publication, a forgotten daguerreotype circa 1859 surfaced in the American press. It was a portrait of what scholars at Amherst College now believe, may show Dickinson sitting next to her friend, Kate Scott Anthon (Turner). If this picture of a robust Dickinson, satisfied, at age 30, is truly the poetess, it provides photographic evidence not only to confirm the hypothesis that she might have had a fulfilling erotic relationship with Turner, as has been suspected by some astute feminist critics, but would support my view also, that she was enjoying the inner spiritual marriage it had catalyzed within her, to bring her to the height of her poetic powers, a consummation we can verify from the poetry she produced at that time. As I see it, through some form of same-sex friendship that would today be called a marriage, Dickinson was conducting her own experiment within individuation in 19th century New England America and doing it in her own way. Her poems, for instance, "The Soul selects Her own Society—" (J 303/F 409) expand our limited notions of partnership and same-sex love in a way that speaks to the debates we are having in America and across the globe about marriage equality for gay and lesbian couples right now. Like Whitman, Dickinson used her poetry to advance an unfamiliar syzygy, just as compelling and important for poetry as the now exhausted trope of the male poet and his other sex muse, which essentially had lost its movement and its force with Wordsworth's "Lucy."

F I think it is important to ask today what is the "psychic cosmic center," the "supreme pole of consciousness" towards which all of the "elementary consciousness of the world shall converge towards the rising of a God"? What is the image of God that is rising? Is the rising God the traditional Christ image, the Bridegroom and the Bride of Revelations, or is that historical image of the last Aion large enough to subsume the All towards which all religions turn? In this regard, Teilhard de Chardin spoke of divinization moving towards a convergence point, an Omega point, which culminates in cosmogenesis in a divine milieu in those in whom the Cosmic Christ Consciousness has been awakened. Dickinson is one of those remarkable souls in whom this marriage with the Cosmos transcended historical Christianity, and embraced the new image of the Divine Feminine and Sacred Masculine, a new union that is exactly where I believe we are today in our spiritual evolution. S. Herrmann, "Teilhard de Chardin: Cosmic Christ." In Encyclopedia of Psychology and Religion.

G Like Whitman, Dickinson sensed the national spirit in bi-erotic love, which she embraced with her full heart, body, and soul. Shamans are not infrequently bi-erotic, as are some poets, but I do not think any other poet-shaman reached the depths or heights of transsexual love that Dickinson in fact did. Today, when the issue of homo *and* heterosexuality has become so pervasively felt within our own nation and world-culture, we would be wise to take instruction from Dickinson as our teacher. The need to explore such feelings as she exposes for us with radical spiritual freedom is urgent. If we do so, we may find that the issue is not so much which erotic form better supports a patriarchal adjustment to love in contemporary persons, but which *loves* can lead us to spiritual marriage, a real psychological achievement whose prerogative will be Spiritual Democracy. This is the destiny Dickinson embraced and what she made it her fate to experience and to offer us: the bi-erotic.

H In this book, I use the term Medicine Woman to connote a trans-national poet who transmits a psychological and physical cure to the United States and the World by way of her innovative method of holding and transcending opposite categories of gender (what I call *bi-erotic*, for instance, Dickinson's equal usage of the words "Boy" and "Girl," "Woman" and "Man,") nationality "This ecstatic Nation / Seek—it is Yourself" (J 1354/F 1381), ethnicity and race, i.e., the "Ethiop within" (J 422/F 415), to arrive at a new creative synthesis, a healing symbol of a *trans-cultural union* that is beyond space and time. Jung called the emotionally-toned causes of our human suffering "personal" and "national complexes." More recently, a contemporary term for such ailments of spirt, body, and soul are personal and *cultural complexes*, Ref.: T. Singer and S. Kimbles, *The Cultural Complex: Contemporary Jungian Perspectives on Psyche and Society.* New York: Brunner-Routledge, 2004. Psychotherapists perform a type of surgery on personal and cultural complexes that can open them up to analysis through forms of fantasy and "talking cure." Jungian scholars do something similar through political, literary, and social analysis. Likewise, Emily Dickinson speaks of a sacred medicine administered to the world through a mytho-poetic mode of imagination: "It knew no Medicine—It was not sickness—then / Nor any need of Surgery— / And therefore—'twas not Pain" (J 559). Her medicine (in a patriarchal Judeo-Christian culture that excluded equal rights for women and the Divine Feminine) required no negotiation on her part. She felt she owed nothing to Heaven, in terms of a traditional belief in a paternal Divinity or a Church-centric concept of an afterlife. For Dickinson, who combined the opposites of sex and gender, her resolution, through what Jung called the *transcendent function,* was essentially in the area of a *trans-theistic* solution: "Is Heaven a Physician? / They say that he can heal— / But Medicine Posthumous / Is unavailable— (J 1270). If the-istic medicine was "unavailable" to her, then what was Dickinson's answer in a culture that placed its premium in a royal treasury of an all-beneficent "Father" in Heaven? In my view, Dickinson is an exchequer. She remains today as one of our greatest *national and trans-national treasuries.* She is a this-world Medicine Woman (a Woman-Man who arrived at a union with a cosmic Divinity transcendent of genders), a shaman-poet who I recommend to readers during a time when we most sorely need her word-cure. For I think that our current xenophobic political system in Washington is in radical need of a feminist medicament at this time, one that can truly heal us. To be sure, all rites of passage require entrance into some kind of neutral zone that is sacred. Whoever enters such a zone of neutrality is in a special situation of standing between two worldviews. In 1908, a year before C.G. Jung traveled to America for the first time, Arnold van Gennep (1873-1957) published *Les Rites de Passage,* where he called such zones of sacredness *transitional, or liminal.* One of the greatest and most universal symbols for such zones of liminality is the passage through a special door-way. Writes van Gennep: "Precisely: the door is the boundary between… the profane and the sacred worlds in the case of a temple. Therefore, to cross the threshold is to unite oneself with a new world" (A. van Gennep,

The Rites of Passage, p. 20, Chicago: The University of Chicago Press, 1960). Therefore, to receive Dickinson's word-treatment, it is necessary to first accept her guidance as a dispenser of sacred Medicine. It is not post-mortem Medicine that she offers us. It can heal us preceding death. She invites readers to crouch within her Door and to drink her remedy in the Now. Entering liminal space with Emily, walking on the sacred steps she walked on, entails a shifting of ego boundaries, a crossover into an unspecified territory, a transliminal space that is fluid and capable of assimilating new complex forms in spacetime that are beyond all pairs of psychic opposites. Dickinson did not want to make herself "invisible" by exposing herself to in-group "shaming" for her radically progressive spiritual views on transnational union (The San Francisco Jungian analyst Samuel Kimbles spoke in "The Cultural Complex and the Myth of Invisibility" about invisibility-making as a form of shaming; cited in T. Singer, *The Vision Thing: Myth, Politics, and Psyche in the World*, p. 164, Routledge: London and New York, 2000). Invisibility for Dickinson was a myth that had been created by the sexism and prejudices of her culture. Sexism is perhaps the central cultural illness her poems were meant to heal, yet, she was also very concerned with racial equality and the abolition of slavery. Rather than compromise her individuality as a poet by the sacrifice of her style, she accented her personal and poetic integrity to the utmost. After the shaming she received by editors for being a woman of genius and tremendous wit, she wrote simply and with irony: "I'm Nobody! Who are You? / Are you—nobody—Too?" (J 288). She did not need the men of her generation to celebrate her as an equal. She unshackled herself from the chains of slavery to patriarchal categories of style and syntax. In post-liminal space, beyond the traditional doors of safety, she was fearless. Her poem "Snake" shows us that she went beyond the fear of the unknown; she stepped into the domain of the shaman who seeks solitude in the vastness of inner and outer space. In Gnosticism and Medieval alchemy, Jung wrote, "the serpent" was considered to be "an alexipharmic and the thing that brings all things into maturity and perfection" (*CW* 12: ¶ 529). Thus, the poem she would not sacrifice her style on—"Snake"—became her fate and destiny. For Dickinson, like everyone with a call to follow the Self-path: "the right way to wholeness is made up, unfortunately, of fateful detours and wrong turnings. It is a *longissima via*, not straight but snakelike, a path that unites the opposites in the manner of the guiding caduceus, a path whose labyrinthine twists and turns are not lacking in terrors" (*CW* 12: ¶ 6).

I After a recent fall at dusk, on November 11, 2016, I experienced a new level of awareness about Emily Dickinson's poem: "Because I could not stop for

Death— / He kindly stopped for me—" During the first 48 hours, when I was still dealing with the initial impact of a concussion, dislocated jaw, back injury, and loss of balance, the first quatrain of this amazing poem kept repeating itself in my mind. The opening four lines repeated themselves over and over again. They kept repeating, without my willing them. What did this quatrain want from me? What was it trying to tell me about my life, fate, and vocation? After my head hit the pavement, I sustained a puncture wound, but I did not lose consciousness. I was shaken and dizzy but I stayed fully aware. The fall occurred in my sixtieth year. "What's the meaning of this fall?" I wondered. Whatever it was, I'm very, very lucky, very fortunate indeed that I fell the way I did. The injury could have been much worse. As I contemplated Dickinson's words for the first couple of days I was icing the back of my head to bring the swelling down, I realized that I hadn't been giving enough time in my life to just simply doing nothing, simply being, simply stopping to contemplate death. That Dickinson refers to death as "kindly" strikes me as particularly moving, because kindness is an attribute of the Buddha, of bodhisattva's, and Christian monks and nuns and saints. The goddesses of compassion, Quan Yin and the Virgin Mary— the feminine principle and the healing powers of the body are very kindly. *We can help our bodies facilitate healing, but ultimately, it is the Self that heals us.* That the Self produces healing powers in the body and psyche is simply miraculous. The curative powers of our bodies are compassion-in-action, balm, indeed. Death is an archetypal reality, a friend, who accompanies us throughout life, counsels us, and walks patiently by our sides. Death provides us with instructions about transience, about impermanence, about the value of relationships, family, friendships, vocation, and love. Death kindly stops for us and invites us in the poem to enter into his carriage and to go on a leisurely ride through life's memories towards Eternity. What a work of genius this poem of Emily's is, what a jewel in her crown! Her main function as a poet-shaman was to heal us from the sickness of modern civilized life, from banality, noise, and obsession with the news. I'm grateful to Dickinson for having transmitted to me the *medicine of solitude*; stopping for death and allowing death to take me on a leisurely carriage ride through fields of meaningful reveries. I did zero intellectual work for six days. I did not read any newspapers, nor gaze at the TV, or the Internet, during our post-election coverage in the USA. I simply let Nature take her healing course. During my healing process, I quietly planted rosemary along the east and south sides of our property. The blue blossoms were in full flower and pungent with healing fragrance and the worker bees were wild with ecstasy. What a beautiful aroma they emitted! I can still smell the oily tincture on my hands as I write this. Rosemary is so ecstatic when it bursts into full bloom, so extraordinary. The honeybees love it and sip its sweet pollen. I am happy to report that four weeks after my fall, I managed to bring this book to completion, notes and all. There is nothing like a blow of Fate to lead one to fulfill one's tasks and write out the true meaning of one's destiny.

J   I owe a tribute of thanks to Henri Ellenberger for helping me to understand the phenomenon of the creative illness as it applies the field of depth psychology. Ellenberger's book *The Discovery of the Unconscious* is a masterpiece. When I first read it in 1998, I was so impressed with it I couldn't put it down. I have since used it in my teaching at the C.G. Jung Institute in San Francisco, in my clinical work and in my writing. In Ellenberger's view, Freud and Jung succeeded shamans in the discovery of the unconscious (p. 9). It was Ellenberger's "hypothesis that Freud's and Jung's systems originated mostly from their respective creative illness (of which their self-analysis was but one aspect)" (p. 889). "Both of them," Ellenberger says, "underwent a creative illness in a spontaneous and original form, and both of them made it a model to be followed by their disciples under the name of training analysis" (p. 890). Jungians, according to Ellenberger, were the first psychologists to consider the training analysis that Jung promoted and which Freudians accepted "as being a kind of initiatory malady comparable to that of the shaman" (p. 890). Freud and Jung unleashed an explosion of psychic energy from the core of the shamanic archetype that would lead them through an "intense preoccupation with an idea" to "a permanent transformation" of their personalities and to "the conviction" that they "have discovered a great truth or a new spiritual world" (pp. 447-448). Ellenberger tells us that throughout the period of creative illness, "the subject never loses the thread of his dominating preoccupation...he is almost entirely absorbed with himself. He suffers from feelings of utter isolation, even when he has a mentor who guides him through the ordeal (like the shaman apprentice with his master)" (p. 448). After he "emancipated himself from the influence" of Charcot, Ellenberger tells us that Freud began to identify "himself" primarily with the figure of "Goethe" (p. 447). A remarkable transformation of consciousness took place in him that may have been attributable to the influence of the shaman-poet archetype. Freud was not only looking for a new system of psychological analysis, he was looking for a style of speech; a mythopoetic language through which the technique of psychoanalysis could be made available for all people. His vehicle for this was not to be found in identification with the founders of the first dynamic psychiatry alone, but in his identification with poets who had preceded depth psychologists in the discovery of the unconscious. In order to write his great Traumdeutung in 1899, Freud was led to make an historic break with all of his early "masters" who were not also poets. As Freud pointed out, it was really "the great poets and writers who" had "preceded psychologists in the exploration of the human mind." Ellenberger says: "He [Freud] often quoted the Greek tragedians, Shakespeare, Goethe, Schiller, Heine, and many other writers. "No doubt," Ellenberger continues, "Freud could have been one of the world's foremost writers, but instead of using his deep, intuitive knowledge of the human soul for the creation of literary works, he attempted to formulate it and systematize it." When the playwright Lenormand went to visit Freud at his office in Vienna, moreover, Freud is reported to have pointed to the works of Shakespeare and the Greek tragedians as his source, saying: "Here are my masters." "He maintained" Ellenberger concluded, "that the essential themes of his theories were based on the intuitions of the poets" (pp. 460, 466-467). The "creative illness" culminates when a great artistic, religious, scientific, or philosophic truth is discovered and revealed for the benefit humanity (p. 447), H. Ellenberger, *The Discovery of the Unconscious: The History and Evolution of Dynamic Psychiatry.*

INDEX

You might also enjoy reading:

Marked By Fire: Stories of the Jungian Way edited by Patricia Damery & Naomi Ruth Lowinsky, 1st Ed., Trade Paperback, 180pp, Biblio., 2012
— ISBN 978-1-926715-68-1

The Dream and Its Amplification edited by Erel Shalit & Nancy Swift Furlotti, 1st Ed., Trade Paperback, 180pp, Biblio., 2013
— ISBN 978-1-926715-89-6

Shared Realities: Participation Mystique and Beyond edited by Mark Winborn, 1st Ed., Trade Paperback, 270pp, Index, Biblio., 2014
— ISBN 978-1-77169-009-6

Pierre Teilhard de Chardin and C.G. Jung: Side by Side edited by Fred Gustafson, 1st Ed., Trade Paperback, 270pp, Index, Biblio., 2014
— ISBN 978-1-77169-014-0

Jungian Child Analysis edited by Audrey Punnett, 1st Ed., Trade Paperback, 240pp, Index, Biblio., 2018
— ISBN 978-1-77169-038-6

Re-Imagining Mary: A Journey Through Art to the Feminine Self by Mariann Burke, 1st Ed., Trade Paperback, 180pp, Index, Biblio., 2009
— ISBN 978-0-9810344-1-6

Advent and Psychic Birth by Mariann Burke, Revised Ed., Trade Paperback, 170pp, 2014
— ISBN 978-1-926715-99-5

Sea Glass: A Jungian Analyst's Exploration of Individuation & Suffering by Gilda Frantz, 1st Ed., Trade Paperback, 240pp, Index, Biblio., 2014
— ISBN 978-1-77169-020-1

Transforming Body and Soul by Steven Galipeau, Rev. Ed., Trade Paperback, 180pp, Index, Biblio., 2011
— ISBN 978-1-926715-62-9

Lifting the Veil: Revealing the Other Side by Fred Gustafson & Jane Kamerling, 1st Ed., Trade Paperback, 170pp, Biblio., 2012
— ISBN 978-1-926715-75-9

Resurrecting the Unicorn: Masculinity in the 21st Century by Bud Harris, Rev. Ed., Trade Paperback, 300pp, Index, Biblio., 2009
— ISBN 978-0-9810344-0-9

The Father Quest: Rediscovering an Elemental Force by Bud Harris, Reprint, Trade Paperback, 180pp, Index, Biblio., 2009
— ISBN 978-0-9810344-9-2

Like Gold Through Fire: The Transforming Power of Suffering by Massimilla & Bud Harris, Reprint, Trade Paperback, 150pp, Index, Biblio., 2009 — ISBN 978-0-9810344-5-4

The Art of Love: The Craft of Relationship by Massimilla and Bud Harris, 1st Ed., Trade Paperback, 150pp, 2010
— ISBN 978-1-926715-02-5

Emily Dickinson: A Medicine Woman for Our Times by Steven Herrmann, 1st Ed., Trade Paperback, 290pp, Index, Biblio., 2018
— ISBN 978-1-77169-041-6

Divine Madness: Archetypes of Romantic Love by John R. Haule, Rev. Ed., Trade Paperback, 282pp, Index, Biblio., 2010
— ISBN 978-1-926715-04-9

Tantra and Erotic Trance in 2 volumes by John R. Haule

   Volume 1 - Outer Work, 1st Ed., Trade Paperback, 215pp, Index, Bibliography, 2012 — ISBN 978-0-9776076-8-6

   Volume 2 - Inner Work, 1st Ed., Trade Paperback, 215pp, Index, Bibliography, 2012 — ISBN 978-0-9776076-9-3

War of the Ancient Dragon: Transformation of Violence in Sandplay by Laurel A. Howe, 1st Ed., Trade Paperback, 166pp, Index, Biblio., 2016 — ISBN 978-1-77169-034-8

Eros and the Shattering Gaze: Transcending Narcissism by Ken Kimmel, 1st Ed., Trade Paperback, 310pp, Index, Biblio., 2011
— ISBN 978-1-926715-49-0

A Jungian Life by Thomas B Kirsch, 1st Ed., Trade Paperback, 224pp, 2014
— ISBN 978-1-77169-024-9

The Motherline: Every Woman's Journey to Find Her Female Roots by Naomi Ruth Lowinsky, Reprint, Trade Paperback, 252pp, Index, Biblio., 2009 — ISBN 978-0-9810344-6-1

The Sister From Below: When the Muse Gets Her Way by Naomi Ruth Lowinsky, 1st Ed., Trade Paperback, 248pp, Index, Biblio., 2009 — ISBN 978-0-9810344-2-3

The Rabbi, The Goddess, and Jung: Getting the Word from Within by Naomi Ruth Lowinsky, 1st Ed., Trade Paperback, 242pp, Index, Biblio., 2017 — ISBN 978-1-77169-036-2

The Dairy Farmer's Guide to the Universe in 4 volumes by Dennis L. Merritt:

   Volume 1 - Jung and Ecopsychology, 1st Ed., Trade Paperback, 242pp, Index, Biblio., 2011 — ISBN 978-1-926715-42-1

   Volume 2 - The Cry of Merlin: Jung the Prototypical Ecopsychologist, 1st Ed., Trade Paperback, 204pp, Index, Biblio., 2012
— ISBN 978-1-926715-43-8

Creases in Culture: Essays Toward a Poetics of Depth
by Dennis Patrick Slattery, 1ˢᵗ Ed., Trade Paperback, 424pp, Biblio., 2014
— ISBN 978-1-77169-006-5

Our Daily Breach: Exploring Your Personal Myth Through Herman Melville's Moby-Dick by Dennis Patrick Slattery, 1ˢᵗ Ed., Trade Paperback, 424pp, Biblio., 2015 — ISBN 978-1-77169-029-4

The Guilt Cure
by Nancy Carter Pennington & Lawrence H. Staples, 1ˢᵗ Ed., Trade Paperback, 200pp, Index, Biblio., 2011 — ISBN 978-1-926715-53-7

Guilt with a Twist: The Promethean Way
by Lawrence Staples,1ˢᵗ Ed., Trade Paperback, 256pp, Index, Biblio., 2008
— ISBN 978-0-9776076-4-8

Our Creative Fingerprint
by Nancy Carter Pennington & Lawrence H. Staples, 1ˢᵗ Ed., Trade Paperback, 92pp, Index, Biblio., 2017— ISBN 978-1-77169-040-9

The Creative Soul: Art and the Quest for Wholeness
by Lawrence Staples, 1ˢᵗ Ed., Trade Paperback, 100pp, Index, Biblio., 2009
— ISBN 978-0-9810344-4-7

Deep Blues: Human Soundscapes for the Archetypal Journey
by Mark Winborn, 1ˢᵗ Ed., Trade Paperback, 130pp, Index, Biblio., 2011
— ISBN 978-1-926715-52-0

The Dream: The Vision of the Night
by Max Zeller, Rev. Ed., Trade Paperback, 202pp, 2015
— ISBN 978-1-77169-028-7

Phone Orders Welcomed
Credit Cards Accepted
International call +1-831-238-7799
www.fisherkingpress.com

Made in the USA
Middletown, DE
01 December 2018